CELEBRATING
CELESTIAL
marriage

RICHARD K. SCOTT

CFI
Springville, Utah

ISBN:1-55517-853-7
v.1

Published by CFI,
an imprint of Cedar Fort, Inc.
925 N. Main Springville, Utah, 84663
www.cedarfort.com

Distributed by:

Cover design by Nicole Williams
Cover design © 2005 by Lyle Mortimer

Printed in the United States of America
10 9 8 7 6 5 4 3 2 1

Printed on acid-free paper

Dedication

To the Lord and His prophets, who have given us so much counsel. To my wife, Janice, who has been my companion and tutor in the quest for charity. And to my children, who are still teaching me what it means to be a parent.

acknowledgments

I would like to thank the many people at Cedar Fort who have been so cordial to work with and who have helped this project come to fruition. Special thanks are due to Lee Nelson, who approved the manuscript, and to Michael Morris and his staff, who improved my initial draft and have been patient in tutoring me on creating a finished project.

I would also like to thank all of the people who have taught me and helped me catch the vision of what marriage is meant to be: my parents, my wife's parents, and many authors, lecturers, and students.

contents

introduction

Celestial marriage is intended to be a joy, a celebration. This celebration, however, is not a single event but an ongoing, transforming process. Celestial marriages are born in the temples but are nurtured and tutored to maturity in homes.

The Latter-day Saint doctrine of celestial marriage is unique to The Church of Jesus Christ of Latter-day Saints and is central to the Church's focus on the eternal family and on eternal progression. Elder Bruce R. McConkie said:

> Marriages performed in the temples for time and eternity, by virtue of the sealing keys restored by Elijah, are called *celestial marriages.* The participating parties become husband and wife in this mortal life, and if after their marriage they keep all the terms and conditions of this order of the priesthood, they continue on as husband and wife in the celestial kingdom of God.
>
> If the family unit continues, then by virtue of that fact the members of the family have gained eternal life (exaltation), the greatest of all the gifts of God, for by definition exaltation consists in the continuation of the family unit in eternity. Those so inheriting are the sons and daughters of God, the members of his family, those who have made their callings and elections sure.

> They are joint-heirs with Christ to all that the Father hath, and they receive the fulness of the glory of the Father, becoming gods in their own right.[1]

Temple marriage is not eternal life, the greatest of all gifts (D&C 14:7). Rather, it is an ordinance that authorizes a couple to commence on a quest toward the vision of what their marriage may become. This marvelous potential cannot be realized with efforts that are telestial—adultery, lying, and so forth (D&C 76:103). Nor can it be achieved through terrestrial efforts performed by honorable people who are blinded by the craftiness of men (D&C 76:75). Celestial marriage requires living on a much higher plane in accordance with celestial laws. It requires the companionship of the Holy Ghost, faith to overcome, and sealing by the Holy Spirit of Promise (D&C 76:52–53). The Lord said:

> If a man marry a wife by my word, which is my law, and by the new and everlasting covenant, and it is sealed unto them by the Holy Spirit of promise, by him who is anointed, unto whom I have appointed this power and the keys of this priesthood; . . . and if ye abide in my covenant, . . . it shall be done unto them in all things whatsoever my servant hath put upon them, in time, and through all eternity; and shall be of full force when they are out of the world; and they shall pass by the angels, and the gods, which are set there, to their exaltation and glory in all things, as hath been sealed upon their heads, which glory shall be a fulness and a continuation of the seeds forever and ever.
>
> Then shall they be gods, because they have no end; therefore shall they be from everlasting to everlasting, because they continue; then shall they be above all, because all things are subject unto them. Then shall they be gods, because they have all power, and the angels are subject unto them. Verily, verily, I say unto you, except ye abide my law ye cannot attain to this glory. For strait is the gate, and narrow the way that leadeth unto the exaltation and continuation of the

lives, and few there be that find it. (D&C 132:19–22)

Most marriage books are not written with this exalted vision of what marriages may become. Marriage books and theories are often written in response to serious marital problems resulting from telestial behaviors. It should not be too surprising, therefore, that the theorized solutions are honorable, but still only terrestrial. Certainly learning how to give "*I* messages" or knowing the "Rules for fair fighting" have their place in raising a telestial relationship to a terrestrial level.

This book will also offer some down-to-earth suggestions for improving struggling marriages. However, marriage has the potential to be so much more than simply tolerable or acceptable. As a graduate student in family therapy, I was disappointed to see that the philosophical goal of the university seemed to be little more than helping couples divorce amicably. Surely Latter-day Saints, especially those married in the temple, have loftier expectations and are committed by covenant to create a marriage that brings happiness in mortality and promises beyond comprehension in the eternities. The law of the harvest teaches that we cannot put forth minimum effort and expect maximum blessings. Eternal marriage is the highest of all blessings and therefore requires extraordinary effort on our part.

Latter-day prophets have given us a vision of marriage worth celebrating. President Spencer W. Kimball said, "Honorable, happy, and successful marriage is surely the principal goal of every normal person. . . . Marriage is perhaps the most vital of all the decisions and has the most far-reaching effects, for it has to do not only with immediate happiness, but also with eternal joys. . . . Marriage can be more an exultant ecstasy than the human mind can conceive. This is within the reach of every couple, every person."[2]

Elder Bruce R. McConkie declared, "The whole aim and purpose of the gospel is to enable men and women—united as one in the Lord—to create for themselves eternal family units in eternity. Celestial marriage prepares us for the greatest joy and happiness known to mortals and for eternal life in the realms ahead."[3]

President James E. Faust stated, "Happiness in marriage and parenthood can exceed a thousand times any other happiness."[4] A true celestial marriage is indeed a celebration!

President Gordon B. Hinckley has said, "I wish with all my heart that every marriage might be a happy marriage. I wish that every marriage might be an eternal partnership. I believe that wish can be realized if there is a willingness to make the effort to bring it to pass."[5]

This book is written for Latter-day Saint couples who do not want to simply endure a marriage or merely accept an honorable marriage. It is written for those who are willing to make the extraordinary effort to bring to pass a godly marriage, one that through the atonement and grace of Christ may eventually be worthy of exaltation.

"What we want is eternal life in families," said Elder Henry B. Eyring. "We don't just want it if that is what works out, nor do we want something approaching eternal life. We want eternal life, whatever its cost in effort, pain, and sacrifice."[6]

Most of this volume is a compilation of what LDS Church leaders have said or written on pertinent marriage topics. Because the Brethren teach what is right and not necessarily what is popular, some of their counsel may initially seem bold and challenging. I hope the reader will have the Spirit and recognize that that is the value of having inspired leaders. As President Boyd K. Packer declared, "Somebody has to stand, face the storm, declare the truth, and let the winds blow, and be serene and composed and steady in the doing of it."[7] How grateful we ought to be for such watchmen upon the towers.

Revealed principles of the gospel of Jesus Christ are the foundation of any happy marriage. However, I am not a spokesman for the Church. Therefore, I must acknowledge responsibility for what is presented here, including the selection of General Authority quotations and the contexts in which they are used. I also feel an obligation to clarify that though my name may have a ring of

familiarity to it, I am not related to Elder Richard G. Scott, a
member of the Quorum of the Twelve Apostles.

Each chapter of this book discusses a distinct topic. Therefore,
the reader could browse through the table of contents and select
the chapters of most interest. Each chapter, however, is written to
strengthen a different aspect of marriage. So the reader is invited
to enjoy the entire book and listen carefully for promptings of the
Spirit that will bear witness to the principles that are true. I hope
there will be many.

Notes

1. McConkie, *Mormon Doctrine*, 117.

2. Kimball, *Marriage and Divorce*, 143, 146.

3. McConkie, "The Mystery of Mormonism," *Ensign*, November 1979,
55.

4. Faust, "The Enriching of Marriage," *Ensign*, November 1977, 11.

5. Hinckley, "Rise to the Stature of the Divine within You," *Ensign*,
November 1989, 97.

6. Eyring, *To Draw Closer to God: A Collection of Discourses*, 161.

7. Packer, *That All May Be Edified*, 269.

SECTION ONE:
gospel foundations

Happiness in marriage, now and eternally, is conditioned upon obedience to gospel truths. No marriage can experience true and lasting happiness unless it is based on gospel foundations. Therefore, the foundation of any happy marriage is the revealed gospel of Jesus Christ—specifically those principles that pertain to the eternal relationship between husband and wife.

The more completely a couple understands the gospel foundations of their marriage, the more likely they will be to enjoy their marriage in mortality and qualify to be married eternally.

President Boyd K. Packer stated, "True doctrine, understood, changes attitudes and behavior. The study of the doctrines of the gospel will improve behavior quicker than a study of behavior will improve behavior."[1]

To the hypothetical question, "How can you receive the greatest happiness and blessings from this earth experience?" Elder Richard G. Scott proposed the following answer:

- Learn the doctrinal foundation of the great plan of happiness by studying the scriptures, pondering their content and praying to understand them. Carefully study and use the proclamation of the First Presidency and the Twelve on the family. It was inspired of the Lord.

- Listen to the voice of current and past prophets. Their declarations are inspired. You may verify that counsel in your own mind and heart by praying about it as it applies to your special circumstances. Ask the Lord to confirm your choices, and accept accountability for them.

- Obey the inner feelings that come as promptings from the Holy Ghost. Those feelings are engendered by your righteous thoughts and acts and your determination to seek the will of the Lord and to live it.

- When needed, seek counsel and guidance from parents and your priesthood leaders.[2]

This section will explore the gospel foundations of the doctrine of celestial marriage and attempt to convey the marvelous vision of what marriage is supposed to be, as well as the motivation to make it such.

Notes

1. Packer, "Little Children," *Ensign*, November 1986, 17.

2. Scott, "The Joy of Living the Great Plan of Happiness," *Ensign*, November 1996, 75.

1

MARRIAGE AND THE PLAN OF
happiness

We sometimes refer to an especially good marriage as a marriage "made in heaven." However, we might more accurately say these marriages will "continue in heaven." An awareness that life continues after mortal death, and that family relationships may also extend into the eternities, is essential to understanding the concept of celestial marriage. The scriptures clearly teach about a plan of salvation or, as Alma called it, "the great plan of happiness" (Alma 42:8). This plan of happiness includes the potential for husbands and wives to experience marital bliss eternally.

President George Q. Cannon taught:

> We believe in the eternal nature of the marriage relation, that man and woman are destined, as husband and wife, to dwell together eternally. We believe that we are organized as we are, with all these affections, with all this love for each other, for a definite purpose, something far more lasting than to be extinguished when death shall overtake us. We believe that when a man and woman are united as husband and wife, and they love each other, their hearts and feelings are one,

that that love is as enduring as eternity itself, and that
when death overtakes them it will neither extinguish
nor cool that love, but that it will brighten and kindle
it to a purer flame, and that it will endure through
eternity.[1]

Not only can family relationships extend into the eternities,
but this very fact is one of the most critical reasons for the existence of eternity. "Marriage and the family unit are the central
part of the plan of progression and exaltation," explained Elder
Bruce R. McConkie. "All things center in and around the family
unit in the eternal perspective. Exaltation consists in the continuation of the family unit in eternity."[2]

Other prophets have also taught that marriage is central to
the plan of progression. President John Taylor noted that celestial
marriage "is one of the greatest blessings that ever was conferred
upon the human family. It is an eternal law which has always
existed in other worlds as well as in this world."[3]

Elder L. Tom Perry taught, "The union between husband and
wife is sacred to the Lord, something not to be trifled with. The
marriage covenant was essential to the Lord God to accomplish
his mission and purposes for which he created the heavens and
the earth."[4]

President Brigham Young observed that the full significance
of marriage may not yet be fully understood:

> But the whole subject of the marriage relation is
> not in my reach, nor in any other man's reach on this
> earth. It is without beginning of days or end of years;
> it is a hard matter to reach. We can tell some things
> with regard to it; it lays the foundations for worlds; for
> angels, and for the Gods; for intelligent beings to be
> crowned with glory, immortality, and eternal lives. In
> fact, it is the thread which runs from the beginning to
> the end of the holy Gospel of salvation—of the Gospel
> of the Son of God; it is from eternity to eternity.[5]

Eternal marriage and godhood are synonymous. The First Presidency taught:

> Man is the child of God, formed in the divine image and endowed with divine attributes, and even as the infant son of an earthly father and mother is capable in due time of becoming a man, so that undeveloped offspring of celestial parentage is capable, by experience through ages and aeons, of evolving into a God.[6]

Godhood is all about teamwork. Elder McConkie noted:

> If righteous men have power through the gospel and its crowning ordinance of celestial marriage to become kings and priests to rule in exaltation forever, it follows that the women by their side (without whom they cannot attain exaltation) will be queens and priestesses (Revelation 1:6; 5:10). Exaltation grows out of the eternal union of a man and his wife. Of those whose marriage endures in eternity, the Lord says, "Then shall *they* be gods" (D&C 132:20; emphasis added); that is, each of them, the man and the woman, will be a god.[7]

Our ultimate potential is exaltation in the celestial kingdom. This potential can only be attained through the ordinance and subsequent processes of temple marriage. Many prophets have spoken boldly about this doctrine. Elder Parley P. Pratt wrote:

> All persons who attain to the resurrection, and to salvation, without these eternal ordinances, or sealing covenants, will remain in a single state, in their saved condition, without the joys of eternal union with the other sex, and consequently without a crown, without a kingdom, without the power to increase. Hence, they are angels, and are not gods; and are ministering spirits, or servants, in the employ and under the direc-

tion of The Royal Family of heaven—the princes, kings and priests of eternity."[8]

President Joseph Fielding Smith taught:

> Since marriage is ordained of God, and the man is not without the woman, neither the woman without the man in the Lord, there can be no exaltation to the fulness of the blessings of the celestial kingdom outside of the marriage relation. A man cannot be exalted singly and alone; neither can a woman. Each must have a companion to share the honors and blessings of this great exaltation. Marriage for time and all eternity brings to pass the crowning glory of our Father's kingdom, by which his children become his heirs, into whose hands he gives all things. If a man and his wife are saved in separate kingdoms, for instance, the celestial and terrestrial, automatically the sealing is broken; it is broken because of the sins of one of the parties. No one can be deprived of exaltation who remains faithful. In other words, an undeserving husband cannot prevent a faithful wife from an exaltation and vice versa. In this case the faithful servant would be given to someone who is faithful.[9]

President Spencer W. Kimball reinforced the critical nature of eternal marriage when he taught:

> Clearly, attaining eternal life is not a matter of goodness only. That is one of the two important elements, but one must practice righteousness and receive the ordinances. People who do not bring their lives into harmony with God's laws and who do not receive the necessary ordinances either in this life or (if that is impossible) in the next, have thus deprived themselves, and will remain separate and single in the eternities. There they will have no spouses, no children. If one is going to be in God's kingdom of exaltation, where God dwells in all his glory, one will be there as a

husband or a wife and not otherwise. Regardless of his virtues, the single person, or the one married for this life only, cannot be exalted. All normal people should marry and rear families. To quote Brigham Young: "No man can be perfect without the woman, so no woman can be perfect without a man to lead her. I tell you the truth as it is in the bosom of eternity. If he wishes to be saved, he cannot be saved without a woman by his side." Celestial marriage is that important.[10]

President Kimball reiterated this principle in other teachings. In 1968, he taught a group of educators that eternal marriage "is the gateway to exaltation, and the Lord says through John, 'Verily, verily, I say unto you, He that entereth not by the door into the sheepfold, but climbeth up some other way, the same is a thief and a robber.' (John 10:1.) In fact, there is only one door. You all know it. I hope you are indoctrinating each and every boy and girl that comes into your presence. Only one door—no other—and that is eternal marriage, for no soul will enter the portals of exaltation alone. There will be no singles. There will always be doubles, and those doubles will be a man and a woman who will love each other intensely and who will have adjusted themselves to each other in a totaling perfection—nothing short of that!"[11]

Over and over, we see Church leaders teaching this essential fact. "Men are not saved alone and women do not gain an eternal fulness except in and through the continuation of the family unit in eternity," said Elder McConkie. "Salvation is a family affair. . . . That is, the man and his wife together, and not either one of them alone, shall be exalted. They shall have eternal life; they shall fill the full measure of their creation; they shall inherit, receive, and possess all things."[12]

Elder Erastus Snow referred to the creation of Adam and Eve to teach us better about the nature of the Gods. He said:

> But he created them male and female, for they were one, and he says not unto the woman multiply, and to

the man multiply, but he says unto them, multiply and reproduce your species, and replenish the earth. He speaks unto them as belonging together, as constituting one being, and as organized in his image and after his likeness. . . . There is no great mystery about it; no more mystery about it than there is about ourselves, and our own relationship to our father and mother, and the relationship of our own children to us. That which we see before our eyes, and which we are experiencing from time to time, day to day, and year to year, is an exemplification of Deity. . . . 'What,' says one, 'do you mean we should understand that deity consists of man and woman?' Most certainly I do. If I believe anything that God has ever said about himself, and anything pertaining to the creation and organization of man upon the earth, I must believe that Deity consists of man and woman. . . . I only repeat what he says of himself; that he created man in the image of God, male and female created he them, and he called their name Adam, which signifies in Hebrew, the first man. So that the beings we call Adam and Eve were the first man placed here on this earth, and their name was Adam, and they were the express image of God. . . . I sometimes illustrate this matter by taking up a pair of shears, if I have one, but then you all know they are composed of two halves, but they are necessarily parts, one of another, and to perform their work for each other, as designed, they belong together, and neither one of them is fitted for the accomplishment of their work alone. And for this reason says St. Paul, "the man is not without the woman, nor the woman without the man in the Lord." In other words, there can be no God except he is composed of the man and woman united, and there is not in all the eternities that exist, nor ever will be, a God in any other way. I have another description: There never was a God, and there never will be in all eternities, except they are made of these two component parts; a man and a woman; the male and the female.[13]

An essential aspect of eternal marriage is eternal increase. The prophets have also taught powerfully about this important doctrine. President Lorenzo Snow said:

> When two Latter-day Saints are united together in marriage, promises are made to them concerning their offspring that reach from eternity to eternity. They are promised that they shall have the power and the right to govern and control and administer salvation and exaltation and glory to their offspring, worlds without end. And what offspring they do not have here, undoubtedly there will be opportunities to have them hereafter. What else could man wish? A man and a woman in the other life, having celestial bodies, free from sickness and disease, glorified and beautified beyond description, standing in the midst of their posterity, governing and controlling them, administering life, exaltation and glory worlds without end![14]

President George Q. Cannon wrote:

> And this is the blessing that God has promised to every faithful man and woman—that to the increase of their seed there shall be no end. This will constitute the great glory of eternity—the man presiding over his family and being lord over them. Thus it is that Jesus is called Lord of lords. He is Lord of lords because His brethren will exercise this power and authority over their posterity.[15]

Of this parent-child relationship, President George Q. Cannon said:

> If we have offspring they will be with us and our mutual associations will be one of the chief joys of the heaven to which we are hastening. . . . God has restored the everlasting priesthood, by which ties can

be formed, consecrated and consummated, which shall be as enduring as we ourselves are enduring, that is, as our spiritual nature; and husbands and wives will be united together, and they and their children will dwell and associate together eternally, and this, as I have said, will constitute one of the chief joys of heaven; and we look forward to it with delightful anticipation.[16]

Elder James E. Talmage wrote:

Neither of the sexes is complete in itself as a counterpart of Deity. We are expressly told that God is the Father of spirits, and to apprehend the literalness of this solemn truth we must know that a mother of spirits is an existent personality. . . . Grand as may seem the achievements of a man who is truly great, the culmination of his glorious career lies in his leaving posterity to continue, and enhance the triumphs of their sire. And if such be true of mortals with respect to the things of earth, transcendently greater is the power of eternal increase, as viewed in the light of revealed truth concerning the unending progression of the future state.[17]

President Marion G. Romney wrote:

The plan provides that couples so married shall in eternity persist as husbands and wives and there progress until they eventually reach perfection and themselves become parents of spirit children.[18]

Elder Melvin J. Ballard asked: "What do we mean by endless or eternal increase?" He answered:

We mean that through the righteousness and faithfulness of men and women who keep the commandments of God they will come forth with celestial bodies, fitted and prepared to enter into their great, high and eternal glory in the celestial kingdom of

God; and unto them, through their preparation, there will come children, who will be spirit children. I don't think that is very difficult to comprehend and understand. The nature of the offspring is determined by the nature of the substance that flows in the veins of the being. When blood flows in the veins of the being, the offspring will be what blood produces, which is tangible flesh and bone, but when that which flows in the veins is spirit matter, a substance which is more refined and pure and glorious than blood, the offspring of such beings will be spirit children. By that I mean they will be in the image of the parents. They will have a spirit body and have a spark of the eternal or divine that always did exist in them. . . .

Unto such parentage will this glorious privilege come, for it is written in our scriptures that "the glory of God is to bring to pass the immortality and eternal life of man." So, it will be the glory of men and women that will make their glory like unto his. When the power of endless increase shall come to them, and their offspring, growing and multiplying through ages that shall come, they will be in due time, as we have been, provided with an earth like this, wherein they too may obtain earthly bodies and pass through all the experiences through which we have passed, and then we shall hold our relationship to them, the fulness and completeness of which has not been revealed to us, but we shall stand in our relationship to them as God, our Eternal Father, does to us, and thereby is this the most glorious and wonderful privilege that ever will come to any of the sons and daughters of God.[19]

As we work on creating our family heaven on earth, it is helpful to keep heaven and these sacred doctrines in mind. It is far too easy to become focused on the day-to-day matters that demand our attention, consequently failing to do those things necessary to establish a family fit for the eternities. Elder Neal A. Maxwell stated, "Someday, when we look back on mortality, we will see that so many of the things that seemed to matter so much at the moment will be seen not to have mattered at all."[20]

Elder Maxwell reinforced this concept when he wrote:

> A mere hundred years from now today's seeming deprivations and tribulations will not matter unless we let them matter too much now! A thousand years from now, for instance, today's serious physical ailment will be but a fleeting memory. A million years from now, those who today worry and are anguished because they are unmarried will, if they are faithful, have smiles of satisfaction on their faces in the midst of a vast convocation of their posterity.[21]

President Ezra Taft Benson noted:

> We all have our difficulties, our problems. "Whom the Lord loveth He chasteneth." (Heb. 12:6.) It is in the depths that men and women learn the lessons that help to build strong men and women, not at the pinnacle of success. In the hour of a man's success is his greatest danger. It sometimes takes a reversal to make us appreciate our blessings and to develop us into strong, courageous characters. We can meet every reversal that can possibly come with the help of the Lord. Every reversal can be turned to our benefit and blessing and can make us stronger, more courageous, more godlike.[22]

Elder Maxwell has given us much wonderful counsel on dealing with adversity. "I believe with all my heart that because God loves us there are some particularized challenges that he will deliver to each of us," Elder Maxwell observed. "He will customize the curriculum for each of us in order to teach us the things we most need to know. He will set before us in life what we need; not always what we like. And this will require us to accept with all our hearts the truth that there is divine design in each of our lives and that we have rendezvous to keep, individually and collectively."[23]

Elder Maxwell added, "Trials and tribulations tend to squeeze the artificiality out of us, leaving the essence of what we really are and clarifying what we really yearn for."[24]

"A few individuals may appear to have no trials at all—which, if it were so, would be a trial in itself. If, as do trees, our souls had rings to measure the years of greatest personal growth, the wide rings would likely reflect the years of greatest moisture—but from tears, not rainfall."[25]

"God is a loving Father who wants us to have the happiness that results from proven righteousness, not from mere innocence. At times, he will not deflect life's harsh learning experiences that may come to each of us, even though he will help us cope with them."[26]

With the help of the Lord, we can deal with challenge and disappointment in marriage. Though our marriage may not be ideal, we must be true to the ideal of marriage. Elder Neal A. Maxwell explained:

> "Why is non-endurance a denial of the Lord? Because giving up is a denial of the Lord's loving capacity to see us through 'all these things'! Giving up suggests that God is less than He really is. . . . So much of life's curriculum consists of efforts by the Lord to get and keep our attention. Ironically, the stimuli He uses are often that which is seen by us as something to endure. Sometimes what we are being asked to endure is His 'help'—help to draw us away from the cares of the world; help to draw us away from self-centeredness; attention-getting help when the still, small voice has been ignored by us; help in the shaping of our souls; and help to keep the promises we made so long ago to Him and to ourselves. . . . Whether the afflictions are self-induced, as most of them are, or whether they are of the divine-tutorial type, it matters not. Either way, the Lord can help us so that our afflictions, said Alma, can be 'swallowed

up in the joy of Christ' (Alma 31:38). Thus, afflictions are endured and are overcome by joy. The sour notes are lost amid a symphony of salvational sounds. Our afflictions, brothers and sisters, may not be extinguished. Instead, they can be dwarfed and swallowed up in the joy of Christ. This is how we overcome most of the time—not the elimination of affliction, but the placing of these in that larger context."[27]

This larger context, this eternal perspective, can help us maintain our celestial bearings and endure mere mortal deprivations, as well as motivate us to create a marriage worthy of continuing into the eternities. "The greatest motivator that we have in the Church is to have Church members understand the plan of salvation," said Elder M. Russell Ballard.[28]

For the plan to be of most benefit to us, we must abide by eternal laws. "There is a law, irrevocably decreed in heaven before the foundations of this world, upon which all blessings are predicated—and when we obtain any blessing from God, it is by obedience to that law upon which it is predicated" (D&C 130:20–21). President Boyd K. Packer observed that "our destiny is not based on *chance*. It is based on *choice!* It was planned that way before the world was. It all works according to the plan, the great plan of happiness."[29]

President Packer also taught, "Without a knowledge of the gospel plan, transgression seems natural, innocent, even justified. There is no greater protection from the adversary than for us to know the truth, to know the plan!"[30]

Receipt of promised blessings is all contingent upon obedience to established laws. However, it is interesting to note that when we keep the plan of happiness in mind, eternal laws are easier to live because they make sense. Commandments are blessings; we discover this powerful truth often in the scriptures:

"Thou shalt keep therefore his statutes, and his commandments, which I command thee this day, that it may go well with thee" (Deuteronomy 4:40).

"For this is the love of God, that we keep his commandments: and his commandments are not grievous" (1 John 5:3).

"Yea, blessed are they whose feet stand upon the land of Zion, who have obeyed my gospel; for they shall receive for their reward the good things of the earth, and it shall bring forth in its strength. And they shall also be crowned with blessings from above, yea, and with commandments not a few, and with revelations in their time—they that are faithful and diligent before me" (D&C 59:3–4).

"And again, I say unto you, I give unto you a new commandment, that you may understand my will concerning you; Or, in other words, I give unto you directions how you may act before me, that it may turn to you for your salvation" (D&C 82:8–9).

It is significant that Alma observed, "God gave unto them commandments, *after* having made known unto them the plan of redemption" (Alma 12:32; emphasis added). Thus, knowledge of the plan makes it easier to abide by the stipulations.

However, the plan cannot compensate for lack of compliance. Elder Neal A. Maxwell observed, "The plan cannot bring true happiness to anyone whose life is grossly inconsistent with its standards."[31]

On another occasion, he stated, "How can we expect to enjoy eternally that which we neglect in mortality?"[32]

And Elder Richard G. Scott observed, "Obedience to the plan is a requisite for full happiness in this life and a continuation of eternal joy beyond the veil."[33]

If we are obedient to the plan, we are assured that the prospect of marriage blessings in eternity blesses marriages in the here-and-now. "One can assume that the longer the view a woman and man have regarding the marital relationship, the greater the probability of success," said Elder Merrill J. Bateman. "The divorce rate for temple marriage is well below that of civil marriages, and civil divorce rates are exceeded by separation rates for open marriages. A view of marriage and the family based on eternal principles increases the probability of success. When one takes the long view, one tries harder to be patient, long-suffering, kind, gentle, and meek. These characteristics, in turn, strengthen the marriage."[34]

Daniel K Judd, an associate professor at Brigham Young University, published research that shows Latter-day Saints have a much lower divorce rate than those belonging to other religions and those who claim no affiliation. His report notes that Brigham Young University Professor Tim Heaton and research analyst Kristen Goodman conducted a major research study that looked at divorce rates among Latter-day Saints living in the United States and Canada. Their review of the research on divorce and the results of their own study indicate that "the high divorce rate characterizing the United States does not appear to be endemic to any particular religion. Those with no religious preference, however, have by far the highest divorce rates: 39 percent of the men and 45 percent of the women have experienced at least one divorce. Mormons have the lowest percentage ever divorced with values of 14 for men and 19 for women." It is important to note that these numbers represent both active and inactive Latter-day Saints and those who were married outside of the temple as well as those with temple marriages.

Professor Judd points out that Heaton and Goodman report that "non-temple marriages are about five times more likely to end in divorce than are temple marriages. The divorce rate for Latter-day Saints who marry in the temple is 5.4 percent for men and 6.5 percent for women." Religious beliefs in general, and especially the beliefs and practices of the Church of Jesus Christ of Latter-day Saints, are a great blessing to the lives of people everywhere.[35]

Our belief that marriage lasts forever helps us make important marital decisions. Such decisions might include whether or not to marry, who to marry, where to marry, and other equally important questions affecting marriage and family. Elder M. Russell Ballard said:

> By focusing on and living the principles of Heavenly Father's plan for our eternal happiness, we can

separate ourselves from the wickedness of the world. If we are anchored to the correct understanding of who we are, why we are here on this earth, and where we can go after this mortal life, Satan cannot threaten our happiness through any form of temptation. If we are determined to live by Heavenly Father's plan, we will use our God-given moral agency to make decisions based on revealed truth, not on the opinions of others or on the current thinking of the world.[36]

President Spencer W. Kimball taught that "if we live in such a way that the considerations of eternity press upon us, we will make better decisions."[37] The value of eternal focus is also touted by Elder Maxwell:

We have a tendency to get ourselves caught in peering through the prism of the present and then distorting our perspective about things. Time is of this world; it is not of eternity. We can, if we are not careful, feel the pressures of time and see things in a distorted way. How important it is that we see things as much as possible through the lens of the gospel with its eternal perspectives. . . . *It is very important that we not assume the perspectives of mortality in making the decisions that bear on eternity! We need the perspective of the gospel to make decisions in the context of eternity!* We need to understand we cannot do the Lord's work in the world's way.[38]

Understanding the plan of happiness enables a couple to approach their marriage from a more spiritual perspective and higher level of commitment. Elder Dallin H. Oaks said it well: "The pure in heart have a distinctive way of looking at life. Their attitudes and desires cause them to view their experiences in terms of eternity. This eternal perspective affects their choices and priorities. As they draw farther from worldliness they feel closer to our Father in Heaven and more able to be guided by his Spirit. We call this state of mind, this quality of life, spirituality."[39]

When looking at the complete plan of salvation, we can see that this phase of mortality is crucial to all of eternity that follows. And in mortality, there is one pivotal ordinance—celestial marriage. Elder McConkie said:

> From the moment of birth into mortality to the time we are married in the temple, everything we have in the whole gospel system is to prepare and qualify us to enter that holy order of matrimony which makes us husband and wife in this life and in the world to come. Then from the moment we are sealed together by the power and authority of the holy priesthood . . . everything connected with revealed religion is designed to help us keep the terms and conditions of our marriage covenant, so that this covenant will have . . . force in the life to come. Thus celestial marriage is the crowning ordinance of the gospel, the . . . most important organization in time or in eternity. . . . We should have more interest in and concern for our families than for anything else in life. . . . There is nothing in this world as important as the creation and perfection of family units.[40]

Because the doctrine of eternal marriage is that critical, it demands our highest level of commitment. "I know of no more complete or important commitment, in time or in eternity, than marriage,"[41] said Elder Richard L. Evans. And Elder Dean L. Larsen observed:

> I am convinced that there is something so absolutely sacred in the eyes of the Lord about the marriage covenant that he expects us to devote every energy and resource in our power to make our marriages endure. For those who do, even in the face of great challenges and difficulties, I am certain there will be ultimate blessings realized that are beyond our present comprehension.[42]

That great marriages are built in the "face of great challenges and difficulties" is an awareness that each couple must recognize and humbly accept. Elder Neal A. Maxwell asked:

> How can you and I really expect to glide naively through life, as if to say, "Lord, give me experience, but not grief, not sorrow, not pain, not opposition, not betrayal, and certainly not to be forsaken. Keep from me, Lord, all those experiences that made Thee what Thou art! Then, let me come and dwell with Thee and fully share Thy joy!"[43]

To what end must we have these difficult experiences? President Boyd K. Packer answers us: "Marriage is not without trials of many kinds. These tests forge virtue and strength. The tempering that comes in marriage and family life produces men and women who will someday be exalted."[44]

President John Taylor quotes Joseph Smith, the Prophet, who said:

> You will have all kinds of trials to pass through. And it is quite as necessary for you to be tried as it was for Abraham and other men of God, and (said he) God will feel after you, and He will take hold of you and wrench your very heart strings, and if you cannot stand it you will not be fit for an inheritance in the Celestial Kingdom of God.[45]

Marriage joys and challenges are designed to temper, forge, and fit us to one day become like Heavenly Father and Heavenly Mother. There is no other way. Let us never lose sight of the ultimate end, and let us celebrate the process!

Notes

1. Cannon, in *Journal of Discourses*, 14:320.
2. McConkie, *Doctrinal New Testament Commentary*, 1:546.
3. Taylor, in *Journal of Discourses*, 24:229.

4. Perry, "They Will Not Endure Sound Doctrine," *Ensign*, November 1975, 131.

5. Young, *Discourses of Brigham Young*, 195.

6. Heber J. Grant, Anthony W. Ivins, Charles W. Nibley, in Clark, *Messages of the First Presidency*, 5:244.

7. McConkie, *Mormon Doctrine*, 613.

8. Pratt, *Key to the Science of Theology*, 169–70.

9. Smith, *Doctrines of Salvation*, 2:65.

10. Kimball, *The Miracle of Forgiveness*, 245.

11. Kimball, "Circles of Exaltation," in *Charge to Religious Educators*, 42.

12. Conference Report, Tonga Area Conference 1976, 34.

13. Snow, in *Journal of Discourses*, 19:270–71.

14. Snow, in *Deseret Evening News*, 27 March 1897, 9.

15. Cannon, *Gospel Truth*, 2:117.

16. Cannon, in *Journal of Discourses*, 14:321.

17. Talmage, *Articles of Faith*, 442–43.

18. Romney, "Scriptures As They Relate to Family Stability," *Ensign*, February 1972, 58.

19. Ballard, *Sermons and Missionary Services of Melvin J. Ballard*, 239–40.

20. Maxwell, *Even as I Am*, 104.

21. Maxwell, *We Will Prove Them Herewith*, 28.

22. Benson, *Teachings of Ezra Taft Benson*, 415.

23. Maxwell, *Neal A. Maxwell Quote Book*, 196.

24. Maxwell, *Things As They Really Are*, 89.

25. Maxwell, *If Thou Endure It Well*, 94.

26. Maxwell, *A Time to Choose*, 47.

27. Maxwell, *Wherefore, Ye Must Press Forward*, 112.

28. Ballard, "The Kingdom Rolls Forth in South America," *Ensign*, May 1986, 15.

29. Packer, "The Great Plan of Happiness," in *Charge to Religious Educators*, 116.

30. Packer, *Our Father's Plan*, 27.

31. Maxwell, "The Great Plan of the Eternal God," *Ensign*, May 1984, 22.

32. Maxwell, *If Thou Endure It Well*, 39.

33. Richard G. Scott, "The Joy of Living the Great Plan of Happiness," *Ensign*, November 1996, 73.

34. Bateman, *Eternal Family*, 115.

35. Religious Studies Center Newsletter, Brigham Young University, 14, no. 1 (September 1999).

36. Ballard, "Answers to Life's Questions," *Ensign*, May 1995, 24.

37. Kimball, *Teachings of Spencer W. Kimball*, 25.

38. Maxwell, *Neal A. Maxwell Quote Book*, 265.

39. Oaks, *Pure in Heart*, 111.

40. McConkie, in Conference Report, April 1970, 27.

41. Richard L. Evans, in Larsen, "Marriage and the Patriarchal Order," *Ensign*, September 1982, 13.

42. Larsen, "Marriage and the Patriarchal Order," *Ensign*, September 1982, 13.

43. Maxwell, "Lest Ye Be Wearied and Faint in Your Minds," *Ensign*, May 1991, 88.

44. Packer, "Marriage," *Ensign*, May 1981, 15.

45. Taylor, in *Journal of Discourses*, 24:197.

2

TEMPLE MARRIAGE AND
beyond

We believe in the eternal nature of the marriage relation, that man and woman are destined, as husband and wife, to dwell together eternally. We believe that we are organized as we are, with all these affections, with all this love for each other, for a definite purpose, something far more lasting than to be extinguished when death shall overtake us. We believe that when a man and a woman are united as husband and wife, and they love each other, their hearts and feelings are one, and that love is as enduring as eternity itself, and that when death overtakes them it will neither extinguish nor cool that love, but that it will brighten and kindle it to a purer flame, and that it will endure through eternity.[1]

This quotation by President George Q. Cannon represents a principle that members of The Church of Jesus Christ of Latter-day Saints are taught from infancy: marriage is good and honorable and should be solemnized in a temple. Such a marriage is intended not just till death do ye part, but to last into life after death, eternally. Elder Bruce R. McConkie declared, "There is not a single thing that any Latter-day Saint will ever do in this world that will compare in importance to marrying the right person, in the right place, by the right authority, because that order and system opens the door to peace and joy here and eternal exaltation hereafter."[2]

For a couple sealed together in temple marriage to reach their eternal potential, certain conditions must be met. President George Q. Cannon stated, "When men go forward and attend to other ordinances, such as receiving their endowments, their washings, their anointings, receiving the promises connected therewith, these promises will be fulfilled to the very letter in time and in eternity—that is, if they themselves are true to the conditions upon which the blessings are promised."[3]

This concept is consistent with a statement by Elder Marvin J. Ashton, "True love is a process. True love requires personal action. Love must be continuing to be real. Love takes time."[4]

Time and one other thing: a sealing ordinance in the temple of the Lord. President Joseph Fielding Smith said:

> If you want salvation in the fullest, that is exaltation in the kingdom of God, so that you may become his sons and his daughters, you have got to go into the temple of the Lord and receive these holy ordinances which belong to that house, which cannot be had elsewhere. No man shall receive the fulness of eternity, of exaltation, alone; no woman shall receive that blessing alone; but man and wife, when they receive the sealing power in the temple of the Lord, if they thereafter keep all the commandments, shall pass on to exaltation, and shall continue and become like the Lord.[5]

Elder John A. Widtsoe reiterated the importance of a temple sealing:

> In the temple, and only there, the bridal couple are

wedded for time and eternity. The contract is endless. Here and hereafter, on earth and beyond, they may travel together in loving companionship. This precious gift conforms to the Latter-day Saint belief that existence in the life after this may be active, useful, progressive. Love, content to end with death, is perishable, poor, and helpless. Marriage that lasts only during earth life is a sad one, for the love established between man and woman, as they live together and rear their family, should not die, but live and grow richer with the eternal years. True love hopes and prays for an endless continuation of association with the loved one. To those who are sealed to each other for all existence, love is ever warm, more hopeful, believing, courageous, and fearless. Such people live the richer, more joyful life. To them happiness and the making of it have no end: Dismal, dreary, full of fear, is the outlook upon love that ends with death.[6]

However, the sealing ceremony in the temple is not all there is to an eternal marriage. On numerous occasions, Elder McConkie taught that continued devotion and growth is required after the temple ceremony. "If righteous men have power through the gospel and its crowning ordinance of celestial marriage to become kings and priests to rule in exaltation forever," he said, "it follows that the women by their side (without whom they cannot attain exaltation) will be queens and priestesses (Revelations 1:6; 5:10). Exaltation grows out of the eternal union of a man and his wife."[7]

And on another occasion: "Marriages performed in the temples for time and eternity, by virtue of the sealing keys restored by Elijah, are called celestial marriages," Elder McConkie taught. "The participating parties become husband and wife in this mortal life, and if after their marriage they keep all the terms and conditions of this order of the priesthood, they continue on as husband and wife in the celestial kingdom of God."[8] Note that exaltation "grows out of the eternal union" and will be realized only "if after their marriage they keep all the terms and conditions" of the temple marriage covenant.

President Spencer W. Kimball expounded on this even more, saying, "Now, all Latter-day Saints are not going to be exalted. All people who have been through the holy temple are not going to be exalted. The Lord says, 'Few there be that find it.' For there are the two elements: (1) the sealing of a marriage in the holy temple, and (2) righteous living through one's life thereafter to make that sealing permanent. Only through proper marriage—and I repeat that—only through proper marriage can one find that strait way, the narrow path."[9]

Lest anyone think that merely getting married in the temple defines proper marriage, President Spencer W. Kimball also said, "Without proper and successful marriage, one will never be exalted."[10] Once a couple have found that path, they must then proceed down it until the journey is complete.

President Marion G. Romney expressed concern that married couples understand that more than a temple sealing is required. He stated:

> I am persuaded that we take too much for granted. We assume that because we are members of the Church, we shall receive as a matter of course all the blessings of the gospel. I have heard people contend that they have a claim upon them because they have been through the temple, even though they are not careful to keep the covenants they there made. I do not think this will be the case. . . . We might take a lesson from an account given by the Prophet of a vision of the resurrection, in which he records that one of the saddest things he had ever witnessed was the sorrow of members of the Church who came forth to a resurrection below that which they had taken for granted they would receive.[11]

As members of The Church of Jesus Christ of Latter-day Saints, we do all we can to motivate our young people to marry in the temple. However, we must be cautious that in so doing, we do not give the false impression that the temple is the destination. Temple marriage is not a final destination but part of the journey leading to something far more glorious. Certainly we can enjoy the journey; however, it is helpful to remember that after marriage in the temple, we are still striving for a oneness with Christ that is not endowed on our wedding day but must be developed. Our ultimate destination is expressed thus by President Joseph Smith:

> Here, then, is eternal life—to know the only wise and true God; and you have got to learn how to be Gods yourselves, and to be kings and priests to God, the same as all Gods have done before you, namely, by going from one small degree to another, and from a small capacity to a great one; from grace to grace, from exaltation to exaltation, until you attain to the resurrection of the dead, and are able to dwell in everlasting burnings, and to sit in glory, as do those who sit enthroned in everlasting power. . . . When you climb up a ladder, you must begin at the bottom, and ascend step by step, until you arrive at the top; and so it is with the principles of the Gospel—you must begin with the first, and go on until you learn all the principles of exaltation.[12]

To marry in the temple is a wonderful step toward the ultimate goal of creating a celestial marriage. However, there are additional steps yet to be taken. The needed ascent is not accomplished with a quantum leap, but by "going from one small degree to another, and from a small capacity to a great one." We appreciate each rung on the ladder, but we cannot stop climbing. There are marvelous plateaus and vistas yet to be experienced, and the ascent must continue.

Perhaps this story will illustrate a possible misconception: A young friend of mine, still growing in her gospel knowledge and experience, once asked me to settle an argument between her and her visiting foster mother. The foster parents had been married in the temple, but the marriage ended in divorce. The estranged parents were not on good speaking terms, but my friend contended that they would still have to live together in the next life because they had been sealed in the temple.

At that point I had the impression that the daughter's inaccurate understanding of sealed was more like chained. The daughter did not yet understand that temple marriage makes an eternal family possible but does not guarantee it. Certainly temple marriage will not be used as a weapon for inflicting punishment upon those who no longer want to be married or who no longer merit that privilege.

With divorce being quite common these days, many wonder how this dissolution of vows affects having been sealed in the temple. Wilford Woodruff wrote in his journal:

> In speaking of giving divorces (Brigham) said [that] when he sealed a woman to a man he asked nothing for it but if they asked for a divorce I charge him $10 for his folly for it is no better than a piece of white paper. For when I seal a woman to a man it takes a higher power than I am to take her away. Some women say I do not want to live with my husband in eternity. They need not trouble themselves about it for she will not be troubled with him in eternity unless he keeps the commandments of God and if he goes to the celestial kingdom and she is not worthy of it, she will not be troubled with him for she will not go there.[13]

We must always remember that temple blessings are contingent upon our faithfulness in keeping the commandments and available only through the grace of Christ; these two things qualify us to live in exaltation. Only individuals meeting these requirements need worry about who was sealed to whom. We would all do well to spend less time worrying about others and more time repenting so that we might qualify for exaltation. Such attitude and behavior will most likely help transform us into more loving, and more lovable, partners, and thus more likely to be someone that our spouse would want to be with eternally.

"An eternal bond doesn't just happen as a result of sealing covenants we make in the temple," noted Elder Robert D. Hales. "How we conduct ourselves in this life will determine what we will be in all the eternities to come. To receive the blessings of the sealing that our Heavenly Father has given to us, we have to keep the commandments and conduct ourselves in such a way that our families will want to live with us in the eternities."[14]

Marriages performed in the temple can be eternal, but initially they are conditional. What we do after leaving the sacred temple determines the ultimate status of our marriage. President Joseph Fielding Smith explained:

> The Holy Spirit of Promise is the Holy Ghost who places the stamp of approval upon every ordinance: baptism confirmation, ordination, marriage. The promise is that the blessings will be received through faithfulness. . . . If a person violates a covenant, whether it be baptism, ordination, marriage or anything else, the Spirit withdraws the stamp of approval, and the blessings will not be received. . . . Every ordinance is sealed with a promise of a reward based upon faithfulness. The Holy Spirit withdraws the stamp of approval where covenants are broken.[15]

Elder McConkie defined the Holy Spirit of Promise for us:

> The Holy Spirit of Promise is the Holy Spirit promised the saints, or in other words, the Holy Ghost. This name-title is used in connection with the sealing and ratifying power of the Holy Ghost, that is, the power given him to ratify and approve the righteous acts of men so that those acts will be binding on earth and in heaven. . . .
>
> To seal is to ratify, to justify, or to approve. Thus an act which is sealed by the Holy Spirit of Promise is one which is ratified by the Holy Ghost; it is one which is approved by the Lord; and the person who has taken

the obligation upon himself is justified by the Spirit in the thing he has done. . . .

The ratifying seal of approval is put upon an act only if those entering the contract are worthy as a result of personal righteousness to receive the divine approbation. They "are sealed by the Holy Spirit of promise, which the Father sheds forth upon all those who are just and true" (D&C 76:53). If they are not just and true and worthy the ratifying seal is withheld. . . .

When any ordinance or contract is sealed by the Spirit, it is approved with a promise of reward, provided unrighteousness does not thereafter break the seal, remove the ratifying approval, and cause loss of the promised blessing. . . . Seals are placed on contracts through righteousness. . . . Thus if both parties are "just and true," if they are worthy, a ratifying seal is placed on their temple marriage; if they are unworthy, they are not justified by the Spirit and the ratification of the Holy Ghost is withheld. Subsequent worthiness will put the seal in force, and unrighteousness will break any seal.[16]

Breaking that seal is, of course, cause for considerable concern. Elder Matthew Cowley noted, "We men of the priesthood who have knelt at the sacred altar and on that altar clasped the hand of a sainted companion and have entered an eternal triangle, not a companionship of two, but of three—the husband, the wife, and God—the most sacred triangle man and woman can become a part of. But my heart sinks in despair when I witness so many who have and are withdrawing that hand from one another. They don't do that until they first divorce God from that triangle, and after divorcing God, it is practically impossible for them to stay together side by side."[17]

An equilateral triangle is a good illustration of the relationship between God, a husband, and a wife. As the husband draws closer to God, he automatically draws closer to his wife. As the wife draws closer to God, she automatically draws closer to her husband. The more the two become one with God, the more they become one with each other.

A couple wanting their temple marriage to be ratified would keep all the basic commandments—and more! "Therefore not leaving the principles of the doctrine of Christ, let us go on unto perfection; not laying again the foundation of repentance from dead works, and of faith toward God. Of the doctrine of baptisms, of laying on of hands, and of the resurrection of the dead, and of eternal judgment. And we will go on unto perfection if God permit" (JST, Hebrews 6:1–3).

Beyond these foundation doctrines, the couple must "go on unto perfection." This ongoing process toward perfection is explained by the Apostle Paul: "Though I speak with the tongues of men and of angels, and have not charity, I am become as sounding brass, or a tinkling cymbal,

"And though I have the gift of prophecy, and understand all mysteries, and all knowledge; and though I have all faith, so that I could remove mountains, and have not charity, I am nothing.

"And though I bestow all my goods to feed the poor, and though I give my body to be burned, and have not charity, it profiteth me nothing" (1 Corinthians 13:1–3). Thus we see that the ultimate attribute to be developed in marriage, as in all things, is charity, the pure love of Christ.

Moroni also taught that if a man "have not charity he is nothing; wherefore he must needs have charity.

"And charity suffereth long, and is kind, and envieth not, and is not puffed up, seeketh not her own, is not easily provoked, thinketh no evil, and rejoiceth not in iniquity but rejoiceth in the truth, beareth all things, believeth all things, hopeth all things, endureth all things.

"Wherefore, my beloved brethren, if ye have not charity, ye are nothing, for charity never faileth. Wherefore, cleave unto charity, which is the greatest of all, for all things must fail—

"But charity is the pure love of Christ, and it endureth forever, and whoso is found possessed of it at the last day, it shall be well with him.

"Wherefore, my beloved brethren, pray unto the Father with all the energy of heart, that ye may be filled with this love, which he hath bestowed upon all who are true followers of his Son, Jesus Christ; that ye may become the sons of God; that when he shall appear we shall be like him, for we shall see him as he is; that we may have this hope; that we may be purified even as he is pure" (Moroni 7:44–48).

Thus, the scriptures provide us with a list of Christlike attributes sufficient to keep any couple busy for many decades following their marriage in the temple.

For that radiant couple just leaving the temple, it may seem senseless to suggest that their greatest need is to develop more love! At that moment, they most likely feel overflowing to the brim with love and could not imagine any lack. We celebrate with them and rejoice in their love. However, we also know that as they are tutored by God who "is love" (1 John 4:8), they can develop capacities to love far more, and far more purely. The Savior commanded his disciples "that ye love one another, as I have loved you. Greater love hath no man than this, that a man lay down his life for his friends" (John 15:12–13). Note that this pure love of Christ is one of giving, even to point of giving one's life if necessary.

Similarly, Elder McConkie noted that "baptism is the gate to the celestial kingdom; celestial marriage is the gate to an exaltation in the highest heaven within the celestial world (D&C 131:1–4). To gain salvation after baptism; it is necessary to keep the commandments of God and endure to the end (2 Nephi 13:17–21); to gain exaltation after celestial marriage the same continued devotion and righteousness is required."[18]

Likewise, Elder Richard G. Scott said, "After you have received all of the temple ordinances, you will continue to grow by keeping the covenants made and faithfully 'endure to the end.'"[19]

Certainly, Church leaders agree that marriage takes work. Elder Dean L. Larsen wrote, "Marriage is not an easy venture. It is largely a one-time through, do-it-yourself project for the husband and wife. I repeatedly encounter the illusion today, especially among younger people, that perfect marriages happen simply if the right two people come together. This is untrue. Marriages don't succeed automatically. Those who build happy, secure, successful marriages pay the price to do so. They work at it constantly."[20]

It is no small accomplishment to worthily marry the right person in the temple. But that is an event, and after that significant event, the process of marriage requires additional daily investments be made to create a celestial marriage. After a temple marriage, a couple must work on keeping their covenants, going from the "justification" of the ordinance toward the "sanctification" of overcoming pride and selfishness. Temple marriage is not a graduation ceremony; it is the entrance into the celestial marriage process.

Certainly, it is critical to get married in the temple. It is equally important to return to the temple to do vicarious work for others. While performing this service, we can review our own covenants and more fully grasp the vision of our own potential. Said Elder F. Enzio Busche, "The temple is the only 'university' for men to prepare spiritually for their graduation to eternal life."[21] Arthur Henry King observed that "only through regular temple work can a marriage be sanctified and become an eternal partnership on this earth."[22]

Elder J. Ballard Washburn worded it succinctly: "We go to the temple to make covenants, but we go home to keep the covenants that we have made. The home is the testing ground. The home is the place where we learn to be more Christlike. The home is the place where we learn to overcome selfishness and give ourselves in service to others."[23]

It may not be till after the temple sealing that the couple becomes aware of the areas of their lives that need changing before they can develop a marriage worthy of becoming eternal. But the realizations will come. President Spencer W. Kimball observed:

> Two people coming from different backgrounds soon learn after the ceremony is performed that stark reality must be faced. There is no longer a life of fantasy or of make-believe; we must come out of the clouds and

put our feet firmly on the earth. Responsibility must be assumed and new duties must be accepted. Some personal freedoms must be relinquished and many adjustments, unselfish adjustments, must be made. . . . One comes to realize very soon after the marriage that the spouse has weaknesses not previously revealed or discovered. The virtues which were constantly magnified during courtship now grow relatively smaller, and the weaknesses which seemed so small and insignificant during courtship now grow to sizable proportions.

The hour has come for understanding hearts, for self-appraisal, and for good common sense, reasoning, and planning. The habits of years now show themselves; the spouse may be stingy or prodigal, lazy or industrious, devout or irreligious, may be kind and cooperative or petulant and cross, demanding or giving, egotistical or self-effacing. The in-law problems comes closer into focus, and the relationships of the spouses to them is again magnified.[24]

True, much must be done after getting married in the temple. But it is also true that a couple who have taken this righteous first step have every right to expect their marriage to get even better as they mature and develop capacities beyond what they started with as newlyweds. Marriage is not for enduring, but for growing, for developing, for edification, for becoming—becoming a celestial marriage.

President Harold B. Lee said:

Those who go to the marriage altar with love in their hearts, we might say to them in truth, if they will be true to the covenants that they take in the temple, fifty years after their marriage they can say to each another; "We must have not known what true love was when we were married, because we think so much more of each other today!" And so it will be if they will follow the counsel of their leaders and obey the holy, sacred instructions given in the temple ceremony; they will grow more perfectly in love even to a fullness of love in the presence of the Lord Himself.[25]

President Gordon B. Hinckley has also painted a word picture for us of a temple marriage growing into a celestial marriage. He said:

> How beautiful is the marriage of a young man and a young woman who begin their lives together kneeling at the altar in the house of the Lord, pledging their love and loyalty one to another for time and all eternity. When children come into that home, they are nurtured and cared for, loved and blessed with the feeling that their father loves their mother. In that environment they find peace and strength and security. Watching their father, they develop respect for women. They are taught self-control and self-discipline, which bring the strength to avoid later tragedy. . . .
>
> The years pass. The children eventually leave the home, one by one. And the father and the mother are again alone. But they have each other to talk with, to depend on, to nurture, to encourage, and to bless. There comes the autumn of life and a looking back with satisfaction and gladness. Through all of the years there has been loyalty, one to the other. There has been deference and courtesy. Now there is a certain mellowness, a softening, an effect that partakes of a hallowed relationship. They realize that death may come anytime, usually to one first with a separation of a season brief or lengthy. But they know also that because their companionship was sealed under the authority of the eternal priesthood and they have lived worthy of the blessings, there will be a reunion sweet and certain.[26]

When a couple is married in the temple, it is as if the ordinance worker celebrates their newly married status by handing them an empty canning jar.[27] The couple are then challenged to go home, enter the real world outside of the temple, and begin to collect fruit. The fruit includes learning to be selfless, couple prayer, family prayer, scripture reading and family scripture reading, tithing, service, developing, repenting, forgiving, patience, cheerfulness, kindness, endurance, faith, commitment, adaptability, thrift, compassion, joy and rejoicing in posterity, and so forth. This process takes decades or even longer, into life after mortal death. But eventually the striving couple achieves sanctification individually and as a partnership. Through the grace of Christ, they have created a celestial marriage.

Now that the canning jar is filled to overflowing, there is definitely something to preserve. Now the Holy Spirit of Promise can truly seal that marriage by the priesthood keys restored by Elijah. Now that promised ordination to King and Queen can take place. What began as a temple marriage is now a celestial marriage, an eternal marriage.

"In a manner of speaking we have, here and now, probationary families even though we have been married in the temple, because our marriage in the temple is conditional," said Elder McConkie. "It is conditioned upon our subsequent compliance with the laws, the terms, the conditions of the covenant that we then make. And so when I get married in the temple, I am put in a position where I can strive and labor and learn to love my wife with the perfection that must exist if I am going to have a fulness of the glory that attends this covenant in eternity, and it puts her in a position to learn to love me in the same way."[27]

Notes

1. Cannon, in *Journal of Discourses*, 14:320–21.

2. McConkie, "The New and Everlasting Covenant of Marriage," in *Brigham Young University Speeches of the Year*, 20 April 1960, 7.

3. Cannon, in *Journal of Discourses* 26:249.

4. Ashton, "Love Takes Time," *Ensign*, November 1975, 108.

5. Smith, *Doctrines of Salvation*, 2:43–44, 58.

6. Widtsoe, *Evidences and Reconciliations*, 297–301.

7. McConkie, *Mormon Doctrine*, 613.

8. McConkie, *Mormon Doctrine*, 117.

9. Kimball, "Marriage Is Honorable," in *Brigham Young University Speeches of the Year, 1972–73*, 265–66.

10. Kimball, *Marriage and Divorce*, 24.

11. Romney, in Conference Report, October 1949, 43.

12. Smith, *Teachings of the Prophet Joseph Smith*, 346–48.

13. Woodruff, *Wilford Woodruff's Journal*, 1833–1898.

14. Hales, "The Eternal Family," *Ensign*, November 1996, 65.

15. Smith, *Doctrines of Salvation*, 1:45

16. McConkie, *Mormon Doctrine*, 361–62.

17. Cowley, in Conference Report, October 1952, 27.

18. McConkie, *Mormon Doctrine*, 118.

19. Scott, "Jesus Christ, Our Redeemer," *Ensign*, May 1997, 54.

20. Larsen, "Enriching Marriage," *Ensign*, March 1985, 20.

21. Busche, "University for Eternal Life," *Ensign*, May 1989, 71.

22. King, "A Testimony of My Conversion," *New Era*, February 1971, 34.

23. Washburn, "The Temple Is a Family Affair," *Ensign*, May 1995, 12.

24. Kimball, *Teachings of Spencer W. Kimball*, 305.

25. Smith, *Teachings*, 243.

26. Hinckley, "Our Solemn Responsibilities," *Ensign*, November 1991, 52.

27. Wilcox, *House of Glory*, 74.

28. McConkie, "How Do I Love Thee?" in *Brigham Young University Devotional Speeches of the Year, 1977*, 173.

3

SERVICE: THE FOUNDATION OF
celestial marriage

Janice had always wanted to be a nurse. She dreamed of it and prepared academically for it, knowing that in this career she would find self-fulfillment and self-esteem. However, while at college she fell in love and married. Soon she was "with child," and she and her husband decided that she would temporarily forego her career goal and stay home to nurture their little family.

Years passed, and the opportunity to earn her nursing degree never again materialized. Though Janice longed to complete her education, she chose a higher path of raising her thirteen children (and husband!). However, over the ensuing years, her circumstances led her into an in-depth study of nutrition for pregnant mothers and growing children, emergency first-aid treatment, pediatric care, foster-parent training, and the hormonal needs of women of all ages. Through all of this, she found little time to dedicate to self-pursuits; what little free time Janice had, she dedicated to genealogical research—and seemed energized by giving this service.

Even in her golden years, Janice continues to nurture her children and grandchildren (and husband!); she also frequently responds to the requests of various individuals desperately suffering from medical, emotional, nutritional, hormonal, or marital problems.

Janice rarely thinks of her long-ago dreams of becoming a nurse; she is simply too busy caring for others. In rare moments of quiet contemplation, she feels a deep contentment and wonders how she would ever have had enough time to be the nurse she thought she once wanted to be. By placing others ahead of herself, she has done more than she could have ever done by focusing on herself. In fact, she has found self-fulfilment through not seeking it.

In contrast, venture into the self-help section of a bookstore and notice the sea of books. Taking care of self first seems to be a very marketable product. However, since the enormous number of self-esteem lessons and self-help books have not produced the advertised results of happiness and peace, we need to ask some questions: Does focusing on self truly make a person happier? If praise from others and self-congratulations are good, why do their effects seem so short-lived? Why is self-esteem such a high-maintenance commodity?

In truth, the pursuit of self-esteem does not result in enhanced self-esteem and certainly does not strengthen a marriage. So what does?

As always, the scriptures provide insight and guidance. In the council in heaven, Satan exposes his self-centeredness by saying, "Behold, here am I, send me, I will be thy son, and I will redeem all mankind, that one soul shall not be lost, and surely I will do it; wherefore give me thine honor" (Moses 4:1). It would take incredible creative effort to make more references to oneself in only one sentence. Satan seems to see life through a pair of self-esteem glasses that have mirrors in place of lenses.

In that same premortal council, the Savior says, "Father, thy will be done, and the glory be thine forever" (Moses 4:2). In the Savior's mortal life and Atonement, we see numerous evidences that Jesus truly did place God and others before Himself. While few would refute this, we might fail to emulate it by thinking,

"Yes, but I must love myself first; then I can better serve God and others. Besides, isn't there some scripture that says I must come first?"

Most likely the person trying to justify such self-focus has a vague recollection of Matthew 22:35–40. The setting is the egotistical Pharisees trying to trap Christ in a then-popular debate. "Then one of them, which was a lawyer, asked him a question, tempting him and saying, Master which is the great commandment in the law? Jesus said unto him, Thou shalt love the Lord thy God with all thy heart, and with all thy soul, and with all thy mind. This is the first and great commandment. And the second is like unto it, Thou shalt love thy neighbor as thyself. On these two hang all the law and the prophets."

Too often, the two commandments mentioned by the Lord are given but passing notice, and the self-esteem lecturer gives almost an entire lesson on the "as thyself" phrase. However, this is not a commandment to love yourself first but a chastisement of the Pharisees who were already guilty of that sin! They loved themselves first and, therefore, had little room in their hearts for others, even God.

On another occasion Jesus "spake this parable unto certain which trusted in themselves that they were righteous, and despised others: Two men went up into the temple to pray; the one a Pharisee, and the other a publican. The Pharisee stood and prayed thus with himself, God, I thank thee, that I am not as other men are, extortioners, unjust, adulterers, or even as this publican. I fast twice in the week, I give tithes of all that I possess. And the publican, standing afar off, would not lift up so much as his eyes unto heaven, but smote upon his breast, saying, God be merciful to me a sinner. I tell you, this man went down to his house justified rather than the other: for every one that exalteth himself shall be abased; and he that humbleth himself shall be exalted" (Luke 18:9–14).

To the more spiritually mature disciples, the Lord said, "A new commandment I give unto you, that ye love one another; as I have loved you, that ye also love one another" (John 13:34).

John further taught, "Beloved, let us love one another: for love is of God; and every one that loveth is born of God, and knoweth God. He that loveth not knoweth not God; for God is love. . . . And this commandment have we from him, That he who loveth God love his brother also" (1 John 4:7–8, 21).

Paul cautioned, "I beseech you therefore, brethren, by the mercies of God, that ye present your bodies a living sacrifice, holy, acceptable unto God, which *is* your reasonable service. And be not conformed to this world: but be ye transformed by the renewing of your mind, that ye may prove what *is* that good, and acceptable, and perfect, will of God. For I say, through the grace given unto me, to every man that is among you, not to think of himself more highly than he ought to think; but to think soberly, according as God hath dealt to every man the measure of faith" (Romans 12:1–3).

On another occasion, Paul said, "Let nothing be done through strife or vainglory; but in lowliness of mind let each esteem other better than themselves" (Philippians 2:3). He also warned that "in the last days perilous times shall come. For men shall be lovers of their own selves" (2 Timothy 3:1–2).

Regardless of good intentions, it may be that self-esteem gurus in our day have not only fulfilled this prophecy but have also even made people feel worse about themselves. Individuals blinded by a myopic vision are not helped by glasses that have mirrors instead of lenses. Spouses focused on self have a hard time thinking of their mates and wonder why the relationship is not more self-fulfilling.

President Ezra Taft Benson observed that "selfishness is one of the more common faces of pride. 'How everything affects me' is the center of all that matters—self-conceit, self-pity, worldly self-fulfillment, self-gratification, and self-seeking."[1] Notice that the common denominator among all these signs of pride is a focus on self.

But what if one of the individuals in a marriage suffers from low self-esteem? Isn't the solution to focus on self until those feelings of inadequacy and discouragement disappear? In her book *Confronting the Myth of Self-Esteem*, Ester Rasband points out that "self-love is not the antidote for self-condemnation. It is simply the opposite manifestation of the same spiritual disease; self-consciousness. Self-hatred, as a matter of fact, is the most intense form of self-love because it is total self-absorption, total preoccupation with seeking our own comfort. . . . It is still as true as it ever was that we must lose ourselves to find ourselves. There is no 'I' in peace."[2]

Daniel K Judd observed:

> The adversary's philosophy is one of deception. Whatever gospel truth is being taught, he provides both its opposite and its counterfeit. Personally, I have come to believe "high self-image" is the adversary's counterfeit of what the scriptures describe as "confidence" and is the opposite of meekness. "Low self-image" is the adversary's counterfeit of meekness and is the opposite of confidence. Having a "high self-image" or a "low self-image" is generally based upon the prideful presence or absence of things temporal, such as physical appearance (1 Samuel 16:7), wealth (Proverbs 13:7), and learning (2 Nephi 9:28). Godly confidence is a spiritual gift that develops from recognizing our own nothingness (Mosiah 4:5; Moses 1:10). If we do the will of our Father in heaven, our "confidence" shall "wax strong." (D&C 121:45)[3]

James E. Faulconer similarly stated:

> A poor self-image—like every self-image including a good one—is selfish. To be selfish is, by definition, to be self-centered, to place oneself at the center of things. But to be concerned about self-image—good or bad—is also to place oneself at the center; it is to act contrary to the admonition given in Doctrine and Covenants 4:1, 2, and 5: "Now behold, a marvelous work is about to come forth among the children of men. Therefore, O ye that embark in the service of

God, see that ye serve him with all your heart, might, mind and strength, that ye may stand blameless before God at the last day. . . . And faith, hope, charity and love, with an eye single to the glory of God, qualify him for the work."⁴

President Gordon B. Hinckley observed:

He who lives only unto himself withers and dies, while he who forgets himself in the service of others grows and blossoms in this life and in eternity. . . . For, generally speaking, the most miserable people I know are those who are obsessed with themselves; the happiest people I know are those who lose themselves in the service of others. . . . By and large, I have come to see that if we complain about life, it is because we are thinking only of ourselves. . . . The most effective medicine for the sickness of self-pity is to lose ourselves in the service of others. . . . My plea is—if we want joy in our hearts, if we want the Spirit of the Lord in our lives, let us forget ourselves and reach out. Let us put in the background our own personal, selfish interests and reach out in service to others. In so doing, we will find the truth of the Master's great promise of glad tidings: "Whosoever will save his life, shall lose it; or whosoever will save his life, shall be willing to lay it down for my sake; and if he is not willing to lay it down for my sake, he shall lose it. But whosoever shall be willing to lose his life for my sake, and the gospel, the same shall save it" (JST, Mark: 8:37–38).⁵

This so greatly contradicts the philosophies of men that it is called the Christian Paradox. Nonetheless, it is true and the great secret to personal happiness and a celestial marriage. We would do well to heed the Prophet Joseph Smith's counsel: "Let every selfish feeling be not only buried, but annihilated; and let love to God and man predominate, and reign triumphant in every mind, that their hearts may become like unto Enoch's of old."⁶

In his teachings, President Spencer W. Kimball observed that "we did not come on earth to love ourselves."[7]

Similarly, President Ezra Taft Benson taught:

> "Thou shalt love thy wife with all thy heart, and shalt cleave unto her and none else" (D&C 42:22). To my knowledge there is only one other thing in all scripture that we are commanded to love with all our hearts, and that is God Himself. Think what that means!
>
> This kind of love can be shown for your wives in so many ways. First and foremost, nothing except God Himself takes priority over your wife in your life—not work, not recreation, not hobbies. Your wife is your precious, eternal helpmate—your companion.
>
> What does it mean to love someone with all your heart? It means to love with all your emotional feelings and with all your devotion. Surely when you love your wife with all your heart, you cannot demean her, criticize her, find fault with her, or abuse her by words, sullen behavior, or actions.
>
> What does it mean to "cleave unto her"? It means to stay close to her, to be loyal and faithful to her, to communicate with her, and to express your love for her.
>
> Love means being sensitive to her feelings and needs. She wants to be noticed and treasured. She wants to be told that you view her as lovely and attractive and important to you. . . .
>
> You should be grateful that she is the mother of your children and the queen of your home, grateful that she has chosen . . . to bear, to nourish, to love, and to train your children—as the noblest calling of all. . . .
>
> Flowers on special occasions are wonderful, but so is your willingness to help with the dishes, change diapers, get up with a crying child in the night, and leave the television or newspaper to help with the

dinner. Those are the quiet ways we say "I love you" with our actions. They bring rich dividends for such little effort.[8]

The prophets teach that in order to grow, to expand, we must forget ourselves. In contrast, today's pop-psychology theme of putting oneself first may actually be self-diminishing, a self-absorbed atrophy. As Elder Maxwell observed, "Each spasm of selfishness narrows the universe that much more by shutting down our awareness of others and by making us more and more alone."[9]

The happiness and peace that we desire in our marriages are achievable. But they can only be obtained by seeking them in the Lord's way. President Benson counseled:

> Would we not do well to have the pleasing of God as our motive, rather than to try to elevate ourselves above our brother and outdo another? . . . The proud depend upon the world to tell them whether they have value or not. Their self-esteem is determined by where they are judged to be on the ladders of worldly success. They feel worthwhile as individuals if the numbers beneath them in achievement, talent, beauty, or intellect are large enough. Pride is ugly. It says: "If you succeed, I am a failure." If we love God, do His will, and fear His judgment more than men's, we will have self-esteem. Pride is a damning sin, in a true sense of the word: it limits or stops progression.[10]

Korihor exemplifies the extreme example of focus and reliance upon self-esteem. He taught that "every man fared in this life according to the management of the creature; therefore every man prospered according to his genius, and that every man conquered according to his strength" (Alma 30:17). Korihor focused on self-esteem to the point of even rejecting Christ and His Atonement!

We would do better to remember the words of Jacob, who said

"there is no flesh that can dwell in the presence of God, save it be through the merits, and mercy, and grace of the Holy Messiah" (2 Nephi 2:8).

Even a casual study of the Sermon on the Mount reveals an emphasis on good works and an absence of focus on self-image or even positive self mantras. We are not to tell ourselves that we are good, we are to be good. To be blessed (happy), we must love God, serve others, and forget ourselves. Paul warned that "the time will come when they will not endure sound doctrine; but after their own lusts shall they heap to themselves teachers, having itching ears; and they shall turn away their ears from the truth, and shall be turned unto fables" (2 Timothy 4:3–4). It is a fable to believe that seeking self-esteem will better prepare us to love God and our neighbors.

Nephi foresaw a day of great wickedness in which "they have all gone astray save it be a few, who are the humble followers of Christ; nevertheless, they are led, that in many instances they do err because they are taught by the precepts of men" (2 Nephi 28:14). Humble discipleship is the only safe route.

Nephi warned that "cursed is he that putteth his trust in man, or maketh flesh his arm, or shall hearken unto the precepts of men" (2 Nephi 28:31). Believing primarily in oneself is a form of "putting [our] trust in man."

A true disciple believes primarily in Christ. Elder Theodore Tuttle explained it this way: "We're not going to survive in this world, temporally or spiritually, without increased faith in the Lord—and I don't mean a positive mental attitude—I mean downright solid faith in the Lord Jesus Christ. That is the one thing that gives vitality and power to otherwise rather weak individuals."[11]

Consider carefully what Nephi says:

"And now, my beloved brethren, after ye have gotten into this strait and narrow path, I would ask if all is done? Behold, I say unto you, Nay; for ye have not come thus far save it were by the word of Christ with unshaken faith in him, relying wholly upon the merits of him who is mighty to save.

"Wherefore, ye must press forward with a steadfastness in Christ, having a perfect brightness of hope, and a love of God and of all men. Wherefore, if ye shall press forward, feasting upon the word of Christ, and endure to the end, behold, thus saith the Father: ye shall have eternal life. And now, behold, my beloved brethren, this is the way; and there is none other way nor name given under heaven whereby man can be saved in the kingdom of God. . . . And now, behold, this is the doctrine of Christ" (2 Nephi 31:19–21).

In a devotional address at Brigham Young University, BYU professor M. Catherine Thomas questioned the value of today's obsessive pursuit of self-esteem. She suggests it is a misguided effort to correct our disease with our spiritual shortcomings. She said:

> Like Adam and Eve, we feel our self-consciousness or spiritual nakedness. The scriptures teach about this nakedness as a feeling of guilt or shame (see 2 Nephi 9:14, Mormon 9:5). . . . Is it possible that in our efforts to find security, we have fallen into a number of errors? Is it possible that we have created the whole issue of self-esteem in an attempt to soothe this fallen, home-sick self? . . .
>
> I suggest that at the base of much low self-esteem lies not only spiritual conflict but a deep self-disap-proval, whether conscious or not, over neglect of the spiritual laws that govern happiness and freedom. . . . But the pursuit of self-esteem will not solve the prob-lems of the self that is in conflict because of sin. It will not even solve the problems of those who suffer from others' sins against them. . . .
>
> Have you noticed that the pursuit of self-esteem seems to produce anxiety, whereas increasing humility and faith in the Lord produces consolation and rest? . . . Now, I ask you, as various doors open and close, as the Lord Jesus Christ orchestrates even the details of our lives, where is the need to pursue self-esteem? We

don't need it. Faith in the Lord Jesus Christ will take us farther. . . . I have become aware of how demanding of attention the self is. What a lot of prayer and deliberate living it will take for me to remove my self as the force in my life. I have become aware that all my sins rise out of the self-absorption of my heart—impulses rising like the ticking of a clock in their persistent quest for self-promotion, self-defense, and self-gratification. It seems as though a change is needed at the very fountain of my heart out of which all thought and emotion rise. Could I actually come to the point where I could act without calculating my own self-interest all the time? Could I really live my daily life so that I was constantly searching out the Lord's will and drawing down his grace to accomplish it? . . .

I propose that self-esteem becomes a nonissue for the person who is perfecting his faith in the Lord Jesus Christ. . . . So many issues that revolve around the subject of self fade like the dew in the sun as one cultivates faith in the Savior. Without him, nothing else matters. No amount of self-esteem or anything else can adequately fill the void. . . . One who practices faith in the Lord Jesus Christ will find relief from the stresses and anxieties of the pursuit of self-esteem.[12]

Taking the focus off self and onto Christ and our spouse seems to be the great mystery mentioned by Paul as he counseled husbands to "love your wives, even as Christ also loved the Church, and gave himself for it; . . . so ought men to love their wives as their own bodies. He that loveth his wife loveth himself" (Ephesians 5:25, 28).

Notice, *self* is to be given away. Said Elder Joseph B. Wirthlin:

Stated simply, charity means subordinating our interests and needs to those of others, as the Savior has done for all of us. The Apostle Paul wrote that of faith, hope, and charity, "the greatest of these is charity" (1 Corinthians 13:13), and Moroni wrote that "except

ye have charity ye can in nowise be saved in the kingdom of God" (Moroni 12:21). I believe that selfless
service is a distinctive part of the gospel.[13]

Realizing that we are totally dependent upon Christ is humbling but in no way humiliating. C. S. Lewis offers a number of
insights that help put things in proper perspective:

> If you really get into any kind of touch with Him
> you will, in fact, be humble—delightedly humble,
> feeling the infinite relief of having for once got rid of
> all the silly nonsense about your own dignity which
> has made you restless and unhappy all your life. He
> is trying to make you humble in order to make this
> moment possible.[14]

Lewis also wrote:

> Until you have given up your self to Him you will
> not have a real self. Sameness is to be found most
> among the most "natural" men, not among those who
> surrender to Christ. How monotonously alike all the
> great tyrants and conquerors have been: how glori-
> ously different are the saints. . . . The very first step
> is to try to forget about the self altogether. Your real,
> new self (which is Christ's and also yours, and yours
> just because it is His) will not come as long as you are
> looking for it. It will come when you are looking for
> Him. . . . Nothing that you have not given away will
> ever be really yours. Nothing in you that has not died
> will ever be raised from the dead. Look for yourself,
> and you will find in the long run only hatred, loneli-
> ness, despair, rage, ruin, and decay. But look for Christ
> and you will find Him, and with Him everything else
> thrown in.[15]

Yet again, this insightful author commented:

> In God you come up against something which is

in every respect immeasurably superior to yourself. Unless you know God as that—and therefore, know yourself as nothing in comparison—you do not know God at all. . . . The real test of being in the presence of God is that you either forget about yourself altogether or see yourself as a small dirty object. It is better to forget about yourself altogether.[16]

Again the counsel is to forget yourself and focus on the magnificence, perfection, and competence of God.

The scriptures tell us that King Benjamin's people learned this life-changing lesson:

And now, it came to pass that when king Benjamin had made an end of speaking the words which had been delivered unto him by the angel of the Lord, that he cast his eyes round about on the multitude, and behold they had fallen to the earth, for the fear of the Lord had come upon them.

And they had viewed themselves in their own carnal state, even less than the dust of the earth. And they all cried aloud with one voice, saying: O have mercy, and apply the atoning blood of Christ that we may receive forgiveness of our sins, and our hearts may be purified; for we believe in Jesus Christ, the Son of God, who created heaven and earth, and all things; who shall come down among the children of men.

And it came to pass that after they had spoken these words the Spirit of the Lord came upon them, and they were filled with joy, having received a remission of their sins, and having peace of conscience, because of the exceeding faith which they had in Jesus Christ who should come, according to the words which king Benjamin had spoken unto them. (Mosiah 4:1–3)

ng Benjamin himself seems to be one who had achieved
sired contentment and peace. In studying his counsel, we
see that peace, even for a king, is found not in focusing on self but
in serving others. A portion of his farewell address notes:

> And again, believe that ye must repent of your sins
> and forsake them, and humble yourselves before God;
> and ask in sincerity of heart that he would forgive you;
> and now if you believe all these things see that ye do
> them.
>
> And again I say unto you as I have said before, that
> as ye have come to the knowledge of the glory of God,
> or if ye have known of his goodness and have tasted
> of his love, and have received a remission of your sins,
> which causeth such exceedingly great joy in your souls,
> even so I would that ye should remember, and always
> retain in remembrance, the greatness of God, and your
> own nothingness, and his goodness and long-suffer-
> ing toward you, unworthy creatures, and humble your-
> selves even in the depths of humility, calling on the
> name of the Lord daily, and standing steadfastly in
> the faith of that which is to come, which was spoken
> by the mouth of the angel.
>
> And behold, I say unto you that if ye do this ye
> shall always rejoice, and be filled with the love of God,
> and always retain a remission of your sins; and ye shall
> grow in the knowledge of the glory of him that created
> you, or in the knowledge of that which is just and true.
> (Mosiah 4:10–12)

This theme appears again when the Lord counsels Moroni:
"And if men come unto me I will show unto them their weakness, I give unto men weakness that they may be humble; and my
grace is sufficient for all men that humble themselves before me;
for if they humble themselves before me, and have faith in me,
then will I make weak things become strong unto them" (Ether
12:27).

In genuine humility, we must focus our faith in Christ, serve our spouse, and forget our weak selves. When we do, we become confident and strong. Nephi develops this confidence in Christ, and relies upon it when his father asks him to return to Jerusalem to obtain the plates of Laban, a seemingly impossible mission. "I will go and do the things which the Lord hath commanded," Nephi declares, "for I know that the Lord giveth no commandments unto the children of men, save he shall prepare a way for them that they may accomplish the thing which he commandeth them" (1 Nephi 3:7). Like Nephi, we will be able to keep the commandments, including creating a celestial marriage, not by bolstering our self-esteem but by humbly going forth and serving others with faith in the Lord.

Today, those who rely "alone upon the merits of Christ" (Moroni 6:4) are able to forget about themselves and accomplish much as tools in the hand of the Almighty. Such individuals also enjoy a peace that cannot be found by seeking self-esteem. President Boyd K. Packer shared:

> Perhaps the greatest discovery of my life, without question the greatest commitment, came when finally I had the confidence in God that I would loan or yield my agency to Him—without compulsion or pressure, without any duress, as a single individual alone, by myself, no counterfeiting, nothing expected other than the privilege. In a sense, speaking figuratively, to take one's agency, that precious gift which the scriptures make plain is essential to life itself, and say "I will do as thou directs," is afterward to learn that in so doing you possess it all the more.[17]

Most of us recognize that Jesus is our Savior in the global, eternal sense, such as when he assumes the role of mediator at the final judgment day. However, it is equally important to realize that He is also our daily bread of life, that refreshing living water that makes each day possible and enjoyable. Daily as we ponder upon the magnificence of God and forget about our self-consciousness, we discover that He is the source of true power and happiness. Whether we strive for success and inspiration in missionary work, church callings, or marriage, we must discover that "an eye single to the glory of God, qualify [us] for the work" (D&C 4:5). Though we often feel, and sometimes are, inadequate in what we attempt to do, we can do amazing things when teamed up with the Lord. As Paul said, "I can do all things through Christ which strengtheneth me" (Philip 4:13).

We are, of course, much more likely to receive needed revelations when we look to and rely on God. "The light of the body is the eye: if therefore thine eye be single to the glory of God, thy whole body shall be full of light" (JST, Matthew 6:22). This illumination is not the result of our own masterful reasoning, but the consequence of our obedience in looking to the Master. "And if your eye be single to my glory, your whole bodies shall be filled with light, and there shall be no darkness in you; and that body which is filled with light comprehendeth all things" (D&C 88:67). We are repeatedly reminded that our focus must be outside of ourselves. "Every man seeking the interest of his neighbor, and doing all things with an eye single to the glory of God" (D&C 82:19).

In praising God and serving our spouse, we experience that personal happiness and peace that all the self-help books and self-esteem lectures cannot produce. This truth is illustrated in an early missionary experience of President Hinckley, who arrived in the mission field amid widespread anti-Mormon rhetoric. He was miserable with hay fever and feeling very much alone:

> After he had taken as much as he felt he could, Elder Hinckley wrote his father that he wasn't getting anywhere with missionary work, and that he couldn't see the point in wasting his time and his father's money. Responding as both father and stake president, Bryant Hinckley sent a reply that was brief and to the point: "Dear Gordon, I have your recent letter. I have only one suggestion: forget yourself and go to work."
> Earlier that day he and his companion had studied

the promise recorded in the Gospels: "For whosoever will save his life shall lose it; but whosoever shall lose his life for my sake and the gospel's, the same shall save it" (Mark 8:35). That scripture, combined with his father's counsel, seared his soul. With the letter in hand, he went into his upstairs bedroom at 15 Wadham Road and got on his knees. As he poured out his heart to the Lord, he promised that he would try to forget himself and lose himself in the Lord's service. Many years later he indicated the significance of that series of events: "That July day in 1933 was my day of decision. A new light came into my life and a new joy into my heart. The fog of England seemed to lift, and I saw the sunlight. Everything good that has happened to me since then I can trace back to the decision I made that day in Preston.[18]

Those who forget themselves and have "an eye single to the glory of God" have a radiance about them which conveys peace and Godly confidence. Alma asked, "Have ye received his image in your countenances? Have ye experienced this mighty change in your hearts" (Alma 5:14)? In order to have the image of God in our countenance, we must be looking up, focused on Him and not ourselves.

Therefore, Alma again asked, "I say unto you, can ye look up to God at that day with a pure heart and clean hands? I say unto you, can you look up, having the image of God engraven upon your countenances" (Alma 5:19)? The more we are looking at Him, the more others will see Him in our countenance. As Elder Maxwell explained, "We are sometimes so anxious about our personal images, when it is His image we should have in our countenances."[19]

In the Doctrine and Covenants, the Lord has revealed his formula for celestial family relationships: "Let thy bowels also be full of charity toward all men, and to the household of faith, and let virtue garnish thy thoughts unceasingly; then shall thy confidence wax strong in the presence of God; and the doctrine of the priesthood shall distill upon thy soul as the dews from heaven. The Holy Ghost shall be thy constant companion, and thy scepter an unchanging scepter of righteousness and truth; and thy dominion shall be an everlasting dominion, and without compulsory means it shall flow unto thee forever and ever" (D&C 121:45–46). Thus it is not worldly self-esteem that we need but that confidence in Christ that accompanies the companionship of the Holy Ghost.

Confidence and peace bring joy; this short acronym can help us remember how to find JOY in marriage: Jesus first, Others (spouse) next, and Yourself last. C. Richard Chidester writes, "Marriage is a commitment to put the relationship first—and self second. This doesn't mean we must forget about our individual interests, but that we put them second. In marriage the goal is to become one and to learn to work cooperatively as a team."[20]

We notice this same theme over and over in counsel from the Brethren. President Harold B. Lee observed:

> If young people would resolve at the moment of their marriage that from that time forth they would do everything in their power to please each other in things that are right, even to the sacrifice of their own pleasures, their own appetites, their own desires, the problem of adjustment in married life would take care of itself, and their home would indeed be happy. Great love is built on great sacrifice, and that home where the principle of sacrifice for the welfare of each other is daily expressed is that home where there abides a great love.[21]

Said Elder H. Burke Peterson:

> After a lot of years of counseling in marriage problems, I find marriage problems come because one or the other of the marriage partners are selfish. This is really fact. There are more problems in marriages when one or the other is more concerned about his/herself than they are about the marriage partner. If you want

to be happy in a marriage situation or any other kind, be of service. Be more concerned about other's comforts and happiness than your own. Incidentally, yours will come.[22]

Elder Jeffrey R. Holland noted:

> True love blooms when we care more about another person than we care about ourselves. That is Christ's great atoning example for us, and it ought to be more evident in the kindness we show, the respect we give, and the selflessness and courtesy we employ in our personal relationships.[23]

President Gordon B. Hinckley observed:

> The greatest joys of life are experienced in happy family relationships. . . . We have many failures in the world, but the greatest of these, in my judgment, is that failure which is found in broken homes. . . . The root of most of this lies in selfishness. The cure for most of it can be found in repentance on the part of the offender and forgiveness on the part of the offended. . . . The cultivation of such a home requires effort and energy, forgiveness and patience, love and endurance and sacrifice; but it is worth all of these and more. I have learned that the real essence of happiness in marriage lies not so much in romance as in an anxious concern for the comfort and well-being of one's companion. Thinking of self alone and of the gratification of personal desires will build neither trust, love, nor happiness.[24]

The counsel continues on and on from inspired leaders who recognized the importance of service in strengthening marriage. President Hinckley taught:

> The most important decision of life is the decision concerning your companion. Choose prayerfully. And

when you are married, be fiercely loyal one to another. Selfishness is the great destroyer of happy family life. I have this one suggestion to offer. If you will make your first concern the comfort, the well-being, and the happiness of your companion, sublimating any personal concern to that loftier goal, you will be happy, and your marriage will go on through eternity.[25]

And again, President Hinckley said:

> Of all of the difficult and discouraging responsibilities I have, the most difficult and the most discouraging is handling cancellation of sealings. Most of those requests come from women—women who on their marriage day were in the house of the Lord, in each case with the young man she loved. And then as the years passed there was argument, anger, losing temper, throwing a chair across the room and other such foolish and unnecessary things, until all love was gone and hatred had taken its place. Now, having run their course, there comes a request for a cancellation of a temple sealing. You can trace it all to selfishness, thinking of oneself instead of one's companion. . . . Any man who will make his wife's comfort his first concern will stay in love with her throughout their lives and through the eternity yet to come.[26]

Finally, President Kimball taught:

> I have learned that it is by serving that we learn how to serve. When we are engaged in the service of our fellowmen, not only do our deeds assist them, but we put our own problems in a fresher perspective. When we concern ourselves more with others, there is less time to be concerned with ourselves. In the midst of the miracle of serving, there is the promise of Jesus, that by losing ourselves, we find ourselves. (See Matthew 10:39.) Not only do we "find" ourselves in terms of acknowledging guidance in our lives, but

the more we serve our fellowmen in appropriate ways, the more substance there is to our souls. We become more significant individuals as we serve others. We become more substantive as we serve others—indeed, it is easier to "find" ourselves because there is so much more of us to find![27]

Thus we see that the Christian Paradox (you must lose yourself to find yourself) is indeed the foundation of celestial marriage.

When Janice and I were married, we loved each other dearly, as do most newlyweds. One year later, we rushed to the hospital for the birth of our first child. In those days (1969), the anxious father-to-be was not allowed into the delivery room but was escorted into a fathers' room to await the announcement of the joyous event. I had no idea how long the labor and delivery would take; in the movies these sorts of things lasted for hours or even days. It was 1 a.m. and, with no all-night TV or videos, I wondered what to do with myself. I browsed through a couple of condensed books left behind by previous anxious men, then I noticed one with a swaying palm tree and breaking surf on the cover. Having only been home from my mission to the Polynesian Islands for two years, the cover sparked my interest, and I began reading the short story. In my mind, I was soon with a young Polynesian boy on an outrigger having an adventure that included attacking sharks and battling terrifying storms at sea. I became thoroughly caught up in the reading adventure.

After little more than an hour, a nurse entered the room and announced that Janice had given birth to our son. Janice and baby would soon be going to the recovery room, she said, and if I hurried I could see them in the hall. I was taken by surprise and had more than a little trouble in transition from my fantasy reading back to the significance of the announcement made by the nurse. My first spontaneous thought was something like, "It hasn't been long enough!" My second thought was, "I am right in the middle of a very exciting chapter and—No! I can't think that! Of course,

I want to see them. . . . Besides, I can always mark my spot in the novel and come back and finish it."

The nurse escorted me through those previously forbidden double doors, and there was my wife draped in a clean white sheet with a little child tucked in her right arm. My first notice of the child was that he had a full head of long, dark hair, and you would have thought the nurses would have cleaned him up a little more before presenting him to me! Then I looked into the eyes of my sweet wife. I'm not sure what gave it away, but I had the distinct impression that she had not been enjoying the previous hour in quite the same way I had. So I went to her side and, not knowing what to say, asked, "Did it hurt?" She immediately began to cry, and I thought, "Oh, boy, it hurt!"

Janice quickly regained her composure, however. "It really didn't hurt as much as I feared," she assured me. "It wasn't that bad." So I asked why she was crying, which, of course, she began to do again. Then, through her tears of joy, she explained, "I'm just so happy to give you a son!"

In that instant, my whole life changed. I became totally aware of my self-centeredness and unworthiness of this compassionate, self-sacrificing helpmeet. At that moment, I began to love my wife more than I loved myself. Fortunately, medical policies soon changed, and I have been in the delivery room with my wife for the births of most of our children.

In these experiences, and in the countless examples of loving our children in the home, this woman who had once dreamed of helping others by being a nurse, instead chose to help me—and so many others—understand how to love, serve, and be happier than I ever could have been in my selfish world.

Notes

1. Benson, " Beware of Pride," *Ensign*, May 1989, 6.
2. Rasband, *Confronting the Myth of Self-Esteem*, 74–75.
3. Judd, *Doctrines of Submission and Forgiveness*, 116.
4. Faulconer, "Self-Image, Self-Love, and Salvation," *Latter-day Digest* 2 (June 1993): 1.

5. Hinckley, "Whoever Will Save His Life," *Ensign*, August 1982, 5.

6. Smith, *Teachings of the Prophet Joseph Smith*, 178–79.

7. Kimball, *Teachings of Spencer W. Kimball*, 243.

8. Benson, "To the Fathers in Israel," *Ensign*, November 1987, 50.

9. Maxwell, "Put Off the Natural Man, and Come Off Conqueror," *Ensign*, November 1990, 16.

10. Benson, "Beware of Pride," *Ensign*, May 1989, 6.

11. Tuttle, "Developing Faith," *Ensign*, November 1986, 73.

12. Thomas, *Selected Writings of M. Catherine Thomas*, 237–50.

13. Wirthlin, "Fruits of the Restored Gospel of Jesus Christ," *Ensign*, November 1991, 16.

14. Lewis, *Mere Christianity*, 114.

15. Ibid., 190.

16. Ibid., 111–12.

17. Packer, *That All May Be Edified*, 256–57.

18. Dew, *Go Forward with Faith*, 64.

19. Maxwell, "'Answer Me,'" *Ensign*, November 1988, 31.

20. C. Richard Chidester, "No Place for Pride," Ensign, March 1990, 16.

21. Harold B. Lee, "A Sure Trumpet Sound: Quotations from Harold B. Lee," *Ensign*, February 1974, 77.

22. Hinckley, *Teachings of Gordon B. Hinckley*, 329.

23. Holland, "How Do I Love Thee," in *Brigham Young University 1999–2000 Devotional and Fireside Speeches*, 2000, 158.

24. Hinckley, "I Believe," *Ensign*, August 1992, 2.

25. Hinckley, *Teachings of Gordon B. Hinckley*, 328–29.

26. Ibid., 329.

27. Kimball, "Small Acts of Service," *Ensign*, December 1974, 2.

4

THE PATRIARCHAL
order

Before performing a temple marriage, the ordinance worker counseled the bride and groom to care for each other and keep the commandments associated with this sacred commitment and covenant. Among other things, the newlyweds were counseled to live the patriarchal order in their marriage. Some family members in attendance smiled with approval while others frowned and squirmed in their chairs. Clearly, there is some confusion about the patriarchal order.

Elder Dean L. Larsen shared a similar experience:

> Recently I was visited in my office by a young woman at whose forthcoming temple marriage I had been invited to officiate. . . . She was distraught and tearful and disclosed that she had some serious questions about whether she should go ahead with the marriage. As we discussed the reasons for these questions, the young prospective bride told me of a conversation she had the previous evening with her fiancé. . . . In a fashion uncharacteristic of their relationship, he had, at the insistence of his father, he said, laid down the

law and the conditions that would have to prevail in
their marriage. He was to be the unquestioned authority. His word would be law. She was to be willing to
submit to his rule. . . .

It was interesting to me that this young man, who
had won the hand and the heart of his sweetheart
through a loving and gentle courtship, now was constrained to impose a strict dominion upon her. In so
doing he was appealing to his misunderstanding of the
patriarchal order, for there could hardly have been a
greater distortion or misrepresentation of the actual
conditions that must prevail within that order.[1]

Perhaps others share the misunderstanding and misrepresentation of this young man, and many relationships may benefit by
defining patriarchal order and how it blesses a marriage.

First, let's identify what the patriarchal order is not. Satan
typically combats revealed truths with two strategies. He puts
forth a counterfeit and an opposite. With these two equally sinis-
ter ploys, he seeks to beguile twice the number of deceived souls.
In an attempt to pervert the revealed patriarchal order, Satan
offers his counterfeit, called *patriarchy* (male dominion), and
his opposite, called *matriarchy* (female dominion). Notice that
both methods consist of some inappropriate form of dominion.
Brigham Young taught a principle that applies here: "Show me
one principle that has originated by the power of the devil. You
cannot do it. I call evil inverted good, or a correct principle made
an evil use of."[2]

In this instance, Satan would have us replace service with
unrighteous dominion.

Because Adam and Eve are actual historical figures as well
as types for understanding proper relationships between husbands and wives, let us turn to their experience. To Eve and to
all women, the Lord said, "I will greatly multiply thy sorrow and
thy conception; in sorrow thou shalt bring forth children; and thy
desire shall be to thy husband, and he shall rule over thee" (Genesis 3:16). For our discussion, we will focus on the word *rule* and

determine what it means for husband-wife relationships today.

To better understand any translated word, especially one that has gone through so many languages and cultures, it is helpful to look at the setting, context, and other words with which the word is used. For example, notice how the word *ruler* is used in three other biblical examples:

"When a man shall take hold of his brother of the house of his father, saying, *Thou hast clothing, be thou our ruler*" (Isaiah 3:6; emphasis added).

"Who then is a faithful and wise servant, whom his lord hath made *ruler over his household, to give them meat* in due season?" (Matthew 24:25; emphasis added).

"The same did God send to be *ruler and a deliverer* by the hand of the angel which appeared to him in the bush (Acts 7:35; emphasis added).

From these verses we conclude that to rule means to provide clothing, food, and deliverance. Eve was being reassured that Adam would provide for her needs.

Nephi was told that "inasmuch as thou shalt keep my commandments, thou shalt be made a *ruler and a teacher* over thy brethren" (1 Nephi 2:22; emphasis added). When Nephi's brothers were bothered by Nephi's position, their father, Lehi, counseled them to "rebel no more against your brother, whose views have been glorious, and who hath kept the commandments from the time that we left Jerusalem; and who hath been an instrument in the hands of God, in bringing us forth into the land of promise; for were it not for him, we must have perished with hunger . . . *he hath not sought for power nor authority over you, but he hath sought the glory of God, and your own eternal welfare*" (2 Nephi 1:24–25; emphasis added).

If *to rule* means not to seek for power or authority but to seek for the glory of God and the welfare of family members, then wives would not need to be concerned with unrighteous dominion of husbands striving to be obedient.

Another example of a righteous ruler is King Benjamin. When speaking to his people, he explained that he had been chosen "to serve you with all the might, mind and strength which the Lord hath granted unto me. I say unto you that . . . I . . . *spend my days in your service* . . . And even I, myself, have labored with mine own hands that I might serve you . . . that there should nothing come upon you which was grievous to be borne" (Mosiah 2:11–14; emphasis added). That service and priesthood are synonyms eliminates any place for unrighteous priesthood dominion in a marriage relationship. The priesthood holder rules by giving his life in service to his wife and children.

The patriarchal order is an order of the Melchizedek Priest-hood, and priesthood means giving service. Consider the teach-ings of these two prophets relative to priesthood, and ponder the application in the marriage relationship. President David O. McKay taught that "priesthood means service; it is not given just as a honor. I congratulate you and commend you, that you are worthy to receive it, but it is given to you for service, and you should act as a authorized representative of our Lord Jesus Christ in whatever position you may be assigned."[3] And President Marion G. Romney observed that "the commandments do not pertain alone to one's personal conduct. They put on every bearer of the priesthood the stimulating responsibility to render service—ser-vice in carrying the restored gospel, with all the blessings of the priesthood, to the peoples of the earth; and service in comforting, strengthening, and perfecting the lives of one another and all the Saints of God."[4]

It would therefore appear that scripturally the word *rule* means to provide clothing, food, deliverance, teaching, and service. In this definition, there is no provision for power or authority over another, there is no dominion. These same principles seem to be taught in The Family: A Proclamation to the World: "By divine design, fathers are to preside over their families in love and righ-teousness and are responsible to provide the necessities of life and protection for their children."[5]

If men will "rule over" their wives in this manner, women will not cringe at the idea of being so served. It is because of Satan's counterfeit of male dominion that many wives have been abused and, therefore, cringe at the word *rule*. Husbands must remember that Brigham Young said, "No man can ever become a ruler in the Kingdom of God, until he can perfectly rule himself; then is he capable of raising a family of children who will rise up and call him blessed."[6]

President Gordon B. Hinckley shared these thoughts about the situation:

> [I] call attention to the statement in the scriptures that Adam should rule over Eve. . . . I regrettably recognize that some men have used this through centuries of time as justification for abusing and demeaning women. But I am confident also that in so doing they have demeaned themselves and offended the Father of us all, who, I am confident, loves His daughters just as He loves His sons.
>
> I sat with President David O. McKay on one occasion when he talked about that statement in Genesis. His eyes flashed with anger as he spoke of despotic husbands and stated that they would have to make an accounting of their evil actions when they stand to be judged by the Lord. He indicated that the very essence of the spirit of the gospel demands that any governance in the home must be done only in righteousness.
>
> My own interpretation of that sentence is that the husband shall have a governing responsibility to provide for, to protect, to strengthen and shield the wife. Any man who belittles or abuses or terrorizes, or who rules in unrighteousness, will deserve and, I believe, receive the reprimand of a just God who is the Eternal Father of both his sons and daughters.[7]

And this isn't the only instance where President Hinckley has addressed this issue. Other examples of include:

> Marriage, in its truest sense, is a partnership of equals, with neither exercising dominion over the other.[8]

Some men who are evidently unable to gain respect by the goodness of their lives use as justification for their actions the statement that Eve was told that Adam should rule over her. How much sadness, how much tragedy, how much heartbreak has been caused through centuries of time by weak men who have used that as a scriptural warrant for atrocious behavior! They do not recognize that the same account indicates that Eve was given as a helpmeet to Adam. The facts are that they stood side by side in the garden. They were expelled from the garden together, and they worked together, side by side, in gaining their bread by the sweat of their brows.[9]

Under the gospel plan, marriage is a companionship, with equality between the partners. We walk side by side with respect, appreciation, and love for one another. There can be nothing of inferiority or superiority between the husband and wife in the plan of the Lord. I am satisfied that our Father in Heaven loves his daughters as much as he loves his sons, and any man who demeans or belittles his wife affronts her Father in Heaven.[10]

Other Latter-day prophets have also spoken out against the counterfeit of male dominion. Elder John A. Widtsoe stated, "This doctrine of equality is confirmed in the ordinances of the Church, which are alike for man and woman. . . . The highest attainable glory cannot be won by man or woman alone. Only those who are united, as husband and wife, by the sealing power, can attain exaltation in the celestial glory in the hereafter."[11]

President Boyd K. Packer observed, "Your wife is your partner in the leadership of the family and should have full participation in all decisions relating to your home."[12]

Elder Moses Thatcher taught, "And he who regards his wife as the creature of his sinful pleasure, made and given to gratify his fallen nature, is unworthy of a wife or to be the father of children."[13] Speaking on this subject, Elder Richard G. Scott counsels those from family or cultural traditions where the male dominates. He said:

> Your Heavenly Father assigned you to be born into a specific lineage from which you received your inheritance of race, culture, and traditions. That lineage can provide a rich heritage and great reasons to rejoice. Yet you have the responsibility to determine if there is any part of that heritage that must be discarded because it works against the Lord's plan of happiness. . . .
>
> Is yours a culture where the husband exerts a domineering, authoritarian role, making all of the important decisions for the family? That pattern needs to be tempered so that both husband and wife act as equal partners, making decisions in unity for themselves and their family. No family can long endure under fear or force; that leads to contention and rebellion. Love is the foundation of a happy family.[14]

One year later, Elder Scott also said:

> As a husband and worthy priesthood bearer, you will want to emulate the example of the Savior, whose priesthood you hold. You will make giving of self to wife and children a primary focus of your life. Occasionally a man attempts to control the destiny of each family member. He makes all the decisions. His wife is subjected to his personal whims. Whether that is the custom or not is immaterial. It is not the way of the Lord. It is not the way a Latter-day Saint husband treats his wife and family.[15]

President Spencer W. Kimball addressed this same issue:

> Now, in some places in the world, there are men who do not recognize their wives with full righteousness. The man and the wife are equals; one has to be in authority, and that is the man. That does not mean that

he is superior. He procreates the children; the mother bears the children, and she helps the father to teach those children righteousness. We depend very strongly upon our wives to do that. Now we should be very thoughtful and considerate of our wives. We marry not to satisfy the urges of the human being—that's a second-rate thing. The first thing is to bring children into the world and teach them to become Christlike. Therefore, we men will be very considerate and thoughtful of our wives. We love them better than our own lives; and loving them, we will treat them with distinction and thoughtfulness. You remember that Paul, in some of his epistles to the Saints throughout the world, spent much of his time in teaching men to love their wives. And so that is a responsibility; any good man will love his wife intently. And any young man who is thinking of marriage will anticipate that kind of a marriage relationship.[16]

This wasn't the only time President Kimball referred to Paul's teachings. Earlier, he had said:

One of the most provocative and profound statements in holy writ is that of Paul wherein he directs husbands and wives in their duty to each other and to the family. First, he commands the women:

"Wives, submit yourselves unto your own husbands, as unto the Lord.

For the husband is head of the wife, even as Christ is the head of the church: And he is the Savior of the body.

Therefore as the church is subject unto Christ, so let the wives be to their own husbands in every thing" (Ephesians 5:22–24.)

If you analyze that very carefully, you can see that the Lord is not requiring women to be subject to their husbands if their husbands are bad and wicked and demanding. This is no idle jest, no facetious matter.

Much is said in those few words "as unto the Lord." As the Lord loves his church and serves it, so men should love their wives and serve them and their families.

A woman would have no fears of being imposed upon, nor of any dictatorial measures, nor of any improper demands if the husband were self-sacrificing and worthy. Certainly no sane woman would hesitate to give submission to her own really righteous husband in everything. We are sometimes shocked to see the wife taking over the leadership of the family, naming the one to pray, the place to be, the things to do.

Husbands are commanded: "Love your wives, even as Christ also loved the church, and gave himself for it" (Ephesians 5:25.)

And that is a high ambition. And here is the answer: Christ loved the Church and its people so much that he voluntarily endured persecution for them, suffered humiliating indignities for them, stoically withstood pain and physical abuse for them, and finally gave his precious life for them.

When the husband is ready to treat his household in that manner, not only the wife, but all the family will respond to his leadership.

Certainly if fathers are to be respected, they must merit respect. If they are to be loved they must be consistent, lovable, understanding, and kind and must honor their priesthood.[17]

Brother Robert Millet follows up with:

Too many men have assumed that their position as the head of the home entitled them to some kind of dictatorial following, that the patriarchal order allowed them to rule wife and children by virtue of their divine appointment as supreme officer over the family. This perception is false. It is damning. Unfortunately, too many women have entered into family living with a misperception and have therefore submitted themselves in ignorance to a man who is in reality dishonoring the priesthood he holds and thereby forfeiting the powers of the priesthood.[18]

In teaching against abuses of male dominance, Doctrine and Covenants, Section 121, is frequently quoted.

> Behold, there are many called, but few are chosen. And why are they not chosen?
>
> Because their hearts are set so much upon the thing of this world, and aspire to the honors of men, that they do not learn this one lesson—
>
> That the rights of the priesthood are inseparably connected with the powers of heaven, and that the powers of heaven cannot be controlled nor handled only upon the principles of righteousness.
>
> That they may be conferred upon us, it is true; but when we undertake to cover our sins, or to gratify our pride, our vain ambition, or to exercise control or dominion or compulsion upon the souls of the children of men, in any degree of unrighteousness, behold, the heavens withdraw themselves; the Spirit of the Lord is grieved; and when it is withdrawn, Amen to the priesthood or the authority of that man. (vv. 34–37)

Elder Russell M. Nelson taught that "some temple marriages fail because a husband forgets that his highest and most important priesthood duty is to honor and sustain his wife. The best thing that a father can do for his children is to 'love their mother.' . . . President Gordon B. Hinckley made a statement recently that each Latter-day Saint husband should heed: 'Magnify your [wife],' he said, 'and in so doing you will magnify your priesthood.'"[19]

So how should priesthood holders treat their wives and the other women in their family? President James E. Faust counseled, "Our wives need to be cherished. . . . The Lord values his daughters just as much as he does his sons. In marriage, neither is superior; each has a different primary and divine responsibility."[20]

And President McKay wrote:

> Let us instruct young people who come to us, to know that a woman should be queen of her own body. The marriage covenant does not give the man the right to enslave her or to abuse her or to use her merely for the gratification of his passion. Your marriage ceremony does not give you that right. Second, let them remember that gentleness and consideration after the ceremony [are] just as appropriate and necessary and beautiful as gentleness and consideration before the wedding. Third, let us realize that manhood is not undermined by the practicing of continence, notwithstanding what some psychiatrists claim. Chastity is the crown of beautiful womanhood, and self-control is the source of true manhood, if you will know it, not indulgence. . . . Let us teach our young men to enter into matrimony with the idea that each will be just as courteous and considerate of a wife after the ceremony as during courtship.[21]

Jesse W. Crosby records this recollection of the Prophet Joseph Smith:

> One day when the Prophet carried to my house a sack of flour he had borrowed, my wife remarked that he had returned more than he had received. He answered that it should be so; that anything borrowed should be returned always with interest to the lender. "Thus," he said, "the borrower, if he be honest, is a slave to the lender." Some of the home habits of the Prophet—such as building kitchen fires, carrying out ashes, carrying in wood and water, assisting in the care of the children, etc.—were not in accord with my idea of a great man's self-respect. The above incident of the Prophet carrying the sack of flour gave me the opportunity to give him some corrective advice which I had desired to do for a long time. I reminded him of

every phase of his greatness and called to his mind the multitude of tasks he performed that were too menial for such as he; to fetch and carry flour was too great a humiliation. "Too terrible a humiliation," I repeated, "for you who are the head, and you should not do it."

The Prophet listened quietly to all I had to say, then made his answer in these words: "If there be humiliation in a man's house, who but the head of that house should or could bear that humiliation?"

Sister Crosby was a very hardworking woman, taking much more responsibility in her home than most women take. Thinking to give the Prophet some light on home management, I said to him, "Brother Joseph, my wife does much more hard work than does your wife."

Brother Joseph replied by telling me that if a man cannot learn in this life to appreciate a wife and do his duty to her, in properly taking care of her, he need not expect to be given one in the hereafter.

His words shut my mouth as tight as a clam. I took them as terrible reproof. After that I tried to do better by the good wife I had and tried to lighten her labors.[22]

Lucy Walker Kimball also recalled this story about the Prophet Joseph:

Joseph Smith often referred to the feelings that should exist between husbands and wives, that they, his wives, should be his bosom companions, the nearest and dearest objects on earth in every sense of the word. He said men should beware how they treat their wives, that they were given them for a holy purpose, that the myriads of spirits waiting for tabernacle might have pure and healthy bodies. He also said many would awake on the morning of the resurrection sadly disappointed; for they, by transgression, would have neither wives nor children, for they surely would be taken from them and given to those who should prove themselves worthy. Again he said, a woman would have her choice; this was a privilege that could not be denied her.[23]

More recently, Elder Robert D. Hales taught that "an eternal bond doesn't just happen as a result of sealing covenants we make in the temple. How we conduct ourselves in this life will determine what we will be in all the eternities to come. To receive the blessings of the sealing that our Heavenly Father has given to us, we have to keep the commandments and conduct ourselves in such a way that our families will want to live with us in the eternities."[24]

Men who exercise unrighteous dominion over their wives will discover that they will lose more than the priesthood (D&C 121:37), they will lose their wives!

"Brethren, please remember," counseled Elder Russell M. Nelson, "the highest degree of the celestial glory is available to you only through that order of the priesthood linked to the new and everlasting covenant of marriage. (See D&C 131:1–4.) Therefore, your first priority in honoring the priesthood is to honor your eternal companion."[25]

Another possible misunderstanding comes when people confuse the hierarchical structure of church government with the patriarchal order of family government. Both systems are inspired for their intended use but are not interchangeable. "In the Church there is a distinct line of authority," notes President Packer. "We serve where called by those who preside over us. . . . In the home, it is a partnership with husband and wife equally yoked together, sharing in decisions, always working together. While the husband, the father, has responsibility to provide worthy and inspired leadership, his wife is neither behind him nor ahead of him but at his side."[26]

Of Adam and Eve, who represent all husbands and wives, Hugh Nibley observed, "There is no patriarchy or matriarchy in the Garden; the two supervise each other. Adam is given no arbitrary power; Eve is to heed him only insofar as he obeys their Father—and who decides that? She must keep check on him as much as he does on her. It is, if you will, a system of checks and balances in which each party is as distinct and independent in its sphere as are the departments of government under the Constitution—and just as dependent on each other."[27]

The patriarchal order is one of mutual dependence between husband and wife. As Elder Neal A. Maxwell points out, "Righteousness in not a matter of role, nor goodness a matter of gender. In the work of the kingdom, men and women are not without each other, but do not envy each other, lest by reversals and renunciations of role we make a wasteland of both womanhood and manhood."[28]

Similarly, President Spencer W. Kimball declared that in His wisdom and mercy "our Father made men and women dependent on each other for the full flowering of their potential. Because their natures are somewhat different, they can complement each other; because they are in many ways alike, they can understand each other. Let neither envy the other for their differences; let both discern what is superficial and what is beautifully basic in those differences and act accordingly."[29]

As we denounce patriarchy (male domination), we must be careful to not replace it with an equally satanic matriarchy (female domination). With so many obvious injustices of patriarchy, it may be tempting to get caught up in male bashing. However, we must remember that Satan would be just as pleased to have us succumb to an opposite as a counterfeit of the patriarchal order. It is one thing to denounce the many evidences of injustices upon women. It is another thing altogether to reject the patriarchal order, eternal marriage, eternal lives, and godhood. Unrighteous dominion by either husband or wife leads to unhappiness. Remember that President Hinckley said that "marriage, in its truest sense, is a partnership of equals, with neither exercising dominion over the other."[30]

Elder Orson Hyde warned that, "I will venture the assertion that no man can be exalted to a celestial glory in the Kingdom of

God whose wife rules over him; and as the man is not without the woman nor the woman without the man in the Lord, it follows as a matter of course, that the woman who rules over her husband thereby deprives herself of a celestial glory."[31]

President Faust cautioned, "There are some voices in our society who would demean some of the attributes of masculinity. A few of these are women who mistakenly believe that they build their own feminine causes by tearing down the image of manhood."[32] How sad would be the loss of eternal marital happiness for misdirected revolts against the inequalities of patriarchy.

"We live in a day" said Elder Dallin H. Oaks, "when there are many political, legal, and social pressures for changes that confuse gender and homogenize the differences between men and women. Our eternal perspective sets us against changes that alter those separate duties and privileges of men and women that are essential to accomplish the great plan of happiness. We do not oppose all changes in the treatment of men and women, since some changes in laws or customs simply correct old wrongs that were never grounded in eternal principles."[33]

These are not new challenges. Well over a hundred years ago, very capable women such as Eliza R. Snow struggled with similar issues. She wrote:

> The status of women is one of the questions of the day. Socially and politically it forces itself upon the attention of the world. Some . . . refuse to concede that woman is entitled to the enjoyment of any rights other than . . . the whims, fancies or justice . . . men may choose to grant her. The reasons which they cannot meet with argument they decry and ridicule; an old refuge for those opposed to correct principles which they are unable to controvert. Others . . . not only recognize that woman's status should be improved, but are so radical in their extreme theories that they would set her in antagonism to man, assume for her a separate and opposing existence; and . . . show how entirely independent she should be. Indeed, they would make

her adopt the more reprehensible phases of character which men present, and which should be shunned or improved by them instead of being copied by women. These are the two extremes, and between them is the "golden mean."[34]

Certainly, unrighteous dominion is as unbecoming to the wife as it is the husband.

Having spent much time on what the patriarchal order is not, we still need to understand what it is. Again, we look to Adam and Eve for insights. As revealed to Moses, the scriptural account notes that Adam was to have dominion over the animals (Moses 2:26), but no dominion was indicated relative to Eve. In fact, Adam's life without Eve was "not good" for he was "alone," therefore God would make a "help meet" for him (Moses 3:18). President Joseph Fielding Smith said a helpmeet is a helper suited to, worthy of, or corresponding to him (see footnote to Genesis 2:18)—"a help who would answer all the requirements, not only of companionship, but also through whom the fulness of the purposes of the Lord could be accomplished regarding the mission of man through mortal life and into eternity."[35]

"She is not inferior to him," notes BYU professor Catherine Thomas. "She is, according to the Hebrew, a partner worthy of him. The word for helper connotes not an assistant of lesser status, nor a subordinate, nor an inferior, but one who is at least an equal. . . . The Hebrew says in effect that Adam and Eve were created equal and complementary—that is, each completes the other in the eternal scheme."[36]

Because Adam and Eve had a common origin, they were considered to be of the same bone and flesh (Moses 3:21–23). President Boyd K. Packer observed, "We are told it [the creation story] is figurative insofar as the man and the woman are concerned."[37] Others agree. "The story of the rib," said President Spencer W. Kimball, "of course, is figurative."[38]

Hugh Nibley writes:

> My story begins with Adam and Eve, the arche-
> typal man and woman, in whom each of us is repre-
> sented. . . . Here is a perfect unity between these two
> mortals; they are "one flesh." The word rib expresses
> the ultimate in proximity, intimacy, and identity.
> When Jeremiah speaks of "keepers of my tsela (rib)"
> (Jeremiah 20:10), he means bosom friends, inseparable
> companions. Such things are to be taken figuratively,
> as in Moses 3:22 and Genesis 2:22, when we are told
> not that the woman was made out of the rib or from
> the rib, but that she was the rib, a powerful metaphor.
> So likewise "bone of my bones, and flesh of my flesh"
> (Genesis 2:23), "and they shall cleave together"—as
> "one flesh"—the condition is that of total identity.[39]

Joseph Fielding Smith declared, "From this we understand
that [Adam's] union with Eve was to be everlasting."[40] It therefore
appears that the rib metaphor symbolizes that Adam and Eve
were married by God, who thence considered them to be "one."
President Harold B. Lee further explained:

> In defining the relationship of a wife to her hus-
> band, the late President George Albert Smith put it
> this way: "In showing this relationship, by a symbolic
> representation, God didn't say that woman was to be
> taken from a bone in the man's head that she should
> rule over him, nor from a bone in his foot that she
> should be trampled under his feet, but from a bone in
> his side to symbolize that she was to stand by his side,
> to be his companion, his equal, and his helpmeet in all
> their lives together."
> I fear some husbands have interpreted erroneously
> the statement that the husband is to be the head of
> the house and that his wife is to obey the law of her
> husband. Brigham Young's instruction to husbands
> was this: "Let the husband and father learn to bend
> his will to the will of his God, and then instruct his
> wives and children in this lesson of self-government

by his example as well as by his precept." (*Discourses of Brigham Young*, pp. 306–307.)

This is but another way of saying that the wife is to obey the law of her husband only as he obeys the laws of God. No woman is expected to follow her husband in disobedience to the commandments of the Lord.[41]

President Brigham Young also said, "I never counseled a woman to follow her husband to the Devil."[42]

Adam and Eve seemed to work together as a team; the scriptures teach us that *they* sewed fig-leaves and *they* heard the voice of the Lord and hid themselves (Moses 4:14–15). Eve's mortal probation was to focus on her children and Adam (Moses 4:22), and Adam's mortal probation was to provide for Eve and her children (Moses 4:23–26). *They* were driven out of the garden together and labored side-by-side (Moses 5:1). That selfless, godlike spirit of motherhood is captured in the statement that "she bare unto him sons and daughters" (Moses 5:2). Adam and Eve prayed to the Lord, and *they* heard the Lord, who spoke unto them, for *they* both were cut off from the presence of the Lord (Moses 5:4). *They* were both given commandments that *they* should worship and make an offering to the Lord (Moses 5:5). However, the actual administration of this ordinance was the responsibility of Adam (Moses 5:5–9). Adam said, "Blessed be the name of God, for because of my transgression *my* eyes are opened, and this life *I* shall have joy, and again in the flesh *I* shall see God" (Moses 5:10; emphasis added).

"And Eve, his wife, heard all these things and was glad, saying: were it not for *our* transgression *we* never should have had seed, and never should have known good and evil, and the joy of *our* redemption, and the eternal life which God giveth unto all the obedient" (Moses 5:11; emphasis added). President Spencer W. Kimball reminded modern couples that they too, "must eliminate the 'I' and the 'my' and substitute therefore 'we' and 'our.'"[43]

Adam and Eve praised God, and they taught their children (Moses 5:12). Decades passed, but Adam and Eve continued to call upon God. More children were born, and in them Eve placed her hopes and dreams (Moses 5:16). Although from the creation, they were considered as one being (Moses 6:9), Adam was given a priesthood (Moses 6:7), which was after the order of Jesus Christ (Moses 6:67), which would ultimately lead to a oneness with God (Moses 6:68). "Adam and Eve," observed President Ezra Taft Benson, "provide us with an ideal example of a covenant marriage relationship. They labored together; they had children together; they prayed together; and they taught their children the gospel— together. This is the pattern God would have all righteous men and women imitate."[44]

In all of this, we see nothing but a full partnership of equals. Two totally devoted people dedicating themselves to serving God and each other. Most responsibilities they shared together, though occasionally they served in their assigned gender roles with no hint of jealousy or unrighteous dominion. "Adam held the priesthood," Elder Russell M. Nelson observed, "and Eve served in matriarchal partnership with the patriarchal priesthood."[45]

The *Encyclopedia of Mormonism* records:

> Adam and Eve were given in marriage to each other by God in the Garden of Eden before the Fall (Genesis 2:22–25; Moses 3:22–25). This sacred act of marriage was the crowning act of all creation: 'In the day that God created man, in the likeness of God made he him: Male and Female created he them; and blessed them' (Genesis 5:1–2). With his blessing, they truly could set the pattern for their descendants thereafter who two by two, a man and a woman, could leave father and mother, cleave to each other, and 'be one flesh' (Genesis 2:24). Thus began the great plan of God for the happiness of all his children.[46]

It seems that Adam and Eve were indeed "meet" for each other, well fitted or suited. Together, they selflessly worked as a team, a model of what a husband and wife should be. Of the current status of Adam and Eve, we have a clue from modern revelation. Zebedee Coltrin said, "The heavens gradually opened, and we saw a golden throne, on a circular foundation, and on the throne sat a man and a woman, having white hair and clothed in white garments. Their heads were white as snow, and their faces shone with immortal youth. They were the two most beautiful and perfect specimens of mankind I ever saw. Joseph said, 'They are our first parents, Adam and Eve.'"[47] Sharing a throne, Adam and Eve continue to be examples of what husbands and wives can become in the mutually beneficial relationship called the patriarchal order.

Adam lived in mortality for 930 years! Thus many generations of righteous couples had a firsthand acquaintance with Adam and Eve and looked to them for teaching and inspiration. Our skimpy record tells us little of Seth, Enos, Cainan, Mahalaleel, Jared, Enoch, or Methuselah. However, each of these was ordained high priests by Adam himself (D&C 107:41–53) and was accountable to him for how they honored the priesthood and served their wives. Since these patriarchs were righteous, we must assume that their wives were treated as well as Mother Eve.

We would like to know more about these patriarchal couples, their family dynamics, and how they counseled together on family issues. However, our biblical record is severely lacking. Elder Bruce R. McConkie explained:

> Indeed, we know that the Bible contains only a sliver, a twig, a leaf, no more than a small branch at the most, from the great redwood of revelation that God has given in ages past. There has been given ten thousand times ten thousand more revelations than has been preserved for us in our present Bible. It contains a bucket, a small pail, a few draughts, no more than a small stream at most, out of the great ocean of revealed truth that has come to men in ages more spiritually enlightened than ours. . . .
>
> And even the small portion of truth preserved for us in our present Bible has not come down to us in its original plainness and perfection. An angel told Nephi,

with repetitive emphasis, that the Bible—including both the Old Testament and the New Testament—contained the knowledge of salvation when first written; that it then went through the hands "of that great and abominable church, which is most abominable above all other churches" (1 Nephi 13:26); that many plain and precious parts and many covenants of the Lord were taken away; and that as a result an exceedingly great many did stumble and did not know what to believe or how to act. (See 1 Nephi 13.) . . .

The everlasting gospel; the eternal priesthood; the identical ordinances of salvation and exaltation; the never varying doctrines of salvation; the same Church and kingdom; the keys of the kingdom, which alone can seal men up unto eternal life—all these have always been the same in all ages; and it shall be so everlastingly on this earth and all earths to all eternity. These things we know by latter-day revelation. . . .

Celestial marriage has always existed. Indeed, such is the heart and core of the Abrahamic covenant.[48]

Let us now turn to Father Abraham, who desired to be a prince of peace (see Abraham 1:2) and Sarah, whose name means princess, to gain further insights into how couples who desire to become a king and queen should treat each other. In the revelation given through Joseph Smith the Prophet "relating to the new and everlasting covenant, including the eternity of the marriage covenant" we learn that "Abraham received all things, whatsoever he received, by revelation and commandment, by my word, saith the Lord, and hath entered into his exaltation and sitteth upon his throne" (D&C 132:29).

But as we study the biblical record of Abraham and Sarah, it is strikingly evident that married life held for them many challenges and family struggles. Over decades of marriage, they had to counsel with each other and show much patience, even long-suffering. "Now Sarai Abram's wife bore him no children: and she had an handmaid, an Egyptian, whose name was Hagar.

"And Sarai said unto Abram, Behold now, the Lord hath restrained me from bearing: I pray thee, go in unto my maid; it may be that I may obtain children by her. And Abram hearkened to the voice of Sarai" (Genesis 16:1–2). Can anyone imagine a more difficult test of pride? Sarah was, indeed, a princess, but one who chose to humble herself greatly for the sake of her husband and family. Later, the circumstances changed, and Sarah again asked Abraham to do a very difficult thing, to send Hagar and their son away. To a brokenhearted Abraham, the Lord said, "Let it not be grievous in thy sight because of the lad, and because of thy bondwoman; in all that Sarah hath said unto thee, hearken unto her voice" (Genesis 21:12). In both of these difficult times, Sarah requested difficult things of Abraham, and he hearkened.

But Abraham and Sarah would have even further tests and obstacles that could be surmounted only by mutual counsel, total dependence upon each other, and faith in the Lord. Famine forced them to flee into Egypt, but the Lord knew that the striking beauty of Sarah would make her a target for Pharaoh's idolatry and lust. "And it came to pass when I was come near to enter into Egypt, the Lord said unto me: Behold, Sarai thy wife, is a very fair woman to look upon;

"Therefore it shall come to pass, when the Egyptians shall see her, they will say—She is his wife; and they will kill you, but they will save her alive; therefore see that ye do on this wise:

"Let her say unto the Egyptians, she is thy sister, and thy soul shall live.

"And it came to pass that I, Abraham, told Sarai, my wife, all that the Lord had said unto me—Therefore say unto them, I pray thee, thou art my sister, that it may be well with me for thy sake, and my soul shall live because of thee" (Abraham 2:22–25). One can only imagine the humility with which Abraham petitioned his wife and the complete faith required of both of them to trust in this commandment from the Lord. In the patriarchal order, whatever is "well" for one is also "for thy sake." There was no superior-inferior relationship between this prince and princess, as both dedicated themselves to the well-being of each other and service to the King of Kings.

The biblical account of the subsequent patriarchs and their family issues composes the bulk of the book of Genesis. Repeatedly, we read of family challenges and how ultimately husband and wife arrive at unanimity. Sometimes the husband leads out and sometimes the wife leads out, but eventually they come together and are sustained by the Lord. Observed Brother Millet, "Abraham, Isaac, and Jacob may have qualified for exaltation in the highest heaven, but they did not so achieve on their own; they stand now, with their eternal companions, not as angels but as gods and goddesses (D&C 132:7). The patriarchal order is a partnership."[49]

Although we live in a different time and place than the ancient patriarchs, with different social and marriage customs, we must develop the same attitude—total commitment to family and obedience to the Lord. It may be that the patriarchal order is more than an orderly form of family government. It may also be a demanding process, designed as a tutorial experience to help both husband and wife overcome pride and learn to become one.

Husbands must learn submissiveness to the Lord, then serve in the family as Christ would do. "Let no man think he is ruler; but let God rule him that judgeth" (D&C 58:20). The husband may not want to follow Christ, nor lead out in the family, but that is his need, and assigned role. Noted President Packer:

> It is interesting to know how man is put together—how incomplete he is. His whole physical and emotional, and for that matter, spiritual nature, is formed in such a way that it depends upon a source of encouragement and power that is found in a woman. When man has found his wife and companion, he has in a sense found the other half of himself. He will return to her again and again for that regeneration that exalts his manhood and strengthens him for the testing that life will give him. A woman has the privilege and influence to transform a man into an able and effective LDS priesthood leader. However, for this there are

two prerequisites. First, she must want to, and second, she must know how. Part of knowing how includes the genius of encouraging him to meet his obligations without replacing him in his role, without presiding over him.[50]

Thus the husband must neither abuse authority nor default from serving with it. The wife must resist the temptation to usurp that authority, while serving valiantly in her assignment. President Kimball taught, "When men come home to their families and women devote themselves to their children, the concept will return, that then to be a mother is her greatest vocation in life. She holds in her hand the destiny of nations, for to her comes the responsibility and opportunity of molding the nation's citizens."[51]

As team players, husband and wife must both focus on giving all that they can for the good of the family. They become excellent at helping each other succeed at their respective callings. They take great joy in the growth and development of the other, for when either succeeds, all benefit.

Perhaps words like *preside* and *submit* can never be adequately defined or explained to those still struggling with principles such as humility and faith. It is likely that as we become more sanctified and pure in motive, we will have less reason to take issue with the Lord's way of preparing us to learn how to become kings and queens in His kingdom. Surely no husband could ever become a king who had not learned how to preside, and no wife would be fit as a queen who had not learned how to nurture! These are not necessarily things that we already do well but things that we need to learn to do well.

For those who have "lost themselves" in service (see JST, Mark: 37–38) there is little need for definitions. They are busy, and content, trying to keep the commandments to the best of their understanding. Such valiant saints go forward with faith that the Lord does not require anything of us that is not for our benefit. They have learned that "it is not meet that I should command in all things; for he that is compelled in all things, the same is a slothful and not a wise servant; wherefore he receiveth no reward.

"Verily I say, men should be anxiously engaged in a good cause, and do many things of their own free will, and bring to pass much righteousness; For the power is in them, wherein they are agents unto themselves. And inasmuch as men do good they shall in nowise lose their reward" (D&C 58:26–28).

It might be helpful to remember that this earth was made for us to dwell upon for a purpose. The Lord said, "we will prove them herewith, to see if they will do all things whatsoever the Lord their God shall command them;

"And they who keep their first estate, shall be added upon; and they who keep not their first estate shall not have glory in the same kingdom with those who keep their first estate; and they who keep their second estate shall have glory added upon their heads for ever and ever" (Abraham 3:25–26). Whether we fully understand it or not, this patriarchal order may be part of proving to see if we will do all things whatsoever the Lord our God shall command us.

However, it is more likely that this is more than a test. It is also the process needed for our growth and development. Elder Larsen provided this summary:

> The patriarchal principle in marriage provides for order and a basis for government in the kingdom of God. It places parents, with the father in the leadership role, in a position of accountability for their own direct family kingdom. It is a system of great simplicity and perfect effectiveness. It requires willing compliance with every principle of righteousness. It provides the greatest possible opportunity for individual development within an environment of love and mutual helpfulness, and the ideal framework within which to exercise personal accountability. We understand that exaltation can be achieved in no other state.[52]

As Sister Thomas concluded, "The point of putting the woman in a counseling role to the man is that, as both of them strove for something higher than themselves, their relationship would not founder in a power struggle—but would flower in mutual support and spiritual growth for each. The point of giving priesthood authority to only one of two imperfect people is to create interdependence and at-one-ment between them. The point of the Adam and Eve relationship is to return the man and the woman to at-one-ment before the Lord."[53]

For those not resisting the Lord's ordained patriarchal order of family government, but simply appreciating any direction, the following counsel proves beneficial. President Marion G. Romney said that husband and wife "should be one in harmony, respect, and mutual consideration. Neither should plan or follow an independent course of action. They should consult, pray, and decide together. Remember that neither the wife nor the husband is the slave of the other. Husbands and wives are equal partners, particularly Latter-day Saint husbands and wives. They should so consider themselves and so treat each other in this life, and they then will do so throughout eternity."[54]

President Kimball also provides guidance:

> Fatherhood is leadership, the most important kind of leadership. It has always been so, it always will be so. Father, with the assistance and counsel and encouragement of your eternal companion, you preside in the home. It is not a matter of whether you are most worthy or best qualified, but it is a matter of law and appointment. You preside at the meal table, at family prayer. You preside at family home evening, and as guided by the Spirit of the Lord, you see that your children are taught correct principles. It is your place to give direction relating to all of family life. . . . You give father's blessings. You take an active part in establishing family rules and discipline. As a leader in your home you plan and sacrifice to achieve the blessing of a unified and happy family. To do all of this requires

that you live a family-centered life.[55]

Elder Matthew Cowley reminded sisters of the following:

> You belong to the great sorority of saviorhood. You
> may not hold the priesthood. Men are different, men
> have to have something given to them to make them
> saviors of men, but not mothers, not women. You are
> born with an inherent right, an inherent authority, to
> be the saviors of human souls. You are the co-creators
> with God of his children. Therefore, it is expected of
> you by a right divine that you be the saviors and the
> regenerating force in the lives of God's children here
> upon the earth.[56]

Elder John A. Widtsoe added:

> Woman does not hold the Priesthood, but she is
> a partaker of the blessings of the priesthood. That is,
> the man holds the Priesthood, performs the priest-
> hood duties of the Church, but his wife enjoys with
> him every other privilege derived from the possession
> of the Priesthood. This is made clear, as an example,
> in the Temple service of the Church. The ordinances
> of the Temple are distinctly of Priesthood character,
> yet woman has access to all of them, and the highest
> blessings of the Temple are conferred only upon the
> man and his wife jointly. . . .
>
> The Prophet Joseph Smith made this relationship
> clear. He spoke of delivering the keys of the Priest-
> hood to the Church and said that the faithful mem-
> bers of the Relief Society should receive them with
> their husbands. . . .
>
> This division of responsibility is for a wise and noble
> purpose. Our Father in Heaven has bestowed upon
> His daughters a gift of equal importance and power,
> which gift, if exercised in its fulness, will occupy their
> entire life on earth so that they can have no possible
> longing for that which they don't possess. The "gift"

referred to is that of motherhood—the noblest most soul satisfying of all earthly experiences. If this power is exercised righteously, woman has no time nor desire for anything greater, for there is nothing greater on earth! This does not mean that women may not use to the full their special gifts, for the more woman exercises her innate qualifications the greater is her power for motherhood. Woman may claim other activity but motherhood should take precedence in her entire scheme of life.[57]

Elder Maxwell put it quite concisely: "Priesthood and motherhood are the perfect partnership!"[58]

That the husband and wife must work together in their sacred roles becomes apparent. Neither has a role without the other, for their roles pertain to their relationship to each other. President Hunter taught:

A man who holds the priesthood accepts his wife as a partner in the leadership of the home and family with full knowledge of and full participation in all decisions relating thereto. Of necessity there must be in the Church and in the home a presiding officer (see D&C 107:21). By divine appointment the responsibility to preside in the home rests upon the priesthood holder (see Moses 4:22). The Lord intended that the wife be a helpmeet for man (meet means equal)—that is, a companion equal and necessary in full partnership. Presiding in righteousness necessitates a shared responsibility between husband and wife: together you act with knowledge and participation in all family matters. For a man to operate independently of or without regard to the feelings and counsel of his wife in governing the family is to exercise unrighteous dominion.[59]

Similarly, Elder Larsen taught:

The husband must assume the role of leadership and see his wife as a knowledgeable counselor and partner in decision-making. In every important matter, both have the duty and responsibility to contribute information and insight, and to express their feelings. If a decision is difficult, or if complete accord has not been reached, the couple may decide to delay a decision while more study or prayer is devoted to the decision. If, ultimately, a husband must propose a course of action in the absence of complete agreement, he must sense the great responsibility in taking this role and should do so with great care. It should never be done precipitously, whimsically, or egotistically, but always thoughtfully and with the welfare of those involved uppermost in mind. The powers of inspiration can more easily and readily be brought to bear in this way.[60]

In such an environment, the spirit of mutual concern, respect, and love are evident. In such a home, the Spirit and attending gift of charity assures everyone that their best interests and security will always be defended. The Prophet Joseph Smith taught:

It is the duty of a husband to love, cherish, and nourish his wife, and cleave unto her and none else; he ought to honor her as himself, and he ought to regard her feelings with tenderness, for she is his flesh, and his bone, designed to be an help unto him, both in temporal, and spiritual things; one into whose bosom he can pour all his complaints without reserve, who is willing (being designed) to take part of his burden, to soothe and encourage his feelings by her gentle voice. It is the place of the man, to stand at the head of his family, and be lord of his own house, not to rule over his wife as a tyrant, neither as one who is fearful or jealous that his wife will get out of her place, and prevent him from exercising his authority. It is his duty to be a man of God (for a man of God is a man of wisdom,) ready at all times to obtain from the scriptures, the revelations, and from on high, such instructions as are necessary for the edification, and salvation of his household.—And on the other hand, it is the duty of the wife, to be in subjection to her husband at all times, not as a servant, neither as one who fears a tyrant, or a master, but as one, who, in meekness, and the love of God, regards the laws and institutions of Heaven, looks up to her husband for instruction, edification and comfort.[61]

Both husband and wife must learn to follow. Said President Brigham Young, "I have counseled every woman of this church to let her husband be her file leader; he leads her, and those above him in the Priesthood lead him." Of course, a husband must lead in righteousness, and a wife must be willingly led in righteousness. However, President Young continued, "I never counseled a woman to follow her husband to hell. . . . I am sanguine and most emphatic on that subject. . . . If a man is determined to expose the lives of his friends, let that man go to the devil and to destruction alone."[62]

On another occasion, President Young taught, "Let the father be the head of the family, the master of his own household; and let him treat them as an angel would treat them; and let the wives and children say amen to what he says, and be subject to his dictates, instead of their dictating the man, instead of their trying to govern him."[63]

Sister Thomas writes this:

> The issue here is not who is more capable, men or women, but who will do the work God has appointed? If full priesthood is withheld from women, it is not because they cannot do the work of priesthood—that they are not spiritual enough, nor intelligent enough, nor rational enough, but rather, to foster the conditions in which the man and the woman may achieve interdependence. . . . What makes all of this so hard in practice? It may seem unfair that the man is sub-

ject to a perfect head, and the woman to an imperfect head. But how much humility the man must cultivate to hear the Lord's voice! And how much humility the woman must exercise to encourage and rely on her imperfect husband to make that connection. The man's presidency over the woman is designed to be as much of a tutorial for him as it is for the woman to submit to his presidency. A very fine tuning is required of each. . . . The challenge of perfecting ourselves is great indeed, but the challenge of perfecting ourselves in a relationship is greater.[64]

We can see that the patriarchal order is more than an inspired method of family government; it is also a tutorial experience for perfecting a husband and wife and preparing them to live together, happily ever after. President David O. McKay declared, "Priesthood means service."[65] In the patriarchal order of the priesthood, both husband and wife devote their lives to serving each other.

Reviewing how the priesthood was restored also reveals insights about the patriarchal order. On 21 September 1823, Moroni first visited Joseph Smith, telling the future prophet "Behold, I will reveal unto you the Priesthood, by the hand of Elijah the prophet, before the coming of the great and dreadful day of the Lord" (Joseph Smith–History 1:38–39; also see D&C 2).

The promised restoration of priesthood took place in stages. On 15 May 1829, John the Baptist appeared to Joseph Smith and Oliver Cowdery, declaring, "Upon you my fellow servants, in the name of Messiah, I confer the Priesthood of Aaron, which holds the keys of the ministering of angels, and of the gospel of repentance, and of baptism by immersion for the remission of sins; and this shall never be taken again from the earth until the sons of Levi do offer again an offering unto the Lord in righteousness" (Joseph Smith–History 1:69; also see D&C 13).

John the Baptist "acted under the direction of Peter, James, and John, who held the keys of the Priesthood of Melchizedek, which Priesthood, he said, would in due time be conferred upon us" (Joseph Smith–History 1:72). By June of that same year, the Melchizedek Priesthood was also restored (see D&C 18:9). Yet the promise of priesthood restoration under the hand of Elijah remained unfulfilled.

Years passed before the Lord commanded the newly gathered Saints to "build a house, in the which I design to endow those whom I have chosen with power from on high" (D&C 95:8). Again, the Lord said, "it is expedient in me that the first elders of my church should receive their endowment from on high in my house, which I have commanded to be built unto my name in the land of Kirtland" (D&C 105:33).

And from the dedicatory prayer of this first temple in the latter days, we read, "And we ask thee, Holy Father, that thy servants may go forth from this house armed with thy power, and that thy name may be upon them, and thy glory be round about them, and thine angels have charge over them. . . . Let the anointing of thy ministers be sealed upon them with power from on high" (D&C 109:22, 35). Interestingly, this last verse is cross referenced with Exodus 25:6 and Leviticus 8:12, where a similar anointing took place for the priests who served in the tabernacle constructed by Moses.

On 3 April 1836, a sequence of marvelous manifestations occurred in the newly dedicated Kirtland Temple. The Lord appeared and accepted the building, but that wasn't the end.

> After this vision closed, the heavens were again opened unto us; and Moses appeared before us, and committed unto us the keys of the gathering of Israel from the four parts of the earth, and the leading of the ten tribes from the land of the north.
>
> After this, Elias appeared, and committed the dispensation of the gospel of Abraham, saying that in us and our seed all generations after us should be blessed.
>
> After this vision had closed, another great and glorious vision burst upon us; for Elijah the prophet, who was taken to heaven without tasting death, stood

before us, and said:

Behold, the time has fully come, which was spoken of by the mouth of Malachi—testifying that he [Elijah] should be sent, before the great and dreadful day of the Lord come—

To turn the hearts of the fathers to the children, and the children to the fathers, lest the whole earth be smitten with a curse—

Therefore, the keys of this dispensation are committed into your hands; and by this ye may know that the great and dreadful day of the Lord is near, even at the doors. (D&C 110:11–16)

Now both the Aaronic and Melchizedek Priesthoods had been restored, along with three different sets of keys to unlock and empower the use of those priesthoods. From Doctrine and Covenants, Section 107, often called the revelation on the priesthood, we learn "the power and authority of *the higher, or Melchizedek Priesthood, is to hold the keys* of all the spiritual blessings of the church—

To have the privilege of receiving *the mysteries of the kingdom of heaven,* to have the heavens opened unto them, to commune with the general assembly and church of the Firstborn, and to enjoy the communion and presence of God the Father, and Jesus the mediator of the new covenant.

The power and authority of *the lesser, or Aaronic Priesthood, is to hold the keys of the ministering of angels, and to administer in outward ordinances,* the letter of the gospel, the baptism of repentance for the remission of sins, agreeable to the covenants and commandments. (vv. 18–20; emphasis added)

The Prophet Joseph Smith would later observe that "there are two Priesthoods spoken of in the Scriptures, viz., the Melchisedek and the Aaronic or Levitical. Although there are two Priesthoods, yet the Melchisedek Priesthood comprehends the Aaronic or Levitical Priesthood, and is the grand head. . . . [It] is the highest and holiest Priesthood, and is after the order of the Son of God, and all other Priesthoods are only *parts*, ramifications, powers and blessings belonging to the same, and are held, controlled, and directed by it."[66] Joseph's most concise explanation is that "all priesthood is Melchizedek, but there are different *portions* or *degrees* of it."[67] Regarding the mysteries of the kingdom of heaven mentioned in Doctrine and Covenants, Section 107, President Lee taught:

> It was of this subject that the Prophet Joseph Smith spoke when he said: "The principle of salvation is given us through the knowledge of Jesus Christ" (*Teachings of the Prophet Joseph Smith*, p. 297), and that "knowledge through our Lord and Savior Jesus Christ is the grand key that unlocks the glories and mysteries of the kingdom of heaven." (Ibid., p. 298) . . . These revelations, which are reserved for and taught only to the faithful Church members in sacred temples, constitute what are called the "mysteries of Godliness." The Lord said He had given to Joseph "the keys of the mysteries, and the revelations which are sealed. . . ." (D&C 28:7.) As a reward to the faithful, the Lord promised: "And to them will I reveal all mysteries, yea, all the *hidden mysteries of my kingdom from days of old*. . . ."(D&C 76:7.)[68]

In those days of old, were they aware of temple ordinances? Elder Bruce R. McConkie taught:

> The everlasting gospel; the eternal priesthood; the identical ordinances of salvation and exaltation; the never-varying doctrines of salvation; the same Church and kingdom; the keys of the kingdom, which alone can seal men up unto eternal life—all these have always been the same in all ages; and it shall be so everlastingly on this earth and all earths to all eternity. . . .
> Do not let the fact that the performances of the

Mosaic law were administered by the Aaronic Priesthood confuse you on this matter. Where the Melchizedek Priesthood is, there is the fulness of the gospel;
and all of the prophets held the Melchizedek Priesthood.[69]

To better appreciate the different parts, portions, or degrees
(orders) of the priesthood along with subsequent powers and
blessings, let's return to the Kirtland Temple and the three visions
of Old Testament prophets. It must be remembered that this
sequence of visions occurred within a temple context. After par-
taking of the Lord's Supper, Joseph Smith and Oliver Cowdery
"retired to the pulpit, the veils being dropped" and bowed in
solemn prayer. The Lord Jehovah appeared in all His splendor
and proclaimed that "the hearts of thousands and tens of thousands shall greatly rejoice in consequence of the blessings which
shall be poured out, and the endowment with which my servants
have been endowed in this house" (D&C 110:9). Three Old Testament prophets then appeared and restored needed priesthood
keys for temple ordinances.

Moses

Moses "committed unto us the keys of the gathering of Israel
from the four parts of the earth, and the leading of the ten tribes
from the land of the north" (D&C 110:11). Previous to this event,
baptisms and missionary work had already been taking place. Yet,
the expansion of this effort into foreign lands would now commence with spectacular results, many of which are yet to take
place.

However, we must not forget that these messengers from
heaven were sent to restore keys pertaining to a promised endowment and with a definite temple context. President Joseph Smith
later said:

> What was the object of gathering Jews, or the people
> of God in any age of the world? . . . The main object [of

gathering] was to build unto the Lord a house whereby
He could reveal unto His people the ordinances of His
house and the glories of His kingdom, and teach the
people the way of salvation; for there are certain ordinances and principles, when they are taught and prac-
ticed, must be done in a place or house built for that
purpose. . . . It is for the same purpose that God gathers together His people in the last days, to build unto
the Lord a house to prepare them for the ordinances
and endowments, washings and anointings, etc. . . .
Why gather the people together in this place? For the
same purpose that Jesus wanted to gather the Jew—to
receive the ordinances, the blessings, and glories that
God has in store for His Saints.[70]

This gathering, for the purpose of building temples and participating in temple ordinances, has also been emphasized by other
writers. "Moses appeared in the Kirtland Temple to commit the
keys of the gathering of Israel," observed President Packer. "The
gathering of the people is done so that the temples can be built;
we gather to build temples."[71] President Spencer W. Kimball
taught that "the gathering of Israel consists of joining the true
church and . . . coming to a knowledge of the true God."[72] Such
knowledge can be obtained most fully in temples.

But what does Moses have to do with temples? As spectacular as was the exodus of Israel from Egypt, the bulk of Moses'
ministry actually centered in the tabernacle and attempting to
get Israel worthy of temple blessings. Joseph Smith, the Prophet,
recorded these fascinating insights: "I preached in the grove, on
the keys of the kingdom, charity, &c. The keys are certain signs
and words by which false spirits and personages may be detected
from true, which cannot be revealed to the Elders till the Temple
is completed. The rich can only get them in the Temple, *the poor
may get them on the mountain top as did Moses.*"[73]

The record of Moses' endowment begins in Moses 1 in the
Pearl of Great Price. "The book of Moses is what the Lord permitted him to write of his endowment experience. . . . He was

given an account of the creation of our eternity and our earth. He saw the scenes of the Garden of Eden. He saw the encounter between Adam, Eve, and the great adversary. With this intelligence, and much more, he could return to Egypt with a new identity and power."[74]

The Lord appeared to Moses "face to face," most likely on more than one occasion (see Moses 7:4 and Exodus 33:11). In fact, "there arose not a prophet since in Israel like unto Moses, whom the Lord knew face to face" (Deuteronomy 34:10). A face-to-face meeting with the Lord was also experienced by Abraham (Abraham 3:11), Jacob (Genesis 32:20), Moroni (Ether 12:39), and the brother of Jared (D&C 17:1). These face-to-face experiences seem to symbolize the ultimate goal of the Atonement. Elder Russell M. Nelson notes that "the components are at-one-ment, suggesting that a person is at one with another. . . . In Hebrew, the basic word for atonement is *kaphar*, a verb that means 'to cover' or 'to forgive.' Closely related is the Aramaic and Arabic word *kafat*, meaning 'a close embrace,' no doubt related to the Egyptian ritual embrace."[75]

John the Beloved also foretold of a future day when the righteous would "see his face; and his name shall be in their foreheads" (Revelations 22:4). We too have been counseled to "sanctify yourselves that your minds become single to God, and the days will come that you shall see him; for he will unveil his face unto you" (D&C 88:68). And we have been promised that "it shall come to pass that every soul who forsaketh his sins and cometh unto me, and calleth on my name, and obeyeth my voice, and keepeth my commandments, shall see my face and know that I am" (D&C 93:1).

After leading the Israelites out of Egypt, Moses ascended Mount Sinai to receive further instructions from the Lord. "The Lord opened the heaven to Moses and through him extended to Israel the opportunity to come to a fulness of his glory, taste of his love, and truly become a Zion people" (see Exodus 25:8; 29:43; D&C 84:23–27). During his forty-day fast upon the mount, Moses received every detail needed for the construction of a tabernacle, a house of the Lord, where Israel could come and receive the keys of salvation and exaltation.

The *Old Testament Student Manual* for Institute states:

> Set forth in symbolic representation and beautifully portrayed in progressive splendor, the tabernacle and its court became a school wherein the things of heaven were to be revealed to the Lord's own people. It was originally intended that an Israelite could move from the outer court of the tabernacle to its inner and more holy precincts and observe, in so doing, that the handiwork and ornamentation became progressively more intricate, ornate, and secluded until at last the ritual placed them before the holy presence, even the Holy of Holies. Sacred beyond description, protected from the eyes of the unworthy, these ordinances were designed to be, and could have become, the cement, or bonding agent, between worthy Israel and her God. This symbolic journey, however, was denied Israel because of her own pride and rebellion (see Exodus 20:18–20; 32:1). Therefore, *Israel lost these higher blessings* and became dependent upon the officiating priests who acted as proxy through a lesser order of priesthood. . . . But that loss of privilege in no way implies that the tabernacle lost its significance for Israel. . . . Though *the fulness of the priesthood endowment was withheld from Israel,* the layout and construction of; the tabernacle itself typified, or symbolized, man's progress toward perfection so that he could enter into the presence of God.[76]

Under the leadership of Moses, the Israelites could have experienced the endowment but disqualified themselves.

President Young once commented on what Israel would have enjoyed, had they not proven themselves unworthy. "If they had been sanctified and holy, the children of Israel would not have travelled one year with Moses before they would have received their endowments and the Melchisedec Priesthood," he said. "But they could not receive them, and never did. Moses left them and they did not receive the fulness of that Priesthood. . . . The Lord told Moses that he would show himself to the people; but they begged Moses to plead with the Lord not to do so."[77]

Though Moses had been endowed and held the keys to help others experience the same, Israel proved themselves unworthy:

> And the Lord confirmed a priesthood also upon Aaron and his seed, throughout all their generations, which priesthood also continueth and abideth forever with the priesthood which is after the holiest order of God.
>
> And this greater priesthood administereth the gospel and holdeth the key of the mysteries of the kingdom, even the key of the knowledge of God.
>
> Therefore, in the ordinances thereof, the power of godliness is manifest.
>
> And without the ordinances thereof, and the authority of the priesthood, the power of godliness is not manifest unto men in the flesh;
>
> For without this no man can see the face of God, even the Father and live.
>
> Now this Moses plainly taught to the children of Israel in the wilderness, and sought diligently to sanctify his people that they might behold the face of God;
>
> But they hardened their hearts and could not endure his presence; therefore, the Lord in his wrath, for his anger was kindled against them, swore that they should not enter into his rest while in the wilderness, which rest is the fulness of his glory.
>
> Therefore, he took Moses out of their midst, and the Holy Priesthood also. (D&C 84:18–25)

Because of the rebellion of Israel, the Lord said, "there shall no man among them see me at this time, and live, for they are exceeding sinful. And no sinful man hath at any time, neither shall there be any sinful man at any time that shall see my face and live" (JST, Exodus 33:20). Further, the *Lord took away "the priesthood out of their midst; therefore my holy order, and the ordinances thereof, shall not go before them;* for my presence shall not go up in their midst, lest I destroy them" (JST, Exodus 34:1; emphasis added). Therefore, Joseph Smith observed that the "law revealed to Moses in Horeb never was revealed to the children of Israel as a nation."[78]

So a natural question would be to ask if the priesthood of Melchisedek was taken away when Moses died. "All Priesthood is Melchizedek," answered President Joseph Smith, "but there are different portions or degrees of it. That portion which brought Moses to speak with God face to face was taken away; but that which brought the ministry of angels remained."[79]

When it was time for priesthood keys for the endowment to be restored in the meridian dispensation, Moses was sent to the Mount of Transfiguration. President Joseph Fielding Smith believes that on that mount, Peter, James, and John received their endowments.[80] They may have also received the "more sure word of prophecy" for they were certainly "neither barren nor unfruitful in the knowledge of our Lord Jesus Christ" (see JST, 2 Peter 1:8, 19).

Apparently, Moses was again sent back to the earth to restore these same keys to a latter-day people who would prove themselves worthy of participating in the temple endowment. As part of the restoration of all things, not only the Aaronic but also the Melchizedek endowments would once more be upon the earth. Church history in Kirtland and Nauvoo evidence the practice of restored temple initiatory ordinances and endowments as previously experienced by Moses and others.

Elias

Elias was the next prophet to appear in the Kirtland Temple. He "committed the dispensation of the gospel of Abraham" (D&C 110:12). But what exactly does that mean? Elder Bruce R. McConkie commented extensively on this topic, saying on one occasion that "the gospel of Abraham was one of celestial marriage."[81] On another occasion, Elder McConkie said: "I went to the temple and I took my wife with me, and we kneeled at the altar. There on that occasion, we entered the two of us, into an 'order of the priesthood.' When we did it, we had sealed upon us, on a conditional basis, every blessing that God promised Father Abraham—the blessings of exaltation and eternal increase. The name of that order of priesthood, which is patriarchal in nature because Abraham was a natural patriarch to his posterity, is the New and Everlasting Covenant of marriage."[82]

Again, Elder McConkie writes:

> What, then, is the Abrahamic covenant? It is that Abraham and his seed (including those adopted into his family) shall have all of the blessings of the gospel, of the priesthood, and of eternal life. The gate to eternal life is celestial marriage, which holy order of matrimony enables the family unit to continue in eternity, so that the participating parties may have posterity as numerous as the sands upon the seashore or the stars in heaven. The Abrahamic covenant enables men to create for themselves eternal family units that are patterned after the family of God our Heavenly Father.[83]

And still again, Elder McConkie defines: "All of these promises lumped together are called the *Abrahamic covenant. Those portions of it which pertain to personal exaltation and eternal increase are renewed with each member of the house of Israel who enters the order of celestial marriage;* through that order the participating parties become inheritors of all the blessings of Abraham, Isaac, and Jacob."[84]

That the marriage ordinance is conditional is further explained by President George Q. Cannon, who said:

> When men go forward and attend to other ordinances, such as receiving their endowments, their washings, their anointings, receiving the promise

connected therewith, these promises will be fulfilled to the very letter in time and in eternity—that is, if they themselves are true to the conditions upon which the blessings are promised. And so it is when persons go to the altar and are married for time and eternity. . . . Just as sure as that promise is made, and the persons united (to whom the promise is made) conform with the conditions thereof, just so sure will it be fulfilled.[85]

President Benson taught:

Adam and his descendants entered into the priesthood order of God. Today we would say they went to the House of the Lord and received their blessings. *The order of priesthood* spoken of in the scriptures is sometimes *referred to as the patriarchal order* because it came down from father to son. But this order is otherwise described in a modern revelation as a order of family government where a man and a woman enter into a covenant with God—just as did Adam and Eve—to be sealed for eternity, to have posterity, and to do the will and work of God throughout their mortality. . . .

When our children obey the Lord and go to the temple to receive their blessings and enter into *the marriage covenant,* they enter into the same *order of the priesthood* that God instituted in the very beginning with father Adam.[86]

Of the patriarchal priesthood, President Joseph Fielding Smith said:

The priesthood that was given to Adam was patriarchal and that priesthood continued until the days of Moses, when the Lord took it away . . . he took Moses and the higher priesthood out of their midst. . . . We read from the statement of the Prophet Joseph Smith that all the prophets held the Melchizedek Priesthood and evidently the patriarchal order of priesthood; but that honor was confined to a very few, and each one had to receive the special ordination. . . . The patriarchal priesthood will be the priesthood that will be held by all those who are worthy of exaltation in the celestial kingdom of God, for the whole plan of salvation and exaltation is based upon the patriarchal order. . . . It is an order; it is part of the Melchizedek Priesthood; in fact, all priesthood is, but the patriarchal is an order of priesthood.[87]

Thus Elias restored the keys for a higher order or level of priesthood called the patriarchal order, or celestial marriage. As the Lord explained, "In the celestial glory there are three heavens or degrees; and in order to obtain the highest, a man must enter into *this order of the priesthood* [meaning the new and everlasting covenant of marriage]" (D&C 131:1–2; emphasis added).

President Wilford Woodruff taught that "we could not obtain a fullness of celestial glory without this sealing ordinance or the institution called the patriarchal order of marriage, which is one of the most glorious principles of our religion."[88]

Other LDS authors and books define the patriarchal order of the priesthood. In the *Encyclopedia of Mormonism*, Lynn McKinlay explained:

> To Latter-day Saints, the patriarchal order of the priesthood is the organizing power and principle of celestial family life . . . today dedicated husbands and wives enter this order in the temple in a covenant with God. The blessings of this priesthood is given only to husbands and wives together. Their covenants extend beyond this life (D&C 76:59, 60), beyond death (D&C 132:20–24), and into the resurrection, to eternal lives, the eternal giving and receiving of life. . . . Eventually, through this order, families will be linked in indissoluble bonds all the way back to the first parents, and all the way forward to the last child born into this world.[89]

Brother Millet writes:

In modern times Elias restored the Abrahamic covenant, the patriarchal order, the keys associated with
that order of the priesthood we know as the new and
everlasting covenant of marriage. (D&C 131:1–4.)
Elias conferred the power whereby men and women
who have been gathered out of the world may then,
through temples, be organized into eternal family
units.[90]

On another occasion, Brother Millet noted that:

The patriarchal order, established in the days of
Adam (see D&C 107:40–42), was and is an order of
the Melchizedek Priesthood. It is, in fact, what we
know as the new and everlasting covenant of marriage. . . . The identity of Elias is not given in the
revelation. This heavenly messenger restored the keys
necessary to establish the Abrahamic covenant, making
the Prophet Joseph Smith and the faithful Saints
who receive celestial marriage heirs to the blessings
and promises made to the fathers (see D&C 27:10).
Elias thus restored the patriarchal order, the power by
which eternal families are organized through the new
and everlasting covenant of marriage.[91]

Brother Millet also wrote that "Elias restored the power necessary to organize eternal family units through the new and everlasting covenant of marriage."[92]

Other scholars have come to the same conclusion regarding
the keys restored by Elias. For example, Joseph Fielding McConkie said:

After the appearance of Moses came the appearance of Elias to commit "the gospel of Abraham,
saying that in us and our seed all generations after us
should be blessed" (D&C 110:12.) Thus the covenant
God made with Abraham was restored. As Abraham
had received the promise of the continuation of his

seed and by implication the eternal nature of his union with Sarai, so the doctrine of eternal marriage with the same promise relative to the nature of the family unit is restored to those of the ancient patriarch's family. So central is the family unit to the whole system and plan of salvation that the eternal union of the man and the woman in marriage by the authority of the priesthood is known as an "order of the priesthood" and is thought of as being synonymous with the "new and everlasting covenant" (D&C 131:2).[93]

Byron R. Merrill wrote that "Elias's power was to draw us to the new and everlasting covenant of eternal marriage and to organize us in family units."[94] And Keith Perkins stated that "Elias brought back the dispensation of the gospel of Abraham or the keys of celestial marriage."[95]

These higher orders of priesthood are held only by husband-and-wife teams. President Packer explained:

> Those who tell you that in the kingdom of God a woman's lot is less than that of the man know nothing of the love, akin to worship, that the worthy man has for his wife. He cannot have his priesthood, not the fulness of it, without her. "For no man," the Prophet said, "can get the fulness of the priesthood outside the temple of the Lord" (see D&C 131:1–3). And she is there beside him in that sacred place. She is there and shares in all that he receives. Each, individually, receives the washings and anointings, each may be endowed. But he cannot ascend to the highest ordinances—the sealing ordinances—without her at his side.[96]

On another occasion, President Packer writes:

> No man receives the fulness of the priesthood without a woman at his side. For no man, the Prophet [Joseph Smith] said, can obtain the fulness of the

priesthood outside the temple of the Lord (D&C
131:1–4). And she is there beside him in that sacred
place. She shares in all that he receives. The man and
the woman individually receive the ordinances encom-
passed in the endowment. But the man cannot ascend
to the highest ordinances—the sealing ordinances—
without her at his side. No man achieves the supernal
exalting status of worthy fatherhood except as a gift
from his wife.[97]

Another apostle of the Lord in this dispensation, Elder James
Talmage writes on the subject of eternal womanhood:

> In the restored Church of Jesus Christ, the Holy
> Priesthood is conferred, as an individual bestowal,
> upon men only, and this in accordance with divine
> requirement. It is not given to woman to exercise the
> authority of the Priesthood *independently;* nevertheless,
> in the sacred endowments . . . woman shares with man
> the blessings of the Priesthood. When the frailties and
> imperfections and mortality are left behind, in the glo-
> rified state of the blessed hereafter, husband and wife
> will administer in their respective stations, seeing and
> understanding alike, and cooperating to the full in the
> government of their family kingdom. . . . Then shall
> woman be recompensed in rich measure for all the
> injustice that womanhood has endured in mortality.
> Then shall woman reign by divine right, a queen in the
> resplendent realm of her glorified state, even as exalted
> man shall stand, priest and king unto the Most High
> God. Mortal eye cannot see nor mind comprehend the
> beauty, glory, and majesty of a righteous woman made
> perfect in the celestial kingdom of God.[98]

The principles of the patriarchal order of priesthood, and the
ordinance of celestial marriage, are designed to help both husband and wife develop their full potential. Through priesthood
and motherhood, both are called upon to give service to each

other and their children. Through this process, both are tutored to overcome selfishness and pride. The ultimate goal for this husband-and-wife team is to become like Heavenly Father and Heavenly Mother.

In fact, whenever we are struggling to understand the patriarchal order, it might be helpful to imagine how Heavenly Father and Heavenly Mother would treat each other. That is how we should treat each other, that is the patriarchal order of the Melchizedek Priesthood.

Just as the title *Elias* means forerunner, the temple ordinance (patriarchal order of celestial marriage) restored by Elias is but a forerunner to yet higher experiences. We must therefore live the patriarchal order so that we may progress to even further heights.

Elijah

If Moses restored additional keys for the gathering of Israel and the temple endowment; and if Elias restored the keys used for celestial marriage in our temples, then what is left for Elijah to restore?

The answer is found in Doctrine and Covenants, Section 132:

> And verily I say unto you, that the conditions of this law are these: All covenants, contracts, bonds, obligations, oaths, vows, performances connections, associations, or expectations, that are not made and entered into and sealed by the Holy Spirit of promise, of him who is anointed, both as well for time and all eternity, and that too most holy, by revelation and commandment through the medium of mine anointed, whom I have appointed on the earth to hold this power (and I have appointed unto my servant Joseph to hold this power in the last days, and there is never but one on the earth at a time on whom this power and they keys of this priesthood are conferred), are of no efficacy, virtue, or force in and after the resurrection from the

dead; for all contracts that are not made unto this end have an end when men are dead. . . .

And again, verily I say unto you, if a man marry a wife by my word, which is my law, and by the new and everlasting covenant, and it is sealed unto them by the Holy Spirit of promise, by him whom is anointed, unto whom I have appointed this power and the keys of this priesthood; and it shall be said unto them—Ye shall come forth in the first resurrection; and shall inherit thrones, kingdoms, principalities, and power, dominions, all heights and depths . . .—it shall be done unto them all things whatsoever my servant hath put upon them, in time, and through all eternity; and shall be of full force when they are out of the world; and they shall pass by the angels, and the gods, which are set there, to their exaltation and glory in all things, as hath been sealed upon their heads, which glory shall be a fulness and a continuation of the seeds forever and ever. (vv. 7, 19).

Said the Prophet Joseph Smith:

What is this office and work of Elijah? It is one of the greatest and most important subjects that God has revealed. He should send Elijah to seal the children to the fathers, and the fathers to the children. . . .

I wish you to understand this subject, for it is important; and if you receive it, this is the spirit of Elijah, that we redeem our dead, and connect ourselves with our fathers which are in heaven, and seal up our dead to come forth in the first resurrection; and here we want the power of Elijah to seal those who dwell on earth to those who dwell in heaven. This is the power of Elijah and the keys of the kingdom of Jehovah. . . .

What you seal on earth, by the keys of Elijah, is sealed in heaven; and this is the power of Elijah, and this is the difference between the spirit and power of Elias and Elijah; for while the spirit of Elias is a forerunner, the power of Elijah is sufficient to make our calling and election sure.[99]

Note that the spirit of Elias, or celestial marriage, is a forerunner for an eternal relationship, which must be sealed by the Holy Spirit of Promise. Joseph Smith worded it another way, saying, "this power of Elijah is to that of Elias what in the architecture of the Temple of God those who seal or cement the stone to their places are to those who cut or hew the stones, the one preparing the way for the other to accomplish the work. By this we are sealed with the Holy Spirit of promise. To obtain this sealing is to make our calling and election sure which we ought to give all diligence to accomplish."[100]

President Packer encourages us to seek a more complete understanding of the sacred sealing powers when he said:

> I have thought a dozen times while preparing for tonight how much I wish there could be time to trace the history of how we got the sealing power. For in that account we would find how much the Lord regards it. We would begin to see into the eternities. But that must wait for another day. I will only set the door ajar, hoping that you, on your own, will seek to open it completely. . . .
>
> Thirteen years after Moroni appeared, a temple had been built adequate for the purpose, and the Lord again appeared and Elijah came with Him and bestowed the keys of the sealing power. Thereafter ordinances were not tentative, but permanent. The sealing power was with us. No authorization transcends it in value. That power gives substance and eternal permanence to all ordinances performed with proper authority for both the living and the dead.[101]

Elder McConkie worded it this way: "Celestial marriage has always existed. Indeed, such is the heart and core of the Abrahamic covenant. Elias and Elijah came to restore this ancient order and to give the sealing power, which gives it eternal efficacy."[102] Note that Elias restored the keys to perform the ordinance of celestial marriage, and Elijah restored the keys to ultimately seal that sanctified marriage.

Elder McConkie also stated:

> Unfortunately some are confused on this point because of a misunderstanding of some of the truths revealed in the revelation on marriage [D&C 132]. Because no person can gain exaltation or eternal life alone; because exaltation includes the continuation of the family unit in eternity; because the whole thrust of revealed religion is to perfect and center everything in the family; and because having one's calling and election made sure is the receipt of a guarantee of eternal life—it was the most natural thing in the world for the Lord to reveal both the doctrine of eternal marriage and the doctrine of being sealed up unto eternal life (meaning having one's calling and election made sure) in one and the same revelation. In effect one grows out of the other. The one is a conditional promise of eternal life; the other is an unconditional promise. . . .
>
> That is to say, after celestial marriage; after entering into sacred covenants in the house of the Lord; after receiving the conditional promise of the continuation of the family unit in eternity; after receiving power to gain kingdoms and thrones—we must so live as to receive the guarantees to which we have thus been called, and the assurances that appertain to our election, and which are given on a conditional basis only in celestial marriage. As with baptism, so with celestial marriage; after the glorious promise of eternal life that is part of each of these covenants, we must press forward in righteousness until our calling and election is made sure; and this high achievement grows out of and is the crowning reward of celestial marriage.[103]

The powers of the patriarchal order of priesthood should

manifest themselves in the way we treat our family members in our homes. Through the marriage and parenting processes, we learn to serve and love more purely, and thus approach perfection. Said President Faust:

> Perhaps we regard the power bestowed by Elijah as something associated only with formal ordinances performed in sacred places. But these ordinances become dynamic and productive of good only as they reveal themselves in our daily lives. Malachi said that the power of Elijah would turn the *hearts* of the fathers and the children to each other. The heart is the seat of the emotions and a conduit for revelation (see Malachi 4:5–6). This sealing power thus reveals itself in family relationships, in attributes and virtues developed in a nurturing environment, and in loving service. These are the cords that bind families together, and the priesthood advances their development. In imperceptible but real ways, the "doctrine of the priesthood shall distill upon thy soul [and thy home] as the dews from heaven" (D&C 121:45).[104]

Similarly, President Ezra Taft Benson taught:

> Now let me say something to all who can worthily go to the house of the Lord. When you attend the temple and perform the ordinances that pertain to the house of the Lord, certain blessings will come to you: You will receive the spirit of Elijah, which will turn your hearts to your spouse, to your children, and to your forebearers. You will love your family with a deeper love than you have loved before. You will be endowed with power from on high as the Lord has promised.[105]

Thus we see that the patriarchal order is not about dominion. It is the priesthood order of celestial marriage as practised by the ancient patriarchs and their wives. This order has been restored and is administered once more in holy temples. Worthy couples who enter into this priesthood order, and faithfully spend their lives in serving God and each other will ultimately realize their greatest dreams of being together forever.

Notes

1. Larsen, "Marriage and the Patriarchal Order," *Ensign*, September 1982, 6.

2. Young, in *Journal of Discourses*, 3: 158.

3. McKay, in Conference Report, April 1957, 94.

4. Romney, "The Oath and Covenant Which Belongeth to the Priesthood," *Ensign*, November 1980, 45.

5. The First Presidency and Council of the Twelve Apostles, "The Family—A Proclamation to the World," *Ensign*, November 1995, 102.

6. Young, *Discourses of Brigham Young*, 265.

7. Hinckley, "Daughters of God," *Ensign*, November 1991, 99.

8. ———, "I Believe," *Ensign*, August 1992, 6.

9. Hinckley, "Our Solemn Responsibilities," *Ensign*, November 1991, 51.

10. Hinckley, *Teachings of Gordon B. Hinckley*, 332.

11. Widtsoe, *Evidences and Reconciliations*, 305.

12. Packer, "The Father and the Family," *Ensign*, May 1994, 21.

13. Thatcher, in *Journal of Discourses*, 26:14–15.

14. Scott, "Removing Barriers to Happiness," *Ensign*, May 1998, 85.

15. Scott, "Receive the Temple Blessings," *Ensign*, May 1999, 26.

16. Kimball, "The Lord's Plan for Men and Women," *Ensign*, October 1975, 2.

17. Kimball, *Teachings of Spencer W. Kimball*, 315.

18. Millet, "Restoring the Patriarchal Order," unpublished paper, 12.

19. Nelson, "Endure and Be Lifted Up," *Ensign*, May 1997, 71.

20. Faust, "Keeping Covenants and Honoring the Priesthood," *Ensign*, November 1993, 38–39.

21. McKay, *Gospel Ideals*, 471–72.

22. Andrus and Andrus, *They Knew the Prophet*, 145.

23. Ibid., 139–40.

24. Hales, "The Eternal Family," *Ensign*, November 1996, 65.

25. Nelson, "Honoring the Priesthood," *Ensign*, May 1993, 39.

26. Packer, "The Relief Society," *Ensign*, May 1998, 96.

27. Nibley, *Old Testament and Related Studies*, 92–93.

28. Maxwell, "The Women of God," *Ensign*, May 1978, 10.

29. Kimball, *Teachings of Spencer W. Kimball*, 315.

30. Hinckley, "I Believe," *Ensign*, August 1992, 6.

31. Hyde, in *Journal of Discourses*, 4:258.

32. Faust, "Happiness is Having a Father Who Cares," *Ensign*, January 1974, 23.

33. Oaks, "'The Great Plan of Happiness,'" *Ensign*, November 1993, 73–74.

34. Snow, *Woman's Exponent*, 15 July 1872, 29.

35. Smith, *Doctrines of Salvation*, 2:70.

36. Thomas, *Spiritual Lightening*, 48.

37. Packer, "The Law and the Light," 11.

38. Kimball, "The Blessings and Responsibilities of Womanhood," *Ensign*, March 1976, 71.

39. Nibley, *Old Testament and Related Studies*, 87–88.

40. Smith, *Doctrines of Salvation*, 2:70.

41. Lee, "Maintain Your Place as a Woman," *Ensign*, February 1972, 50.

42. Young, *Discourses of Brigham Young*, 201.

43. Kimball, *Teachings of Spencer W. Kimball*, 306.

45. Nelson, *Power within Us*, 109.

46. *Encyclopedia of Mormonism*, 856.

47. Andrus and Andrus, *They Knew the Prophet*, 28.

48. McConkie, *Sermons and Writings of Bruce R. McConkie*, 293.

49. Millet, *Selected Writings of Robert L. Millet*, 5.

50. "Church Relief Society Conference," *Salt Lake Tribune*, October 2, 1971, B-1.

51. Kimball, "'Why Call Me Lord, and Do Not the Things that I Say,'" Ensign, May 1975, 4.

52. Larsen, "Marriage and the Patriarchal Order," *Ensign*, September 1982, 4.

53. Thomas, *Spiritual Lightening*, 48.

54. Romney, "In the Image of God," *Ensign*, March 1978, 2.

55. Kimball, "The Example of Abraham," *Ensign*, June 1975, 3.

56. Cowley, *Matthew Cowley Speaks*, 109.

57. Widtsoe, *Priesthood and Church Government*, 84.

58. Maxwell, *Deposition of a Disciple*, 82.

59. Hunter, "Being a Righteous Husband and Father," *Ensign*, November 1994, 50.

60. Larsen, "Marriage and the Patriarchal Order," *Ensign*, September 1982, 3.

61. Smith, *Elders Journal*, 1: 61–62.

62. Young, in *Journal of Discourses*, 8:141.

63. Young, in *Journal of Discourses*, 4:55.

64. Thomas, *Spiritual Lightening*, 54.

65. McKay, *Pathway to Happiness*, 231.

66. Smith, *History of the Church*, 4:207.

67. Smith, *Teachings of the Prophet Joseph Smith*, 180–81.

68. Lee, *Ye Are the Light of the World*, 210–11; emphasis added.

69. McConkie, *Sermons and Writings of Bruce R. McConkie*, 292.

70. Smith, *History of the Church*, 5:423, 424, 427.

71. Packer, *Holy Temple*, 217.

72. Kimball, *Teachings of Spencer W. Kimball*, 439.

73. Smith, *History of the Church*, 4:608.

74. Nibley, *Temples of the Ancient World*, 54–55.

75. Nelson, "The Atonement," *Ensign*, November 1996, 34.

76. *Old Testament Student Manual: Genesis–2 Samuel*, 147, 154; emphasis added.

77. Young, in *Journal of Discourses*, 6:100–101.

78. Smith, *History of the Church*, 5:554–55.

79. Smith, *Teachings of the Prophet Joseph Smith*, 180–81.

80. *Doctrines of Salvation*, 2:165.

81. McConkie, *Mormon Doctrine*, 219–20.

82. McConkie, "The Eternal Family Concept," Second Annual Priesthood Genealogical Research Seminar, Brigham Young University, Provo, Utah, 23 June 1967.

83. McConkie, *New Witness for the Articles of Faith*, 505.

84. McConkie, *Mormon Doctrine;* 13, emphasis added.

85. Cannon, in *Journal of Discourses*, 26:249.

86. Benson, "What I Hope You Will Teach Your Children about the Temple," *Ensign*, August 1985, 6–10.

87. Joseph Fielding Smith, address to religious educators, 15 June 1956.

88. Woodruff, in *Journal of Discourses*, 1:13, 167.

89. *Encyclopedia of Mormonism*, 1067.

90. Millet, *LDS Church News*, 1 July 1995.

91. Millet, "The Ancient Covenant Restored," *Ensign*, March 1998, 36.

92. Millet, *The Mormon Faith*, 124.

93. McConkie, *Joseph Smith*, 161.

94. Merrill, *Elijah*, 120–21.

95 Perkins, *LDS Church News*, 28 May 1994.

96. Packer, "The Circle of Sisters," *Ensign*, November 1980, 109.

97. Packer, "The Relief Society," *Ensign*, May 1998, 73.

98. Talmage, "The Eternity of Sex," *Young Woman's Journal* 25 (October 1914): 602–3.

99. Smith, *History of the Church*, 6:251–52.

100. Smith, *Words of Joseph Smith*, 335.

101. Packer, "Ordinances," in *Brigham Young University 1979–80 Devotional and Fireside Speeches*, 12.

102. McConkie, *Sermons and Writings of Bruce R. McConkie*, 293.

103. McConkie, *Doctrinal New Testament Commentary*, 3:332–33.

104. Faust, "Father, Come Home," *Ensign*, May 1993, 35.

105. Benson, *Teachings of Ezra Taft Benson*, 254.

5

THE COURAGE TO BE IMPERFECT
WHILE STRIVING FOR

perfection

Janice shouldered a lot of responsibility—and stress—as the mother in our home. In addition to mothering our large brood of children, my parents came to live with us. Dad had heart problems and was not expected to live more than five years (he actually lived 22 years), and Janice invited them into our home. This noble gesture on her part reflected her genuine compassion and commitment to a life of service.

However, even people who love each other and get along well face difficulties putting two more adults into a small house and kitchen, as well as into the dynamics of raising children. I was busy being a seminary principal, marriage and family counselor, high councilman, runner, and outdoorsman. In addition, due to a job change from military pilot to seminary teacher, I was now earning only one-half the income we'd earned before. Finances were tight, and Janice bore most of the burden of making ends meet.

Life was challenging for all of us. But what I failed to notice was that, after several years of valiant effort, Janice was beginning to suffer an emotional and spiritual breakdown. She felt inadequate as a mother and worried about disappointing her in-laws. She felt guilty for not doing everything she felt like she should be, such as genealogy, journal writing, missionary work, and temple work. Mostly, she simply felt overwhelmed, inadequate, and imperfect.

We attended stake conference and thoroughly enjoyed our regional representative, Brother J. Ballard Washburn. He gave a marvelous talk about doing our very best, even though our best would always prove to be insufficient. We would always come up short, he observed, and discover that in the end we are totally dependent upon the Lord. He promised those in attendance that if we would give our very all, even to the point of falling upon our faces in exhaustion, we would then qualify to petition the Lord for assistance, and He would then carry the load for us. We were not encouraged to slacken our efforts, but we were reassured that total effort, though insufficient, would be accepted by the Lord.

Following the meeting, Janice spent most of the next two hours in tears and prayer. Finally responding to my coaxing, she shared with me her burden and shame. She wanted so much to be a never-ending reservoir of compassion and service, to be perfect. But she had reached the point that there was no more to give, the reservoir had become empty. She wondered if perhaps she had been valiant enough to consider asking the Lord to forgive her imperfection and relieve some of her load.

Realizing that it was I, not she, who was in need of repentance, I immediately took steps to secure a loan so we could build an apartment attached to our house. This provided both parents and grandparents with their own domain and unique relationship to the children. I also began to better monitor my wife's condition, remembering that she needed reassurance that the Lord will accept our best offering, imperfect though it may be. We both came to know more fully that the Savior and the Atonement are for our imperfections as well as our sins.

Later that year, at a Boy Scout Jamboree, I met Brother Washburn. I took the opportunity to thank him for his timely gospel message that so blessed our lives. We visited briefly, he a physician and me a therapist, regarding the many people we knew who seemed so burdened with the guilt of their own imperfections and assumed unworthiness. What to him was probably a forgotten casual conversation became a profound awareness for me into the nature and character of God. Imperfect though we are, God loves us! He is gracious, meaning He is predisposed to bless us. He is not only capable, but anxious, to help. He is already aware of our inadequacies, that is why He makes Himself so available.

We should not be surprised that we are far from perfection; the purpose of life is to grow, progress, and develop. We must be cautious, however, that this awareness does not make us dysfunctional, but more committed to humbly petition the Lord for His help. Without Him, we are hopeless; with Him, we have hope. Building upon that hope, we must press forward with the courage to be imperfect while striving for perfection.

"Anything worth doing is worth doing poorly," (Many motivational speakers and teachers use this saying, but it appears to have originated with G. K. Chesterton.)[1] The point is that some things are so important that they must be done, even if at first we cannot do them well. We can easily see illustrations of this in art, music, sports, and many other endeavors. We can never become good at what we don't work at. There must be a willingness to try, to practice, to improve, to become.

This is certainly true in husband-and-wife relationships, as well as parenting. There is nothing more critical in this earth life, but we don't begin these relationships as experts. We are learning, we are in process. If we are not willing to risk, willing to jump into these learning experiences, we can never develop the skills and attitudes necessary to become the ideal. Life is for becoming. That requires courage and a willingness to participate fully, even while we are still developing the desired traits. We must give our imperfect best, and in so doing, our best will eventually become perfect.

Perhaps we have all experienced, in some facet of our lives, the dysfunction that can result from fear of failure. As a young military pilot, I was disappointed to see how I allowed test anxiety to hamper my flying skills during the required annual test flight. The atmosphere was very demanding and competitive and required serious preparation and performance. Although I always passed, my performance under those pressure circumstances was less than my normal and therefore frustrating. The more fixated I became on perfection, the more it eluded me.

Eventually, I became the check pilot whose job it was to administer the feared test flight to the other pilots. Over and over again, I saw pilots make mistakes that they would not have made under normal conditions. I too still had to be tested annually and continued to see my own performance degrade when under these self-imposed pressure circumstances. By this time, I had served eight years active duty and was flying only one weekend a month in the reserves.

I had served as a bishop for a little over a year when my stake president asked me to resign from the military reserves so I wouldn't be gone so often. I agreed but had to complete my responsibilities by attending the next weekend, as previously scheduled. Ironically, that weekend I was scheduled for my annual qualifications test. Since I was the check pilot in the squadron, arrangements had been made for a check pilot from another squadron to administer the tests to me. The pressure on a check pilot to do well on his own check ride is even greater.

As soon as I reported to the base for my weekend duty, I told the squadron commander that I was resigning. He accepted the news graciously but asked if I would complete the scheduled tests as previously arranged. I was prepared and was actually quite excited to be allowed to fly, for one last time. When the visiting check pilot arrived, I was pleasantly surprised to see that he was an old friend from earlier days when we had been in a squadron together.

He administered a thorough verbal test on procedures and aircraft specifications, quizzed me during the pre-flight inspection of the aircraft, and put me through the paces in flying the required maneuvers and handling emergency situations. During all of this, we had a marvelous reunion and enjoyed sharing updates on our families and our new careers in the civilian world. I was now a seminary teacher, and he worked in his Baptist congregation with youth groups. We spent a most enjoyable afternoon together.

At the conclusion of the flight, we were walking back toward the ready room for debrief, when my friend asked, "How did you do that?" I didn't have any idea what he was referring to and responded, "Do what?"

He said, "That was the finest check flight I have ever seen. How did you manage to do that?" I was shocked by his evaluation because I had not been worrying about my performance or evaluating myself, I was simply enjoying the flight and the friendship. Then I realized why things had gone so well—I was not unduly worried. I hadn't worried about failure, and thus I hadn't created failure. Because I was not overly anxious, I finally flew a check flight at my real level of proficiency.

And so it is in marital and parenting situations. We can become dysfunctional by demanding from ourselves nothing less than a flawless performance. We can become so inflexible in unrealistic demands upon ourselves that we make no provision for development, for improvement, for becoming. Marriage and parenting are not skills that we have already developed and are now being tested on to see if we are still performing perfectly. Marriage and parenting are skills to be attained through the process of learning by experience. If we are not willing to begin, to learn by experience, even failures, and to develop over time, we can never approach the perfection we ultimately desire.

We readily recognize that professionals, musicians, and athletes only become proficient with experience, over time. Why would we think it is any different with becoming an excellent mate or parent? Though imperfect now, we must wholeheartedly devote ourselves to the process, that one day we might become the ideal. Yet, while in process, why not relax, enjoy the growing experience, and watch how our performance and joy increase?

Elder Dean L. Larsen observes:

Some of us create such a complexity of expectations that it is difficult to cope with the magnitude of them. Sometimes we establish so many particulars by which to evaluate and rate ourselves that it becomes difficult for us to feel successful and worthy to any degree at any time. We can drive ourselves unmercifully toward perfection on such a broad plane. When this compulsion is intensified by sources outside ourselves, the problem is compounded. Confronting these demands can bring mental and emotional despair. . . .

Everyone needs to feel successful and worthy in some ways at least part of the time. The recognition of our frailties need not propel us to try to achieve perfection in one dramatic commitment of effort. The best progress sometimes comes when we are not under intense duress. Overzealousness is at least as much to be feared as apathy. Trying to measure up to too many particular expectations without some sense of self-tolerance can cause spiritual and emotional "burn-out."[2]

Psychologist Albert Ellis believes that most mental illness can be traced to irrational ideas. If your views on life includes one of these irrational ideas, you experience psychological and relationship problems. The second most common cause of mental illness, claims Ellis, is the belief that "you must be unfailingly competent and almost perfect in all you undertake: The results of believing you must behave perfectly are self blame for inevitable failure, lowered self- esteem, perfectionistic standards applied to mate and friends, and paralysis and fear at attempting anything."[3]

Paralysis in marriage and parenting is a condition so contrary to the very purpose of our coming to this earth that we must be wary of any attitude that could hamper our development and progress toward our ultimate perfection.

Psychologists specializing in child rearing coined the phrase the "courage to be imperfect." They believed that perfectionism produces psychologically sick children. Parents who create a perfectionistic atmosphere in the home create a setting where competition, superiority, and pride are the motivators. Children in such homes often become constant judges of their own imperfections and are handicapped with a debilitating fear of making mistakes. Anticipating the danger of making mistakes makes them more vulnerable to error, thus validating their fears that they cannot measure up to parental expectations.

Family relationships that are focused on finding fault and pointing out mistakes usually result in discouragement and ineffective, unhappy human beings. On the other hand, we can just as easily create a home where children are encouraged to try, regardless of the results. Helping others and being useful to friends and community are rewarded. Mistakes are not dwelled upon, but what the individual does after the mistake becomes the focal point. Respect for others and self is emphasized. A child reared in this type of environment is more likely to have the courage to successfully cope with the challenges of living.

And naturally, if such an atmosphere is beneficial for the child, would it not be just as beneficial for the parent? Sister Pat Holland taught this concept to Latter-day Saints when she said, "We must have the courage to be imperfect while striving for perfection."[4]

Our expectations for being the perfect mate and the perfect parent exceed even our professional and individual hopes. Nothing in this earth life is as important to us. Therefore, we often experience our greatest frustrations and disappointments in the family realm. If all is not as we would hope, we are inclined to feel that all is lost, there is no hope.

How much better it would if we periodically reminded ourselves that though we, and circumstances, are not all that we would hope or expect, we are heading in the right direction. If we are allowing ourselves to be tutored, we are improving and getting closer to our ultimate goal. We must learn to get on the straight and narrow path, continue to move in the right direction, relax, and thus accelerate down this wondrous journey.

Please understand! I have not said that we should lower standards of personal conduct or slack off in any of our efforts to be valiant. I am only saying that when results are not perfect, do not give up in desperation. Do not quit. Pick yourself up and do better next time. Perfection is our ultimate goal, but it is not currently the minimum acceptable level of performance.

God has provided us with a thorough and lengthy tutorial experience so that we may learn the needed lessons and develop the necessary traits to become a God. To a discouraged student who wanted to become a doctor or dentist, we would offer counsel to stay in school and not drop out as a mere freshman or sophomore in undergraduate work. Similarly, to those of us who want to become perfect mates and parents, the counsel is the same—do not drop out of school. One day, we can be all that we wish we could be now, but that day will never come if we fail to complete the course. We must show more faith in the Master Teacher and enjoy the education.

Besides, our sense of self-worth should be increased, for we have been given a full-ride scholarship to this institution of higher learning. All of God's creations and His work and glory are for our immortality and eternal life (see Moses 1:39). President Spencer W. Kimball said:

> God is your Father. He loves you. He and your Mother in Heaven value you beyond any measure. They gave your eternal intelligence spirit form, just as your earthly mother and father have given you a mortal body. You are unique, one of a kind, made of the eternal intelligence which gives you claim upon eternal life. Let there be no question in your mind about your value as an individual. The whole intent of the gospel plan is to provide an opportunity for each of you to reach your fullest potential, which is eternal progression and the possibility of godhood.[5]

Of course, any discussion of perfection must include the Lord's command to "be ye therefore perfect, even as your Father which is in heaven is perfect" (Matthew 5:48). However, President Joseph Fielding Smith further clarifies:

Salvation does not come all at once; we are commanded to be perfect even as our Father in heaven is perfect. It will take ages to accomplish this end, for there will be greater progress beyond the grave, and it will be there that the faithful will overcome all things, and receive all things, even the fulness of the Father's glory. . . . I believe the Lord means just what he said: that we should be perfect, as our Father in heaven is perfect. That will not come all at once, but line upon line, and precept upon precept, example upon example, and even then not as long as we live in this mortal life, for we will have to go even beyond the grave before we reach that perfection and shall be like God.[6]

Apparently, the race of life is more of a long steeplechase than a sprint, and we must approach it as such.

That we sometimes forget this, and therefore suffer, needlessly, is too often evident. For example, many a bishopric has spent agonizing hours over what to do about Mother's Day. The issue is more significant than choosing between flowers, chocolate, or a poem. Many mothers consider this their least favorite sacrament meeting of the year and even choose to not attend church that day. For too many, what is intended to be a day of honor becomes a day of self-recrimination and heart ache. To the uninitiated in guilt trips, this may not make much sense. But to those sorely afflicted, the pain is real and grates against the most sensitive of exposed emotional nerve endings.

The scenario goes something like this: The well-intended youth speaker tells a series of stories of perfect mothers. Perhaps you have heard the one of the mother who, in compassion for her child born without ears, had her own ears transplanted onto the young child. The mother's beautiful, long auburn hair concealed the truth from the unsuspecting young woman until years later, at her mother's funeral when she stroked her mother's beautiful hair aside and discovered that her mother's ears had been surgically removed at some earlier date. At that moment the daughter realized that her mother had given up her ears for her daughter.

Whether true or not, the story touches hearts and souls and usually gets the desired response as many in the congregation shed tears. However, the tears of the mothers in the congregation are, more often than not, tears of guilt and shame. After all, they still have their ears! And therefore, they must not be perfect, or even good, mothers. For some mothers, it is less painful to skip church on Mother's Day than to be so cruelly reminded that they are not perfect mothers.

Well-intended Relief Society lessons sometimes have the same undesired results. One Sunday morning after a mother education lesson, I noticed a higher than normal percentage of women leaving the Relief Society meeting with tears streaming down their faces. These did not appear to be tears of joy or appreciation, so I asked one of the sisters about it. She responded that the teacher had just taught such a wonderful lesson on how to be the perfect mother. I asked why this would make her cry tears of sorrow. This sister explained that she fell so far below the ideal described by the teacher that she was overcome with her own inadequacies. She would not be comforted and left the building brokenhearted.

I stepped into the Relief Society room to visit with the teacher, who had brought so many to tears. There, alone, leaning against the wall sobbing, was the teacher! I told her that her lesson seemed to touch many sisters and wondered why she would be so downhearted. She exclaimed through her tears that she felt like such a hypocrite! She had spent the entire month preparing and gave the lesson as outlined, but she knew that she was not living those principles she espoused, and thus she wept in shame and guilt.

Both teacher and class members had misunderstood. The ideals being presented were standards to which we must strive, but they are not standards of minimum performance for which we condemn ourselves. This is not the final judgment day! And, fortunately, we are not the judge. Somehow, we must motivate others and ourselves in ways that inspire enhanced performance and not recrimination and spiritual paralysis.

It is common for a woman who compares herself to others to

conclude that she does not measure up. However, at such a time, the distraught woman is usually not listening to the loving Spirit, which is applauding her goodness and encouraging continued growth. In addition, when such comparisons are made, a woman is more likely comparing herself to an imaginary, perfect woman who does not exist. Margaret B. Black and Midge W. Nielsen labeled this woman of fiction Patti Perfect:

> Many LDS women unconsciously compete with an idealized image of the already perfect wife and mother who successfully incorporates all the demands of family, church, and society into her life. Although we have never met such a woman, we persist in believing she's out there somewhere. We can just imagine what she must accomplish in a day. . . .
>
> Patti gets up very early and says her personal prayers. She zips her slim, vigorous body into her warmup suit and tiptoes outside to run her usual five miles (on Saturday she does ten). Returning home all aglow, she showers and dresses for the day in a tailored skirt and freshly starched and ironed blouse. She settles down for quiet meditation and scripture reading, before preparing the family breakfast. The morning's menu calls for whole-wheat pancakes, homemade syrup, freshly squeezed orange juice, and powdered milk (the whole family loves it).
>
> With classical music wafting through the air, Patti awakens her husband and 10 children. She spends a quiet moment with each and helps them plan a happy day. The children quickly dress in clothes that were laid out the night before. They cheerfully make their beds, clean their rooms, and do the individual chores assigned to them on the Family Work Wheel Chart. They assemble for breakfast the minute mother calls.
>
> After family prayer and scripture study, the children all practice their different musical instruments. Father leaves for work on a happy note. All too soon it is time for the children to leave for school. Having

brushed (and flossed) their teeth, the children pick up coats, book bags, and lunches, which were prepared the night before and arrive at school five minutes early.

With things more quiet, Patti has story-time with her pre-schoolers and teaches them a cognitive reading skill. She feeds, bathes, and rocks the baby before putting him down for his morning nap. With baby sleeping peacefully and the three-year-old twins absorbed in creative play, Patti tackles the laundry and housework. In less than an hour, everything is in order. Thanks to wise scheduling and children who are trained to work, her house never really gets dirty.

Proceeding to the kitchen, Patti sets out tonight's dinner: frozen veal parmigiana that she made in quantity from her home-grown tomatoes and peppers. She then mixes and kneads 12 loaves of bread. While the bread rises, Patti dips a batch of candles to supplement her food storage. As the bread bakes, she writes in her personal journal and dashes off a few quick letters: one to her Congressman and a couple of genealogy inquiries to distant cousins. Patti then prepares her mini-class lesson on organic gardening. She also inserts two pictures and a certificate in little Paul's scrapbook, noting with satisfaction that all family albums are attractive and up-to-date. Checking the mail, Patti sees that their income tax refund has arrived—a result of having filed in January. It is earmarked for mission and college savings accounts. Although Patti's hard-working husband earns only a modest salary, her careful budgeting has kept the family debt-free.

After lunch, Patti drops the children off at Grandma's for their weekly visit. Grandma enjoys babysitting and appreciates the warm loaf of bread. Making an extra call, Patti takes a second loaf to one of the sisters she is assigned to visit teach. A third loaf goes to the non-member neighbor on the corner.

Patti arrives at the elementary school where she directs a special education program. A clinical psychologist, Patti finds this an excellent way to stay abreast of her field while raising her family. Before picking up her little ones, Patti finishes collecting for the charity and fund drive.

Home again, Patti settles the children down for their afternoon naps. She spends some quiet time catching up on her reading and filing. As she mists her luxuriant house plants, the school children come through the door. Patti listens attentively to each one as they tell about their day. The children start right in on their homework, with Mother supervising and encouraging them. When all schoolwork is done, Patti and the children enjoy working on one of their projects. Today they work on the quilt stretched on frames in a corner of the family room.

Dinnertime and Father arrives, and it is a special hour for the whole family. They enjoy Patti's well-balanced, tasty meal, along with stimulating conversation. After dinner, Father and the children pitch in to clean up so that mom can relax. She enjoys listening to the sounds of laughter and affection that come from the kitchen.

With the teenaged children in charge at home, Mother and Father attend an evening session at the Temple. During the return trip, they sit close together as in courting days. "Well, Dear," says Paul Perfect, "did you have a good day?" Patti reflectively answers, "Yes, I really did. But I feel I need more challenge in my life. I think I'll contact our Family Organization and volunteer to head up a reunion for August."[7]

We may laugh at such a spoof, but the realities are that many women do compare themselves to such an imaginary perfect woman and, therefore, become very discouraged or even depressed. For them, this little poem may be more accurate:

I am alone,
And the Church is filled with perfect

Mothers and sweet sisters who know their
Role—and
I am alone.
I am alone—sometimes it seems
Every word is directed at me and
For me
Because
My house is unorganized—and I'm often
Impatient—and I feel resentment
Because he has to go so much.
I am alone. And guilty. Because the
Church is filled with perfect mothers and
Sweet sisters who know their role and—
I am alone—and lonely—
Oh, that someone could understand
Without judging—help without criticizing—
For I am alone.[8]

When we judge and condemn ourselves for our imperfections, it is little wonder that we long for peace and a sense of worth. Professionals may attempt to help individuals struggling with such incongruence by suggesting that the troublesome standards be eliminated. Granted, there are certainly times when our expectations may be unrealistic and need to be modified. However, we have no right to do away with revealed standards just because we are not living up to the ideal.

So, if we cannot do away with the standard, yet we feel badly for not living up to that level, what can we do to ease the discontent? We can progress toward the standard! We would all perform at a much higher level, and enjoy the experience, if we would recognize that progression is what is expected of us. In our currently imperfect state, we can always do better. And in doing better, we have the right to feel the encouragement of the Holy Ghost.

The straight and narrow path is to be traveled for improvement, for progress. The path is not the destination, it is for getting to the ultimate destination. However, at this stage in our progression, it is enough to be on the path and headed in the right direction. To become depressed and dysfunctional because we are not yet perfect would be like boarding a plane to an exotic destination but then jumping out the cargo door en-route because we had not yet arrived. Wouldn't it make more sense to complete the journey and actually arrive at the desired destination?

M. Catherine Thomas writes:

> We can be so cruel to ourselves; we destroy ourselves with our negative self-talk. We see only the raw material, much of it yet undeveloped, and we block from our awareness many already godlike qualities in us. We throw a wet blanket over all this divine fire. We steadfastly ignore the fact that many of our goals have been accomplished by our exercising godlike qualities: sacrifice, discipline, creativity, perseverance, love, faith. We decline to acknowledge the divinity that is developing in us through the challenges that life has presented to us for this very purpose. And we are ready to argue—in a most ungodly way—with anyone who tries to tell us something to the contrary. This refusal to accept our developing divinity is a sort of blasphemy and a denial of the purposes of the plan of salvation; it diminishes the effectiveness of our service and inhibits our full surrender to the Lord Jesus Christ. There is no real settled contentment, no real enlarging of the soul to meet great opportunities and possibilities, until we find our own divine fire.[9]

President George Q. Cannon observed the following:

> Now, this is the truth. We humble people, we who feel ourselves sometimes so worthless, so good-for-nothing, we are not so worthless as we think. There is not one of us but what God's love has been expended upon. There is not one of us that He has not cared for and caressed. There is not one of us that He has not desired to save and that He has not devised means to save. There is not one of us that He has not given His

angels charge concerning. We may be insignificant and contemptible in our own eyes and in the eyes of others, but the truth remains that we are children of God and that He has actually given His angels . . . charge concerning us, and they watch over us and have us in their keeping.[10]

How long has God given us to achieve perfection? Is time about up? Is it time to panic or give up? It is comforting to know that the time remaining is not really the issue. We will have plenty of time, if we are diligently doing our best. Sinning or quitting are the real concerns, not running out of time.

Certainly, we should not become lax or slothful. "For behold, this life is the time for men to prepare to meet God; yea, behold the day of this life is the day for men to perform their labors.

"And now, as I said unto you before, as ye have had so many witnesses, therefore, I beseech of you that ye do not procrastinate the day of your repentance until the end; for after this day of life, which is given us to prepare for eternity, behold, if we do not improve our time while in this life, then cometh the night of darkness wherein there can be no labor performed" (Alma 34:32–33).

But what of those who did not procrastinate and did improve, yet still died imperfect? We must be careful not to equate mortality with the second estate (see Abraham 3:26). The second half of the second estate, the spirit world, is also a place for progress, for those who are still learning and growing—which is all of us. The Prophet Joseph Smith taught, "When you climb up a ladder, you must begin at the bottom, and ascend step by step, until you arrive at the top; and so it is with the principles of the Gospel—you must begin with the first, and go on until you learn all the principles of exaltation. But it will be a great while after you have passed through the veil before you will have learned them. It is not all to be comprehended in this world; it will be a great work to learn our salvation and exaltation even beyond the grave."[11]

"Another idea that is powerful to lift us from discouragement," said Elder Dallin H. Oaks, "is that the work of the Church of Jesus Christ of Latter-day Saints to 'bring to pass the . . . eternal life of man' (Moses 1:39) is an eternal work. Not all problems are overcome and not all needed relationships are fixed in mortality. The work of salvation goes on beyond the veil of death, and we should not be too apprehensive about incompleteness within the limits of mortality."[12]

President Joseph Fielding Smith noted that "here we lay the foundation. Here is where we are taught these simple truths of the gospel of Jesus Christ, in this probationary state, to prepare us for that perfection. It is our duty to be better today than we were yesterday, and better tomorrow than we are today. Why? Because we are on that road, if we are keeping the commandments of the Lord, we are on that road to perfection, and that can only come through obedience and the desire in our hearts to overcome the world."[13]

Elder Bruce R. McConkie wrote:

> What we are saying is that when the saints of God chart a course of righteousness, when they gain sure testimonies of the truth and divinity of the Lord's work, when they keep the commandments, when they overcome the world, when they put first in their lives the things of God's kingdom, when they do all these things, and then depart this life though they have not yet become perfect they shall nevertheless gain eternal life in our Father's kingdom; and eventually they shall be perfect as God their Father and Christ His Son are perfect.[14]

Later, he repeated this message:

> Everyone in the Church who is on the straight and narrow path, who is striving and struggling and desiring to do what is right, though is far from perfect in this life; if he passes out of this life while he's on the straight and narrow, he's going to go on to eternal

reward in his Father's kingdom. . . .

We don't need to get a complex or get a feeling that you have to be perfect to be saved. You don't. There's only been one perfect person, and that's the Lord Jesus, but in order to be saved in the Kingdom of God and in order to pass the test of mortality, what you have to do is get on the straight and narrow path—thus charting a course leading to eternal life—and then, being on the path, pass out of this life in full fellowship. I'm not saying that you don't have to keep the commandments. I'm saying that you don't have to be perfect to be saved. If you did, no one would be saved. The way it operates is this: you get on the path that's named the "straight and narrow." You do it by entering the gate of repentance and baptism. The straight and narrow path leads from the gate of repentance and baptism, a very great distance, to a reward that's called eternal life. If you're on that path and pressing forward, and you die, you'll never get off the path. There is no such thing as falling off the straight and narrow path in the life to come, and the reason is that this life is the time that is given to men to prepare for eternity. Now is the time and the day of your salvation, so if you're working zealously in this life—though you haven't fully overcome the world and you haven't done all you hoped you might do—you're still going to be saved. You don't have to do what Jacob said, "Go beyond the mark." You don't have to live a life that's truer than true. You don't have to have an excessive zeal that becomes fanatical and becomes unbalancing. What you have to do is stay in the mainstream of the Church and live as upright and decent people live in the Church—keeping the commandments, paying your tithing, serving in the organizations of the Church, loving the Lord, staying on the straight and narrow path. If you're on that path when death comes—because this is the time and the day appointed, this the probationary estate—you'll never fall off from it, and, for all practical purposes, your calling and election is made sure.[15]

A few months later, in a similar address, Elder McConkie added:

> There are yet others who have an excessive zeal which causes them to go beyond the mark. Their desire for excellence is inordinate. In an effort to be truer than true they devote themselves to gaining a special, personal relationship with Christ that is both improper and perilous. . . . I say perilous because this course, particularly in the lives of some who are spiritually immature, is a gospel hobby which creates an unwholesome holier-than-thou-attitude. In other instances it leads to despondency because the seeker after perfection knows he is not living the way he supposes he should.[16]

Then what should we be doing on a daily basis? We should diligently strive to do our best, live to be worthy of the companionship of the Holy Ghost, and cease to fret over the fact that we are not yet perfect. Consider this counsel from President Heber J. Grant:

> I do not believe that any man lives up to his ideals, but if we are striving, if we are working, if we are trying, to the best of our ability, to improve day by day, then we are in the line of our duty. If we are seeking to remedy our own defects, if we are so living that we can ask God for light, for knowledge, for intelligence, and above all, for His Spirit, that we may overcome our weaknesses, then, I can tell you, we are in the straight and narrow path that leads to life eternal. Then we need have no fear.[17]

This counsel from President Gordon B. Hinckley reveals the attitude of the Lord toward us and thus the attitude we also should have toward ourselves: "Please don't nag yourself with thoughts of failure. Do not set goals far beyond your capacity to achieve. Simply do what you can do, in the best way you know, and the Lord will accept of your effort."[18]

Elder Neal A. Maxwell wrote that "the Church is for the perfecting of the Saints, hence new arrivals are entitled to expect instant community but not instant sainthood—either in themselves or in others."[19] On another occasion, he observed that "though imperfect, an improving person can actually know that the course of his life is generally acceptable to the Lord despite there being much distance yet to be covered."[20]

He also wrote, "Just as God cannot look upon sin with the least degree of allowance (D&C 1:13), as we become more like Him, neither can we. The best people have a heightened awareness of what little of the worst is still in them!"[21]

How can we as imperfect, though improving, individuals know that the Lord is pleased with the course our lives are taking? The Lord's pleasure is manifest by the gift of the Holy Ghost endowed upon each of us. In addition to providing revelation and guidance, the presence of the Holy Ghost is an indication to each of us that our lives, though still needing much improving, are headed in the right direction, and thus pleasing to the Lord. The comfort and peace that accompanies the Holy Ghost encourages continued progress down that same path that has brought us to this point.

Though the task is so great that we will not arrive at perfection while in mortality, we can and should on a daily basis live so as to be worthy of the companionship of the Holy Ghost. What the Lord requires of us is that we be on the path, headed in the right direction, being patient, knowing that He will guide us to our ultimate destination. The straight and narrow path is a lighted path, lighted by the Light of Christ and the Holy Ghost. As long as we stay in the light, we will do fine.

"That which is of God is light; and he that receiveth light, and continueth in God, receiveth more light; and that light groweth brighter and brighter until the perfect day" (D&C 50:24).

Elder John A. Widtsoe said:

> The gift of the Holy Ghost remains inoperative unless a person leads a blameless life. Worthiness determines whether a person shall enjoy the privileges promised when the "gift" is conferred. It is useless to expect this high official assistance unless there is daily conformity to the laws of the gospel. Faith and prayer, out of the heart and unceasing, will fit a person for the presence of the Holy Ghost, and to such a life he will respond in power. Latter-day Saints have received, under the hands of those divinely empowered, this inexpressibly glorious "gift," which will lead them if they are fitted, into the companionship of the Holy Ghost, and win for them intelligence and power to win joy in life and exaltation in the world to come. Those who have been so blessed have not always understood the greatness of that which has been given them, or have not earnestly sought its help. So powerful a gift, with such boundless promise, justifies every attempt to cleanse body and soul. Certain it is, that only with the aid of the Holy Ghost shall we be able to rise to the heights of salvation of which we dream and for which we pray.[22]

The writers of the scriptures acknowledge our imperfection. But rather than concluding that we are totally depraved, as did Augustine and Calvin, these inspired men encourage us to try even harder. Referring to himself, Paul said, "Not as though I had already attained, either were already perfect: but I follow after, if that I may apprehend that for which also I am apprehended of Christ Jesus.

"Brethren, I count not myself to have apprehended: but this one thing I do, forgetting those things which are behind, and reaching forth unto those things which are before, I press toward the mark for the prize of the high calling of God in Christ Jesus" (Philippians 3:12–14).

King Benjamin taught:

> As ye have come to the knowledge of the glory of
> God, or if ye have known of his goodness and have
> tasted of his love, and have received a remission of your
> sins, which causeth such exceedingly great joy in your
> souls, even so I would that ye should remember, and
> always retain in remembrance, the greatness of God,
> and your own nothingness, and his goodness and long-
> suffering toward you, unworthy creatures, and humble
> yourselves even in the depths of humility, calling on
> the name of the Lord daily, and standing steadfastly in
> the faith of that which is to come, which was spoken
> by the mouth of the angel.
>
> And behold, I say unto you that if ye do this ye
> shall always rejoice, and be filled with the love of God,
> and always retain a remission of your sins; and ye shall
> grow in the knowledge of the glory of him that cre-
> ated you, or in the knowledge of that which is just and
> true. . . .
>
> And see that all these things are done in wisdom
> and order; for it is not requisite that a man should run
> faster than he has strength. And again, it is expedient
> that he should be diligent, that thereby he might win
> the prize; therefore, all things must be done in order.
> (Mosiah 4:11–12, 27)

Moroni's closing message in the Book of Mormon consists of
this invitation: "Yea, come unto Christ, and be perfected in him,
and deny yourselves of all ungodliness; and if ye shall deny yourselves of all ungodliness, and love God with all your might, mind,
and strength, then is his grace sufficient for you, that by his grace
ye may be perfect in Christ . . .

"And again, if ye by the grace of God are perfect in Christ,
and deny not his power, then are ye sanctified in Christ by the
grace of God, through the shedding of the blood of Christ, which
is in the covenant of the Father" (Moroni 10:32–33).

Finally, the Lord counseled, "Ye are not able to abide the presence of God now, neither the ministering of angels; wherefore, continue in patience until ye are perfected" (D&C 67:13).

The words of the Lord and His prophets give encouragement to move forward and never give up. The philosophies of men and creeds of Satan lead to discouragement and withdrawing from the race. Elder Bruce C. Hafen noted:

> The person most in need of understanding the grandeur of the Savior's mercy is probably the one who has worked himself to exhaustion in a sincere effort to repent, but who still believes his estrangement from God is permanent and hopeless. . . .
>
> I sense that an increasing number of Church members are weighed down beyond the breaking point with discouragement about their personal lives, even while making sustained and admirable efforts. When we habitually understate the meaning of the Atonement, we take more serious risks than simply leaving one another without comforting reassurances—for some may simply drop out of the race, worn out and beaten down with the inaccurate belief that they are just not celestial material. . . .
>
> Perfection is another category of both our theology and our experience in which we may also be rescued by the Lord's mercy, for perfection is finally made possible through the Atonement. While part of the perfection process involves being cleansed from our sins; there is also an affirmative dimension through which we acquire a Christlike nature, becoming perfect even as the Father and the Son are perfect. . . .
>
> Such a promise throws a wonderful lifeline to the increasing numbers among us who feel discouragement, stress, low self-esteem, and even depression. The Savior desires to save us from our inadequacies as well as our sins. Inadequacy is not the same as being sinful—we have far more control over the choice to sin than we may have over our innate capacity. We sometimes say that the Lord will not save us in our sins, but

from them. It is quite possible, however, that he will save us in our inadequacies as well as from them. A sense of falling short or falling down is not only natural, but also essential to the mortal experience. But, after all we can do, the Atonement can fill that which is empty, straighten our bent parts, and make strong that which is weak.[23]

Thus if we would dwell less upon our imperfections and focus intently upon His perfection and the Atonement, we would be far more inclined to lean further toward His end of the spectrum. Sniveling in our imperfections is an excuse for not trying hard enough and not repenting sincerely enough; it evidences a lack of understanding and perhaps even a lack of faith in our Redeemer and the Atonement!

Stephen E. Robinson wrote:

Perfection comes through the Atonement of Christ. We become one with him, with a perfect being. And as we become one, there is a merger. Some of my students are studying business, and they understand it better if I talk in business terms. You take a small bankrupt firm that's about ready to go under and merge it with a corporate giant. What happens? Their assets and liabilities flow together, and the new entity that is created is solvent. . . .

Spiritually, this is what happens when we enter into the covenant relationship with our Savior. We have liabilities, he has assets. He proposes to us a covenant relationship. I use the word 'propose' on purpose because it is a marriage of a spiritual sort that is being proposed. That is why he is called the Bridegroom. This covenant relationship is so intimate that it can be described as a marriage. I become one with Christ, and as partners we work together for my salvation and my exaltation. My liabilities and his assets flow into each other. I do all that I can do, and he does what I cannot yet do. The two of us together are perfect.[24]

Elder M. Russell Ballard shared this:

> As most of you know, coping with the complex and
> diverse challenges of everyday life, which is not an
> easy task, can upset the balance and harmony we seek.
> Many good people who care a great deal are trying
> very hard to maintain balance, but they sometimes feel
> overwhelmed and defeated. . . .
>
> Another mother of four remarked, "My struggle is
> between self-esteem, confidence, and feelings of self-
> worth versus guilt, depression, and discouragement for
> not doing everything I am told we must do to attain
> the celestial kingdom."
>
> Brothers and sisters, we all face these kinds of
> struggles from time to time. They are common human
> experiences. Many people have heavy demands upon
> them stemming from parental, family, employment,
> church, and civic responsibilities. Keeping everything
> in balance can be a real problem. . . . Set short-term
> goals that you can reach. Set goals that are well bal-
> anced—not too many nor too few, and not too high
> nor too low. Write down your attainable goals and
> work on them according to their importance. Pray for
> divine guidance in your goal setting. . . .
>
> Not long ago, one of my children said, "Dad,
> sometimes I wonder if I will ever make it." The answer
> I gave to her is the same as I would give to you if you
> have had similar feelings. Just do the very best you can
> each day. Do the basic things and before you realize
> it, your life will be full of spiritual understanding that
> will confirm to you that your Heavenly Father loves
> you. When a person knows this, then life will be full
> of purpose and meaning, making balance easier to
> maintain.[25]

Too many have prejudged themselves as irredeemable or forever inadequate and, therefore, default to a life of despair or what-
difference-does-it-make sin. Such an approach severely handicaps

our performance and our happiness. We must remind ourselves that, while perfection may be our ultimate goal, today we focus on improvement, on progress. All great things take time, and perfection is no exception. We recognize this principle in academics, in athletics, in talents. The principle applies equally well to matters of personal mastery, marriage, and parenting. Elder Maxwell masterfully addressed these issues when he said:

> Now may I speak, not to the slackers in the Kingdom, but to those who carry their own load and more, not to those lulled into false security, but to those buffeted by false insecurity, who, though laboring devotedly in the Kingdom, have recurring feelings of falling forever short . . .
>
> The first thing to be said of this feeling of inadequacy is that it is normal. There is no way the Church can honestly describe where we must yet go and what we must yet do without creating a sense of immense distance. Following celestial road signs while in telestial traffic jams is not easy . . .
>
> There is a difference, therefore between being "anxiously engaged" and being over-anxious and thus underengaged. . . .
>
> Brothers and Sisters, the scriptures are like a developmental display window through which we can see gradual growth—along with this vital lesson, it is direction first, then velocity! Enoch's unique people were improved "in process of time" (Moses 7:21). Jesus "received not of the fulness at first, but received grace for grace" (D&C 93:12) and even He grew and "increased in wisdom and stature" (Luke 2:52) . . .
>
> What can we do to manage these vexing feelings of inadequacy? Here are but a few suggestions:
>
> 1. We can distinguish more clearly between divine discontent and the devil's dissonance, between dissatisfaction with self and disdain for self. We need the first and must shun the second, remembering that when conscience calls to us from the next ridge, it is

not solely to scold but also to beckon.

2. We can contemplate how far we have already come in the climb along the pathway to perfection; it is usually much farther than we acknowledge. True, we are "unprofitable servants," but partly because when "we have done that which was our duty to do" (Luke 17:10), with every ounce of such obedience comes a bushel of blessings.

3. We can accept help as well as gladly give it . . .

4. We can allow for the agency of others (including our children) before we assess our adequacy. Often our deliberate best is less effectual because of someone else's worst.

5. We can write down and act upon more of those accumulating resolutions for self-improvement that we so often leave, unrecovered, at the edge of sleep.

6. We can admit that if we were to die today, we would be genuinely and deeply missed . . .

7. We can put our hand to the plow, looking neither back nor around, comparatively. Our gifts and opportunities differ: some are more visible and impactful. The historian Moroni felt inadequate as a writer beside the mighty Mahonri Moriancumer, who wrote overpoweringly. We all have at least one gift and an open invitation to seek "earnestly the best gifts" (D&C 46:8).

8. We can make quiet but more honest inventories of our strengths, since, in this connection, most of us are dishonest bookkeepers and need confirming "outside auditors." He who was thrust down in the first estate delights to have us put ourselves down. Self-contempt is of Satan; there is none of it in heaven. We should, of course, learn from our mistakes, but without forever studying the instant replays as if these were the game of life itself.

9. We can add to each other's storehouse of self-esteem by giving deserved, specific commendation more often, remembering too, that those who are

breathless from going the second mile need deserved praise just as the fallen need to be lifted up.

10. We can also keep moving. Only the Lord can compare crosses, but all crosses are easier to carry when we keep moving.

11. We can know that when we have truly given what we have, it is like paying a full tithe; it is, in that respect, all that was asked . . .

12. We can allow for the reality that God is more concerned with growth than with geography . . .

13. We can learn that at the center of our agency is our freedom to form a healthy attitude toward whatever circumstances we are placed in! . . .

14. Finally, we can accept this stunning, irrevocable truth: Our Lord can lift us from deep despair and cradle us midst any care. We cannot tell Him anything about aloneness or nearness! . . .

True, there are no instant Christians, but there are constant Christians![26]

The Prophet Joseph Smith exemplified the attitude we should have relative to ourselves and others. "I told them I was but a man, and they must not expect me to be perfect," he said. "If they expected perfections from me, I should expect it from them, but if they would bear with my infirmities and the infirmities of the brethren, I would likewise bear with their infirmities."[27]

Our contemporary leaders also provide encouragement and guidance as we work to achieve this delicate balance. Elder Richard G. Scott taught, "Throughout your life on earth, seek diligently to fulfill the fundamental purposes of this life *through the ideal family.* While you may not have yet reached that ideal, do all you can through obedience and faith in the Lord to consistently draw as close to it as you are able. Let nothing dissuade you from that objective. . . . Don't become overanxious. . . . Do the best you can while on earth to have an ideal family."[28]

How do we apply these principles to our family life? We must never quit but diligently move forward with balance. We need to recognize that, at this phase of our development, we are expected to be progressing, though absolute perfection will not be attained in mortality. While we can't accept sin or slothfulness, we must be patient with our inadequacies. And ultimately, after all we can do, we must have faith in the Lord and His ability to redeem us from sin and inadequacy. In other words, we must have the courage to be imperfect, while striving for perfection!

Notes

1. Ralph, *The Bible and the End of the World*, 117.

2. Larsen, "The Message: The Peaceable Things of the Kingdom," *New Era*, February 1986, 6.

3. Ellis, *Humanistic Psychotherapy: Rational/Emotive Applications.*

4. Holland, "One Needful Thing: Becoming Women of Greater Faith in Christ," *Ensign*, October 1987, 26–33.

5. Kimball, "Privileges and Responsibilities of Sisters," *Ensign*, November 1978, 105.

6. Smith, *Doctrines of Salvation*, 2:18.

7. Margaret B. Black and Midge W. Nielsen, in Barlow, *Twelve Traps in Today's Marriages*, 148.

8. Mike Zundell, unpublished poem; used with permission.

9. Thomas, *Gospel Scholarship Series*, 254.

10. Cannon, *Gospel Truth*, 1:2.

11. Smith, *Teachings of the Prophet Joseph Smith*, 346–48.

12. Oaks, "Powerful Ideas," *Ensign*, November 1995, 26.

13. Smith, *Doctrines of Salvation*, 2:18–19.

14. McConkie, "The Dead Who Die in the Lord," *Ensign*, November 1976, 107.

15. McConkie, *Here We Stand*, 175.

16. McConkie, *Sermons of Bruce R. McConkie*, 66.

17. Grant, *Gospel Standards*, 184–85.

18. Hinckley, "Rise to the Stature of the Divine within You," *Ensign*, November 1989, 96.

19. Maxwell, "The Net Gathers of Every Kind," *Ensign*, November 1980, 15.

20. Maxwell, *Men and Women of Christ*, 23.

21. Maxwell, *Notwithstanding My Weakness*, 16–17.

22. Widtsoe, *Evidences and Reconciliation*, 150–51.

23. Hafen, *The Broken Heart*, 5–6, 19.

24. Robinson, "Believing Christ," *Liahona*, April 1992, 14.

25. Ballard, "Keeping Life's Demands in Balance," *Ensign*, May 1987, 13–16.

26. Maxwell, "Notwithstanding My Weakness," *Ensign*, November 1976, 12.

27. Ehat and Cook, *Words of Joseph Smith*, 132.

28. Scott, "First Things First," *Ensign*, May 2001, 7.

6

BE OF GOOD

cheer

As we work to develop personality traits and characteristics that will serve us well in a celestial marriage, we should also be looking for these same traits in our future spouse. Eternity is a long time; we want our relationship to be pleasant and exhilarating. In contrast, one day being miserable or being with someone who is miserable can seem like an eternity!

Although you'll most likely identify many important character traits you desire in your spouse, consider this: "The most important characteristic of a marriageable person is the habit of happiness."[1] As we made our lists of characteristics we were looking for in our future spouse, it is very possible that being happy did not show up. However, soon into marriage we begin to recognize that this is a very desirable attribute. And the longer we are married, the more important this trait becomes! In fact, we come to realize fairly quickly that the habit of happiness is not just desirable, but essential, for a happy celestial marriage.

Les Parrott III, a noted marriage therapist, wrote:

> It is no accident that some couples who encounter

marital turbulence navigate it successfully, while others in similar circumstances are buffeted by frustration, disappointment, and eventual despair. It is also no accident that some couples are radiant, positive, and happy, while other couples are beaten down, defeated, and anxiety-ridden. Researchers who have searched for the difference between the two groups have come up with all kinds of explanations for marital success (long courtships, similar backgrounds, supportive families, good communication, well educated, and so on). But the bottom line is that happy couples *decide* to be happy. In spite of the troubles life deals them, they make happiness a habit . . . it is your attitude that will determine whether you and your partner "live happily ever after." . . . Happiness in marriage has nothing to do with luck and everything to do with will.[2]

The simple truth is, we like to be around happy people. Happy people make those around them happy. One day, I surprised one of my seminary students with this question: "Noni, why are you always so happy?" After a few seconds of pondering, she sweetly responded, "I suppose it's because my mother is always happy." What a profound insight! What a marvelous legacy this mother has bequeathed to her daughter and perhaps generations yet unborn.

Ron Enos was a fellow seminary teacher that I saw only a few times each year at area meetings. I looked forward to seeing Ron. His Hawaiian heritage blessed him with a perpetual tan; a deep, mellow voice; and a beautiful countenance that I learned to love as a missionary in New Zealand. "Hi, Ron, how are you?" I would greet him. Without fail, he always responded with a genuine, "I'm happy, thank you. How are you?"

His answer never failed to impress me—and it always cheered me. I often shared my experience with Ron in my classes, and one day in an institute class, a young lady raised her hand. To my surprise, she said, "Ron Enos is my dad!" She then added that even at home he was that way, genuinely happy and striving

☙

to help others enjoy that same happiness. What a blessing—and legacy—to share with others.

"Happiness," said the Prophet Joseph Smith, "is the object and design of our existence." However, far too few couples, even within the Church, seem to really be happy. Often happiness would be significantly increased if we complied with the rest of Joseph's statement, which continues with this caveat: "if we pursue the path that leads to it; and this path is virtue, upright-ness, faithfulness, holiness and keeping all the commandments of God."[3] Certainly Alma was correct when he observed that any time we act "contrary to the nature of God" we are "in a state contrary to the nature of happiness" (see Alma 41:10–11).

Yet even those couples that diligently strive to keep the weight-ier matters of the law sometimes fail to experience this illusive commodity called happiness. To what extent do our *desires* and *will* determine if we are happy? Can we do anything to increase our own happiness?

Yes! In fact, we are ultimately the only ones who can make ourselves happy. Happiness is not something you find or some-thing that others can force upon you. Happiness is something you choose. Happiness is the result of our use of agency and our attitudes. Simply stated, we can choose to be happy and only we can make ourselves unhappy.

Before a person can experience happiness, he or she must have "desires of happiness" (Alma 41:5). Happiness must be something we genuinely desire. It must have more value for us than the dis-torted payoff of wallowing in self-pity and dwelling upon the pes-simistic and negative aspects of life. Being unhappy may result in obtaining sympathy, exercising power over others, or relieving one of much responsibility among peers, but it is not a very satisfying approach to life's challenges. Wise King Solomon observed that, "A merry heart maketh a cheerful countenance: but by sorrow of the heart the spirit is broken" (Proverbs 15:13).

Attitude, like clothing styles, is a matter of choice. We choose, by our perception and paradigm, to be happy or miserable. When caught in a rut of pessimism, we can accomplish much through optimism, gratitude, and changing attitudes. We can accomplish even more through scripture reading, prayer, losing ourselves in the service of others, and praising God. "There are seeds of happiness planted in every human soul," observed President David O. McKay. "Our mental attitude and disposition constitute the environment in which these seeds may germinate. There is as much need for sunshine in the heart as for sunshine in the world."[4]

Happiness, however, should not be understood to be the absence of trials or suffering. In fact, Peter taught that "if ye suffer for righteousness' sake, happy are ye" (1 Peter 3:14). Many difficulties are listed in the Beatitudes, but we can react to each with a conscious decision "to be happy" (Matthew 5:3, footnote a). Happiness seems not to be the result of our circumstances, but the reflection of our righteousness and faith in Christ, in spite of our circumstances. Though in a period of terrible war and destruction, it is said of the people of Captain Moroni "there never was a happier time among the people" (Alma 50:23). To him who was sick of the palsy, Jesus said, "Son, be of good cheer" (Matthew 9:2). To the disciples troubled with fear, "Jesus spake unto them, saying, Be of good cheer" (Matthew 14:26). And to those same disciples who were anxious about His departure, Jesus counseled, "In the world ye shall have tribulation: but be of good cheer; I have overcome the world" (John 16:33).

Similar messages were given to disciples in our day. To those encountering many dangers upon the Missouri River, the Lord said, "Be of good cheer, little children; for I am in your midst, and I have not forsaken you" (D&C 61:36). To concerned elders, the Lord responded, "Be of good cheer, and do not fear, for I the Lord am with you" (D&C 68:6). To those wondering how to provide for the poor, Jesus instructed, "Ye cannot bear all things now; nevertheless, be of good cheer, for I will lead you along" (D&C 78:18). Notice how often we are commanded to be of good cheer because Christ is with us or has one something—or everything—for us.

"We are commanded to be joyful because he has borne our sorrows," wrote noted scholar Hugh Nibley. "He was a man of sorrows and acquainted with grief so that we need not be. Our own sins and limitations are the things that make us sad. He had no sins and limitations: he was not sad for his sake, but wholly for ours. Only one could suffer for others who did not deserve to suffer for himself . . . If we remain gloomy after what he did for us, it is because we do not accept what he did for us. If we suffer, we deserve to suffer because there is no need for it if we only believe in him."[5]

The *Oxford English Dictionary* notes that *cheer* can mean a "disposition, frame of mind, mood, etc. esp. as showing itself by external demeanor, etc., usually with qualifications as 'good,' 'glad,' 'joyful,' or 'sorrowful,' 'heavy' etc."

"Be of good cheer" could therefore mean a charge to have a happy or joyful disposition or attitude.

To be of good cheer is not just a choice, it is a commandment! Keeping this commandment greatly blesses our lives and the lives of our loved ones, especially our spouses. We owe it to these most important individuals in our lives to be of good cheer. It might be well for us to review our attitudes when we are interviewed by our bishop and he asks something like this: "Is there anything in your conduct relating to members of your family that is not in harmony with the teachings of the Church?"

President Gordon B. Hinckley shared these thoughts:

> I enjoy these words of Jenkins Lloyd Jones which I clipped from a column in the *Deseret News* some years ago. I pass them on to you as I conclude my remarks. Said he: "Anyone who imagines that bliss is normal is going to waste a lot of time running round shouting that he's been robbed. . . . Most putts don't drop. Most beef is tough. Most children grow up to be just people. Most successful marriages require a high degree of mutual toleration. Most jobs are more often dull than otherwise. . . . Life is like an old-time rail journey—delays, sidetracks, smoke, dust, cinders, and jolts, interspersed only occasionally by beautiful vistas and thrilling bursts of speed. . . . The trick is to thank

the Lord for letting you have the ride." (*Deseret News*, 12 June 1973.) I repeat, my brothers and sisters, the trick is to thank the Lord for letting you have the ride; and really, isn't it a wonderful ride? Enjoy it! Laugh about it! Sing about it! Remember the words of the writer of Proverbs: 'A merry heart doeth good like a medicine: but a broken spirit drieth the bones.' (Proverbs 17:22)[6]

How characteristic of this incredible prophet. He seems to always want to uplift, to encourage, to share his enthusiasm. Can we be as good-natured and fun, as optimistic and positive as President Hinckley? Yes, of course, we can! But we must achieve this demeanor as he does. This kind of attitude comes as a reward for unflinching faith and tireless service.

Being happy and cheerful is something we must do now, it is not a later reward for a life well lived. Each of us must determine and live to enjoy true happiness now. We cannot wait until eternity. In fact, we are living in eternity today. The principle of restoration teaches that attitudes don't change in the next life. As Moroni explained, "he that is happy shall be happy still; and he that is unhappy shall be unhappy still" (Mormon 9:14).

Decide to be happy and cheerful now, live so as to merit that blessing for which God designed you. President Brigham Young stated, "We want to see every countenance full of cheerfulness and every eye bright with the hope of future happiness."[7]

Being happy is more than personality or style. As we've already determined, it is a commandment. President Marion G. Romney brought the spiritual aspect of this commandment into clear focus when he said simply, "The key to happiness is to get the Spirit and keep it."[8] Thus, we can see that happiness is a consequence of keeping commandments. It therefore follows that we will never be truly happy until our will comes in line with the will of our Heavenly Father.

President Heber C. Kimball left us a marvelous explanation of the relationship between our emotions and the Spirit. He said:

Often when I have been in the presence of brother Brigham, we would feel such a buoyant spirit that when we began to talk we could not express our feelings, and so "Hallelujah," says Brigham, "Glory to God," says I. I feel to say it. . . .

Some of the brethren kind of turn their noses on one side at me when I make such expressions, but they would not do it if they knew God. Such ones do not even know brothers Brigham and Heber; if they did they would not turn a wry face at us. I am perfectly satisfied that my Father and my God is a cheerful, pleasant, lively, and good-natured Being. Why? Because I am cheerful, pleasant, lively, and good-natured when I have His Spirit. That is one reason why I know; and another is—the Lord said, through Joseph Smith, "I delight in a glad heart and a cheerful countenance." That arises from the perfection of His attributes; He is a jovial, lively person, and a beautiful man. . . .

I cannot refer to any man of my acquaintance in my life as being so much like God as was brother Brigham's father. He was one of the liveliest and most cheerful men I ever saw, and one of the best of men. He used to come and see me and my wife Vilate almost every day, and would sit and talk with us, and sing, and pray, and jump, and do anything that was good to make us lively and happy, and we loved him.[9]

Since being cheerful, pleasant, lively, and good-natured are godly attributes, it follows that a celestial marriage will include these attributes. We must work on developing these traits as we would faith, dependability, courage, forgiveness, and other character traits of God.

I remember a research study in graduate school that was trying to determine why some people are happier than others. The conclusion of the study? Happy people are happier! After we chuckle at such an obvious insight, the deeper significance of the statement begins to surface: greater happiness is a consequence of the choice to be happy!

This little story by an unknown author illustrates the advantage of such a positive attitude: There once was a man who woke up one morning, looked in the mirror, and noticed he had only three hairs on his head. 'Well,' he said. 'I think I'll braid my hair today.' So he did, and he had a wonderful day. The next day, he woke up, looked in the mirror, and saw that he had only two hairs on his head. 'Hmm,' he said. 'I think I'll part my hair down the middle today.' So he did, and he had a grand day. The next day, he woke up, looked in the mirror, and noticed he had only one hair on his head. 'Well,' he said, 'Today I'm going to wear my hair in a pony tail.' So he did, and he had a fun, fun day. The next day, he woke up, looked in the mirror, and noticed there wasn't a single hair on his head. 'Yeah!' he exclaimed. 'I don't have to fix my hair today at all!'

Marriage provides numerous opportunities for couples to learn how to make adjustments pleasantly. Someone wisely observed that marriage is sleeping in a room that is too warm, with someone who is sleeping in a room that is too cold. Research reveals that "the level of a couple's joy is determined by each partner's ability to adjust to things beyond his or her control."[10] Every happy couple has learned to find the right attitude in spite of the conditions they find themselves in.

Such an attitude is, in fact, a powerful expression of faith— faith that God will reward the righteous. Today may be very difficult, but the promised rewards of eternity fill us with that positive expectation called hope. "Things will work out," encourages President Hinckley. "Keep trying. Be believing. Be happy. Don't get discouraged. Things will work out."[11]

Truly happy individuals and couples have learned to keep an eternal vision while living in the very real present. Such couples know that most concerns are temporal, or pertaining to the present life or this world, and therefore temporary, or effective for a time only. Elder Neal A. Maxwell has reminded us:

> If the big things that really matter are finally going
> to work out in eternity, then the little things that go

wrong mortally are not cause for desperation . . . It is ungraceful for a human who has been promised an eternal expanse to be genuinely upset with his family upon coming home from work because someone earlier in the day took his preferred parking place! [Furthermore] an economic depression would be grim, but it would not change the reality of immortality. The inevitability of the second coming is not affected by the unpredictability of the stock market. Political despots make this world very ugly, but they cannot touch that better world to come. A case of cancer does not cancel the promises of the temple endowment . . . Thus, the things of which we can be most certain are also those things which matter most . . . we can have a bad day but still have a good life . . . [because] all that matters [most] is gloriously intact. The promises are in place.[12]

President Gordon B. Hinckley has taught:

> For those of you who are married, it is particularly important that you cultivate a positive attitude and constantly look for the virtues in one another. Two students of BYU came to see me some years ago. Six months earlier they had been married. They declared their love for one another. In a sacred place they had pledged their loyalty one to another for time and for eternity. Now, the young man came first. He was disillusioned. He was bitter. He was heartbroken. His wife, he said, did this and did that—simple little things of small consequence, such as leaving the dishes undone when she left for school in the morning. And then came his wife, a beautiful girl of great talent. She spoke of her husband's faults. He was stingy. He did not pick up his clothes. He was careless. Each had his or her faults. Every one of those faults was easily correctable. The problem lay in the fact that there was a stronger inclination to emphasize the faults than

there was to talk of virtues. With a little self-discipline, each could have changed. With a little desire, each could have spoken with a different tone. But neither was willing. They had permitted a negative attitude to destroy the sweetest, richest association of life. They had thrown away with careless and sour words the hopes and dreams of eternity. With criticism and shouting, they had violated the sacred promises that might have taken them on to exaltation. . . . I do not suggest that you simply put on rose-colored glasses to make the world look rosy. I ask, rather, that you look above and beyond the negative, the critical, the cynical, the doubtful, to the positive.[13]

President Brigham Young said this:

If you feel evil, keep it to yourselves until you overcome that evil principle. This is what I call resisting the devil, and he flees from me. . . . When you are influenced by the Spirit of holiness and purity, let your light shine; but if you are tried and tempted and buffeted by Satan, keep your thoughts to yourselves—keep your mouths closed; for speaking produces fruit, either of a good or evil character. . . . You frequently hear brethren and sisters say that they feel so tried and tempted, and have so many cares, and are so buffeted, that they must give vent to their feelings; and they yield to the temptations, and deal out their unpleasant sensations to their families and neighbors. Make up your minds thoroughly, once for all, that if we have trials, the Lord has suffered them to be brought upon us, and he will give us grace to bear them. . . . But if we have light or intelligence—that which will do good, we will impart it. . . . Let that be the determination of every individual, for spirit begets spirit—likeness, likeness; feelings beget their likeness. . . . If then we give vent to all our bad feelings and disagreeable sensations, how quickly we beget the same in others, and load each other down with our troubles, and become sunk in darkness and despair! . . . In all your social communications . . . let all the dark, discontented, murmuring, unhappy, miserable feelings—all the evil fruit of the mind, fall from the tree in silence and unnoticed; and so let it perish, without taking it up to present to your neighbors. But when you have joy and happiness, light and intelligence, truth and virtue, offer that fruit abundantly to your neighbors, and it will do them good, and so strengthen the hands of your fellow-beings.[14]

Similarly, President Heber C. Kimball noted:

It is the duty of every one to labor day by day to promote each other's happiness, and also to study the well-being of mankind. When we take a course opposite to this, we become uneasy, unhappy and discontented; we are not satisfied with anything that is around us. . . . It is the spirit of the world, or that spirit which controls the world, which causes people to feel in this way; and unless they drive it far from them it will lead them down to sorrow, misery and death.[15]

Notes

1. Landis and Landis, *Building a Successful Marriage*, 54.
2. Parrott and Parrott, *Saving Your Marriage*, 54–55.
3. Smith, *Teachings of the Prophet Joseph Smith*, 255–56.
4. McKay, in Conference Report, October 1934, 92.
5. Nibley, *World and the Prophets*, 3:259.
6. Hinckley, *Teachings of Gordon B. Hinckley*, 254.
7. Young, *Discourses of Brigham Young*, 236.
8. Romney, in Conference Report, October 1961, 61.
9. Kimball, in *Journal of Discourses*, 4:222.
10. Parrott and Parrott, *Saving Your Marriage*, 61.
11. Holland, "President Gordon B. Hinckley: Stalwart and Brave He Stands," *Ensign*, June 1995, 4.
12. Maxwell, *Notwithstanding My Weakness*, 50, 57.
13. Hinckley, "The Lord Is at the Helm," in *Brigham Young University*

1993–94 Devotional and Fireside Speeches, 109.

    14. Young, in *Journal of Discourses,* 7:26.

    15. Kimball, in *Journal of Discourses,* 10:240.

SECTION TWO:
Divine Differences

Marriage is a partnership of two individuals, two individuals with many differences. Elder John H. Groberg has reminded us that "the Brethren have spoken clearly and consistently on this subject and have stated over and over again that the best marriages are those that have as many things held in common as possible, especially the same religion, and as far as possible, the same social, cultural, economic, and educational background. The reason is very simple: marriage at its very best is full of potential trials and hazards and it is not only unwise, but very foolish to add extra burdens to any marriage."[1]

Learning how to work with the remaining differences, and even enjoy them, is one of the wonderful challenges of marriage. "Each of us is an individual," observed President Gordon B. Hinckley. "Each of us is different. There must be respect for those differences, and while it is important and necessary that both the husband and the wife strive to ameliorate those differences, there must be some recognition that they exist and that they are not necessarily undesirable. There must be respect one for another, not withstanding such differences. In fact, the differences may make the companionship more interesting."[2]

We must recognize that some differences are essential to marriage and the happiness of both husband and wife. "In his wisdom and mercy," observed President Spencer W. Kimball, "our Father made men and women dependent on each other for the full flowering of their potential. Because their natures are somewhat different, they can complement each other, because they are in many ways alike, they can understand each other. Let neither envy the other for their differences; let both discern what is superficial and what is beautifully basic in those differences, and act accordingly . . . as we help each other along the path to perfection."[3]

Elder Richard G. Scott noted:

> Our Heavenly Father endowed His sons and daughters with unique traits specifically fitted for their individual responsibilities as they fulfill His plan. To follow His plan requires that you do those things He expects of you as a son or daughter, husband or wife. Those roles are different, but entirely compatible. In the Lord's plan, it takes two—a man and a woman—to form a whole. Indeed, a husband and wife are not two identical halves, but a wondrous, divinely determined combination of complementary capacities and characteristics. . . .
>
> Marriage allows these different characteristics to come together in oneness—in unity—to bless a husband and wife, their children and grandchildren. For the greatest happiness and productivity in life, both husband and wife are needed. Their efforts interlock and are complementary. Each has individual traits that best fit the role the Lord has defined for happiness as a man or woman. When used as the Lord intends, those capacities allow a married couple to think, act, and rejoice as one—to grow in love and understanding and through temple ordinances to be bound together as one whole, eternally. That is the plan.[4]

Elder Marvin J. Ashton explained how charity benefits us as we work to accept divine differences in marriage. "Perhaps the greatest charity comes when we are kind to each other, when we don't judge or categorize someone else, when we simply give each other the benefit of the doubt or remain quiet," Elder Ashton observed. "Charity is accepting someone's differences, weaknesses, and shortcomings; having patience with someone who has let us down; or resisting the impulse to become offended when someone doesn't handle something the way we might have hoped. Charity is refusing to take advantage of another's weakness and being willing to forgive someone who has hurt us. Charity is expecting the best of each other."[5]

Elder Merrill J. Bateman adds further insight when he said, "When a man understands how glorious a woman is, he treats her differently. When a woman understands that a man has the seeds of divinity within him, she honors him not only for who he is but for what he may become. An understanding of the divine nature allows each person to have respect for the other. The eternal view engenders a desire in men and women to learn from and share with each other. . . . Men and women have different strengths and weaknesses, and marriage is a synergistic relationship in which spiritual growth is enhanced because of the differences."[6]

This section, titled Divine Differences, focuses on gaining an understanding and appreciation of some basic differences between husbands and wives. Two facets, gender and its subtopic sex, will be discussed in some detail.

However, there are other differences that are not gender specific that play a significant role in relationships. Any two or more individuals (missionary companions, roommates, siblings, and so forth) need to be aware of these differences, especially if they desire to create strong, meaningful, joyful relationships. Only when we understand and like ourselves—and understand and like someone very different from ourselves—can we be truly happy in relationships.

I have found several excellent books on these subjects that are entertaining, beneficial, and readily available at LDS bookstores. I highly recommend that all couples read these books. They contain insights and tools that have the potential to greatly enhance any marriage. To understand your personality and how to accept and communicate with others, I believe Taylor Hartman's *The*

Color Code: A New Way to See Yourself, Your Relationships and Life to be the best book available. The concepts in this book are easily understood and have had a huge positive impact on many individuals and couples.

For decades, LDS couples preparing for marriage have been referred to *The Act of Marriage: The Beauty of Sexual Love*, by Tim and Beverly LaHaye. This is an excellent, moral book on the subject of marital sexual relations. However, it has a slight flavor of male dominion over females that bothers me. As a therapist, bishop, and teacher, I have often wished there was an equally good book written from the LDS paradigm. I even thought that perhaps when I retire I'd have to take on that project. To my relief and pleasure, that will no longer be necessary because *Between Husband and Wife: Gospel Perspectives on Marital Intimacy*, by Stephen E. Lamb and Douglas E. Brinley, has now been published. This book is a must for all couples.

Sex Begins in the Kitchen: Because Love Is an All-Day Affair by Kevin Leman is a fun way to study the concepts of birth order and family style. This may explain to some why they think as they do and empower them to consciously improve relationships and choose to build upon the experiences gained in our families of origin.

To learn how to say "I love you" in a way that a spouse will understand has greatly helped many couples. Two books deal with this concept: John Lund's *Avoiding Legal Divorce by Avoiding Emotional Divorce* and *The Five Love Languages: How to Express Heartfelt Commitment to Your Mate* by Gary Chapman.

Married for time and eternity, or until *debt* do us part is becoming more and more the refrain and behavior that is destroying marriages. One of the most familiar puzzles facing LDS couples and individuals alike is how to successfully combine their finances, interpersonal relationships, and spirituality. In *For Love and Money: How to Share the Same Checkbook and Still Love Each Other*, Bernard E. Poduska shows how personal values, lifestyles, relationships, family types, and birth order impact the way we manage our financial resources.

Of course, there are other books, and you are encouraged to improve your marriage by constantly studying and learning to accept synergistic differences and celebrate your eternal quest for wholeness and, ultimately, oneness.

Notes

1. Groberg, Devotional Speech, Church College of Hawaii, LDS Church Archives, 10 February 1978.

2. Hinckley, *Teachings of Gordon B. Hinckley*, 661.

3. Kimball, *Teachings of Spencer W. Kimball*, 315.

4. Scott, "The Joy of Living the Great Plan of Happiness," *Ensign*, November 1996, 73.

5. Ashton, "The Tongue Can Be a Sharp Sword," *Ensign*, May 1992, 18.

6. Bateman, "The Eternal Family," in *Brigham Young University 1997–98 Devotional and Fireside Speeches*, 111.

7

GENDER
differences

Cartoonists and comedians never tire of commenting about gender differences. We enjoy and laugh at such commentary because we have made similar observations and find these fundamental differences to be a fascinating though illusive topic. One young man boasted, "I've spent a lot of time trying to figure out women. And I finally figured them out—'it all depends'!"

On a familiar and relaxed level, we generally seem to acknowledge gender differences. However, when we feel that Big Brother is listening, we tend to be more constrained by philosophical and political agendas that demand that we keep secret our personal beliefs and bear allegiance to the theory that men and women are basically the same. It would not be correct or acceptable to suggest otherwise. Although this philosophy was more actively promoted a few decades ago, it continues to linger in some minds and textbooks. Many of us may still hesitate to share our observations, wondering if it is yet permissible to disagree or if we still have to pretend that there are no significant gender differences.

In contrast, the Church teaches that there have always been differences in gender. "Gender is an essential characteristic of individual premortal, mortal, and eternal identity and purpose."[1] Elder James E. Talmage declared, "We affirm as reasonable, scriptural, and true, the eternity of sex [gender] among the children of God. The distinction between male and female is no condition peculiar to the relatively brief period of mortal life. It was an essential characteristic of our preexistent condition, even as it shall continue after death, in both disembodied and resurrected states. . . . [The] scriptures attest a state of existence preceding mortality, in which the spirit children of God lived, doubtless with distinguishing characteristics, including the distinction of sex."[2]

Even the departed dead, waiting in the spirit world for the resurrection, are distinguished by gender. This was made very clear by President Joseph F. Smith at the funeral of Sister Mary A. Freeze, when he said:

> Now, among all these millions of spirits that have lived on the earth and have passed away, from generation to generation, since the beginning of the world, without the knowledge of the Gospel—among them you may count that at least one-half are women. Who is going to preach the Gospel to the women? Who is going to carry the testimony of Jesus Christ to the hearts of the women who have passed away without a knowledge of the Gospel? Well, to my mind, it is a simple thing. These good sisters who have been set apart, ordained to the work, called to it, authorized by the authority of the Holy Priesthood to minister for their sex, in the House of God for the living and for the dead, will be fully authorized and empowered to preach the Gospel and minister to the women while the elders and prophets are preaching it to the men. The things we experience here are typical of the things of God, and the life beyond us.[3]

Elder Melvin J. Ballard promised that "when you see men and women in the resurrection, we shall see them in very bloom of their glorious manhood and womanhood, and he has promised all who would keep his commandments and obey the gospel of the Lord Jesus Christ, the restoration of their houses, glorified, immortalized, celestialized, fitted to dwell in the presence of God."[4]

Interestingly, the past few years have witnessed an increasing number of scientific research projects that report a startling "new" discovery—men and women are different! Those not previously deceived by the bizarre social experiment of ignoring gender differences simply smile, pleased that science now affirms what most have always known. Recognizing and accepting those differences is essential if a couple are to fully celebrate their marriage.

Science currently seems to be focusing on biological gender differences such as how the differing male and female brains handle information. However, there are also personality and relationship differences that need to be acknowledged if we want to truly work at creating a celestial marriage.

Biological gender differences typically noted might include the following contrasting generalizations:

- women have better manual dexterity—fine motor skills, an acute sense of touch, and better close-up vision
- men have better depth perception—do better at spacial tasks
- women have the ability to hold abstract feelings
- men can deal better with abstract shapes
- women notice fine details
- men see things in 3-D
- women read feelings better
- men read maps better
- women need less oxygen and food per pound
- men have more upper body strength
- infant girls study faces
- infant boys avoid eye contact
- infant girls sit up sooner
- infant boys crawl away
- infant girls rhythmically mouth
- infant boys startle more easily

- toddler girls kept from their mothers cry for rescue
- toddler boys kept from their mothers attack the barrier
- women navigate by memory of landmarks
- men navigate by a vague sense of north and south
- women have a memory for detail
- men focus more on the big picture
- the woman's month is a hormonal roller coaster
- the man has higher testosterone levels and is therefore more aggressive and stronger
- women's sex drive vacillates and is generally lower
- men's sex drive is constant and higher
- women learn better in group discussion settings
- men score higher on SAT math tests
- women use both sides of the brain in decision making
- men use only one side of the brain in decision making

Gender differences, which more affect impact relationships, might include the following:

- young girls prefer dolls, makeup, and relationship role playing
- young boys prefer action figures and playing war
- girls excel at verbal skills
- boys excel at math
- women are person oriented
- men are task oriented
- women communicate to establish relationships
- men communicate to talk about competition
- women talk more, they use more words per day
- men are more competitive, on task
- women think in terms of relationships
- men think in terms of objects
- women are integrated; everything affects everything else
- men are compartmentalized and can focus on one thing at a time
- women derive self-esteem from home, children
- men derive self-esteem from work, occupation
- women want to be loved, cared for, and reassured

- men want to be respected, won't ask for directions

The point is, men and women are different, far beyond what you would expect from cultural conditioning. We are biologically and emotionally different. We see and think differently. Even though society and governments may struggle to protect the rights of each gender by claiming that there are no gender differences, our personal and now scientific experience suggests otherwise. We must acknowledge gender differences and celebrate the contrasts within the marriage partnership.

Gender differences should not have to be excused, or acknowledged with apology. We are different by divine design! Marriage is better because of the differences. Elder Richard G. Scott explained it this way:

> Our Heavenly Father endowed His sons and daughters with unique traits especially fitted for their individual responsibilities as they fulfill His plan. To follow His plan requires that you do those things He expects of you as a son or daughter, husband or wife. Those roles are different but entirely compatible. In the Lord's plan, it takes two—a man and a woman—to form a whole. Indeed, a husband and wife are not two identical halves, but a wondrous, divinely determined combination of complementary capacities and characteristics. . . .
>
> Marriage allows these different characteristics to come together in oneness—in unity—to bless a husband and wife, their children and grandchildren. For the greatest happiness and productivity in life, both husband and wife are needed. Their efforts interlock and are complementary. Each has individual traits that best fit the role the Lord has defined for happiness as a man or woman. When used as the Lord intends, those capacities allow a married couple to think, act, and rejoice as one—to face challenges together and overcome them as one, to grow in love and understanding, and through temple ordinances to be bound together

as one whole, eternally. That is the plan.[5]

Different, but complementary; that is how the Brethren frequently state it. "Except Adam and Eve by nature be different from one another, they could not multiply and fill the earth," explained President Boyd K. Packer. "The complementing differences are the very key to the plan of happiness."[6]

Elder Merrill J. Bateman wrote:

> When a man understands how glorious a woman is, he treats her differently. When a woman understands that a man has the seeds of divinity within him, she honors him not only for who he is but for what he may become. An understanding of the divine nature allows each person to have respect for the other. The eternal view engenders a desire in men and women to learn from and share with each other. . . . Men and women are created as complements. They complete one another. . . . Men and women complement each other not only physically, but also emotionally and spiritually. . . . Men and women have different strengths and weaknesses, and marriage is a synergistic relationship in which spiritual growth is enhanced because of the differences.[7]

President Ezra Taft Benson said:

> In this pronouncement that it was not good for man to be alone, God declared a fundamental truth. The Lord gave woman a different personality and temperament than man. By nature woman is charitable and benevolent, man is striving and competitive. Man is at his best when complemented by a good woman's natural influence. She tempers the home and marriage relationship with her compassionate and loving influence. . . . Yes, it is not good for man to be alone because a righteous woman complements what may be lacking in a man's natural personality and disposition.

Nowhere is this complementary association more ideally portrayed than in the eternal marriage of our first parents, Adam and Eve.[8]

Another prophet, President Spencer W. Kimball taught that "in his wisdom and mercy, our Father made men and women dependent on each other for the full flowering of their potential. Because their natures are somewhat different, they can complement each other, because they are in many ways alike, they can understand each other. Let neither envy the other for their differences; let both discern what is superficial and what is beautifully basic in those differences, and act accordingly . . . as we help each other along the path to perfection."[9]

President Gordon B. Hinckley noted, "Each of us is an individual. Each of us is different. There must be respect for those differences, and while it is important and necessary that both the husband and the wife strive to ameliorate [to make better or tolerate] those differences, there must be some recognition that they exist and that they are not necessarily undesirable. There must be respect one for another, notwithstanding such differences. In fact, the differences may make the companionship more interesting."[10]

Gender differences noted by scientists and social observers tend to be those associated with the contrasting design of our mortal bodies, including the brain and hormones. However, the Brethren more often make mention of differences that are more intrinsic to the nature of our eternal genders and subsequent roles here in mortality. For example, in speaking to women, President Benson said:

> You were not created to be the same as men. Your natural attributes, affections, and personalities are entirely different from a man's. They consist of faithfulness, benevolence, kindness, and charity. They give you the personality of a woman. They also balance the more aggressive and competitive nature of a man. . . . The business world is competitive and sometimes ruthless. We do not doubt that women have both the

brainpower and skills—and in some instances superior abilities—to compete with men. But by competing they must, of necessity, become aggressive and competitive. Thus their godly attributes are diminished and they acquire a quality of sameness with man.[11]

Caution was expressed by President Packer, who counseled:

> In the home and in the Church, sisters should be esteemed for their very nature. Be careful lest you unknowingly foster influences and activities which tend to erase the masculine and feminine differences nature has established. A man, a father, can do much of what is usually assumed to be a woman's work. In turn, a wife and a mother can do much—and in time of need, most things—usually considered the responsibility of the man, without jeopardizing their distinct roles. Even so, leaders, and especially parents, should recognize that there is a distinct masculine nature and a distinct feminine nature essential to the foundation of the home and the family. Whatever disturbs or weakens or tends to erase that difference erodes the family and reduces the probability of happiness for all concerned.[12]

Unfortunately, history records ample evidence that gender differences have been used as an excuse for one gender exercising unrighteous dominion over the other. This sin needs to be repented of and not perpetuated. However, the solution is not to pretend that there are no gender differences.

"We live in a day," said Elder Dallin H. Oaks, "when there are many political, legal, and social pressures for changes that confuse gender and homogenize the differences between men and women. Our eternal perspective sets us against changes that alter those separate duties and privileges of men and women that are essential to accomplish the great plan of happiness. We do not oppose all changes in the treatment of men and women, since some changes in laws or customs simply correct old wrongs that were never grounded in eternal principles."[13]

Because of these eternal gender differences, husbands and wives have different roles. Both are absolutely critical. These two complementary, though different, partners comprise the whole that is needed for the creation of a marriage and family. "Some roles are best suited to the masculine nature," President Packer stated, "and others to the feminine nature."[14]

President Benson explained it this way: "In the eternal family, God established that fathers are to preside in the home. Fathers are to provide, to love, to teach, and to direct. . . . But a mother's role is also God-ordained. Mothers are to conceive, to bear, to nourish, to love, and to train. So declare the revelations."[15]

The Proclamation on the Family, written by the First Presidency and Quorum of the Twelve Apostles, states: "By divine design, fathers are to preside over their families in love and righteousness and are responsible to provide the necessities of life and protection of their families. Mothers are primarily responsible for the nurture of their children. In these sacred responsibilities, fathers and mothers are obligated to help one another as equal partners. Disability, death, or other circumstances may necessitate individual adaptation. Extended families should lend support when needed."[16]

President Spencer W. Kimball noted that "our roles and assignments differ. These are eternal differences—with women being given many tremendous responsibilities of motherhood and sisterhood and men being given the tremendous responsibilities of fatherhood and the priesthood."[17]

President James E. Faust explained why both a father and a mother are needed to raise children when he said, "Both fathers and mothers do many intrinsically different things for their children. Both mothers and fathers are equipped to nurture children, but their approaches are different. Mothers seem to take a dominant role in preparing children to live within their families (present and future). Fathers seem best equipped to prepare children to function in the environment outside the family."[18]

Elder Neal A. Maxwell added this observation:

> We know so little, brothers and sisters, about the reasons for the division of duties between womanhood and manhood as well as between motherhood and priesthood. These were divinely determined in another time and another place. . . . We men know the women of God as wives, mothers, sisters, daughters, associates, and friends. You seem to tame us and to gentle us, and, yes, to teach us and to inspire us. For you, we have admiration as well as affection, because righteousness is not a matter of role, nor goodness a matter of gender. In the work of the Kingdom, men and women are not without each other, but do not envy each other, lest by reversals and renunciations of role we make a wasteland of both womanhood and manhood.[19]

Our gender roles, different yet complementary, are essential to our personal and marital progress and happiness. It, therefore, should not be surprising that Satan is doing all he can to keep us from reaching our full potentials. "This is a day when the adversary has launched an all-out attack against womanhood, because he knows—he absolutely knows—that the influence of a righteous woman is enormous and that it spans generations," said Sheri L. Dew. "He would have us be disinterested in marriage and motherhood, confused by the world's view of men and women, too harried by the pace of life to really live the gospel and to let it penetrate our souls."[20]

President Kimball also raised a clarion call to women as he observed, "There has never been a time in the world when the role of woman has been more confused. There has never been a time in the Church when women are able to do more to show what their true role in the world can and ought to be. The impact and influence of women and mothers on our world is most important. The thought that 'the hand that rocks the cradle rules the world' is more viable today than ever before."[21]

Many of our inspired leaders have commented on the sacred station of women. President Hinckley observed that "only after the earth had been formed, after the day had been separated from the night, after the waters had been divided from the land, after vegetation and animal life had been created, and after man had been placed on the earth, was woman created; and only then was the work pronounced complete and good."[22]

President Packer stated, "Those who tell you that in the kingdom of God a woman's lot is less than that of the man know nothing of the love, akin to worship, that the worthy man has for his wife."[23]

Such awe of womanhood was also expressed by President Howard W. Hunter, who said:

> Women should maintain their spiritual superiority in marriage. I suppose you would say it is a man's viewpoint to throw a burden upon a woman to maintain the stability and the sweetness of marriage, but this seems to be her divine nature. She has a superior spirituality in the marriage relationship, and the opportunity to encourage, uplift, teach, and be the one who sets the example in the family for righteous living. When women come to the point of realizing that it is more important to be superior than to be equal, they will find the real joy in living those principles that the Lord set out in his divine plan.[24]

In another instance, President Hunter noted:

> We must be careful to not confuse the roles of women and men. It seems strange that women want to enter into professions and into work and into places in society on an equality with men, wanting to dress like men and carry on men's work. I don't deny the fact that women are capable of doing so, but as I read the scriptures, I find it hard to reconcile this with what the Lord has said about women—what he has said about the family, what he has said about children. It seems to me that in regard to men and women, even though they might be equal in many things, there is a differentiation between them that we fully

understand. I hope the time never comes when women will be brought down to the level with men, although they seem to be making these demands in meetings held . . . all over the world.[25]

Elder Scott spoke directly to women during a general conference address wherein he declared:

> I humbly thank our Father in Heaven for His daughters, you who were willing to come to earth to live under such uncertain circumstances. Most men could not handle the uncertainties you are asked to live with. Social customs require that you wait to be asked for marriage. You are expected to go with your husband wherever his employment or call takes him. Your environment and neighborhood are determined by his ability to provide, meager or not. You place your life in the Lord's hands each time you bear a child. Men make no such sacrifice. The blessing of nurturing children and caring for a husband often is intermingled with many routine tasks. But you do all of these things willingly because you are a woman. Generally you have no idea of how truly wonderful and capable you are, how very much appreciated and loved, or how desperately needed, for most men don't tell you as completely and as often as needed.[26]

From the premortal world, women came to mortality with unique qualities. President Faust observed that femininity "is the divine adornment of humanity. It finds expression in your . . . capacity to love, your spirituality, delicacy, radiance, sensitivity, creativity, charm, graciousness, gentleness, dignity, and quiet strength. It is manifest differently in each girl or woman, but each . . . possesses it. Femininity is part of your inner beauty."[27]

Margaret D. Nadauld, who served as Young Women general president, said:

> You can recognize women who are grateful to be

daughters of God by their attitude. They know that the errand of angels is given to women, and they desire to be on God's errand to love His children and minister to them, to teach them the doctrines of salvation, to call them to repentance, to save them in perilous circumstances, to guide them in the performance of His work, to deliver His messages. They understand that they can bless their Father's children in their homes and neighborhoods and beyond. Women who are grateful to be daughters of God bring glory to His name. . . . Women of God can never be like the women of the world. The world has enough women who are tough; we need women who are tender. There are enough women who are coarse; we need women who are kind. There are enough women who are rude; we need women who are refined. We have enough women of fame and fortune; we need more women of faith. We have enough greed; we need more goodness. We have enough vanity; we need more virtue. We have enough popularity; we need more purity.[28]

Of the many roles of women, none is more sacred than the gift of motherhood. Elder John A. Widtsoe called motherhood "the noblest most soul satisfying of all earthly experiences. If this power is exercised righteously, woman has no time nor desire for anything greater, for there is nothing greater on earth! This does not mean that women may not use to the full their special gifts, for the more woman exercises her innate qualification the greater is her power for motherhood. Woman may claim other activity but motherhood should take precedence in her entire scheme of life."[29]

The privilege of bearing God's children fulfills a premortal promise to women "for their exaltation in the eternal worlds" (D&C 132:63). According to President Packer, "the woman, by her very nature, is also co-creator with God and the primary nurturer of the children. Virtues and attributes upon which perfection and exaltation depend come naturally to a woman and are refined through marriage and motherhood."[30]

In addition to their natural attributes, women receive endowments of special traits to assist them in this most sacred of all callings. "From my experience, it would seem that faithful mothers have a special gift that we often refer to as mother's intuition," observed President Harold B. Lee. "Perhaps with the great blessings of motherhood, our Heavenly Father has endowed them with this quality, since the fathers, busy in priesthood callings and with the work of earning a livelihood, never draw quite as close to heavenly beings in matters that relate to the more intimate details of bringing up children in the home."[31]

Speaking of mothers, the First Presidency (consisting of Heber J. Grant, J. Reuben Clark, and David O. McKay) declared the following in a 1942 general conference:

> Motherhood thus becomes a holy calling, a sacred dedication for carrying out the Lord's plans, a consecration of devotion to the uprearing and fostering, the nurturing in body, mind, and spirit, of those who kept their first estate and who come to this earth for their second estate "to see if they will do all things whatsoever the Lord their God shall command them" (Abraham 3:25). To lead them to keep their second estate is the work of motherhood, and "they who keep their second estate shall have glory added upon their heads for ever and ever" (Abraham 3:26). . . .
>
> This divine service of motherhood can be rendered only by mothers. It may not be passed to others. Nurses cannot do it; public nurseries cannot do it; hired help cannot do it—only mother, aided as much as may be by the loving hands of father, brothers, and sisters, can give the full needed measure of watchful care. . . .
>
> The mother who entrusts her child to the care of others, that she may do non-motherly work, whether for gold, for fame, or for civic service, should remember that "a child left to himself bringeth his mother to shame" (Proverbs 29:15). In our day the Lord has said

that unless parents teach their children the doctrines of the Church "the sin be upon the heads of the parents" (D&C 68:25). . . .

Motherhood is near to divinity. It is the highest, holiest service to be assumed by mankind. It places her who honors its holy calling and service next to the angels.[32]

In 1993, President Packer read the above quoted passage and added, "That message and warning from the First Presidency is needed more, not less, today than when it was given. And no voice from any organization of the Church on any level of administration equals that of the First Presidency."[33]

And President Benson cautioned:

We hear much talk—even among some of our own sisters—about so-called "alternative life-styles" for women. It is maintained that some women are better suited for careers than for marriage and motherhood, or that a combination of both family and career is not inimical to either. Some have even been so bold as to suggest that the Church move away from the "Mormon woman stereotype" of homemaking and rearing children. God grant that dangerous philosophy will never take root among our Latter-day Saint women. I repeat: You are elect because you were elected to a certain work. How glorious is the knowledge that you are dignified by the God of heaven to be wives and mothers in Zion.[34]

Clearly gender differences are divine, dictated not by culture or education, but by our very nature. These differences exist for a divine purpose as well, with each gender uniquely equipped to shoulder different roles and responsibilities. As we strive to enjoy a celestial marriage, we should celebrate and embrace these differences.

Notes

1. The First Presidency and Council of the Twelve Apostles, "The Family—A Proclamation to the World," *Ensign*, November 1995, 102.

2. Talmage, "The Eternity of Sex," *Millennial Star*, 24 August 1922, 530.

3. Smith, *Gospel Doctrine*, 320.

4. Hinckley, *Sermons and Missionary Services of Melvin J. Ballard*, 186.

5. Scott, "The Joy of Living the Great Plan of Happiness," *Ensign*, November 1996, 73–74.

6. Packer, "For Time and All Eternity," *Ensign*, November 1993, 21.

7. Bateman, *Eternal Family*, 113.

8. Benson, in *Woman*, 69.

9. Kimball, *Teachings of Spencer W. Kimball*, 315.

10. Hinckley, *Cornerstones of a Happy Home*, 4.

11. Benson, *Teachings of Ezra Taft Benson*, 547–48.

12. Packer, "The Relief Society," *Ensign*, May 1998, 7.

13. Oaks, "'The Great Plan of Happiness,'" *Ensign*, November 1993, 73–74.

14. Packer, "For Time and All Eternity," *Ensign*, November 1993, 21.

15. Benson, *Come, Listen to a Prophet's Voice*, 26.

16. The First Presidency and Council of the Twelve Apostles, "The Family—A Proclamation to the World," 102.

17. Kimball, *Teachings of Spencer W. Kimball*, 315.

18. Faust, "Fathers, Mothers, Marriage," *Ensign*, August 2004, 3.

19. Maxwell, "The Women of God," *Ensign*, May 1978, 10.

20. Dew, "'Are You the Woman I Think You Are?'" *Ensign*, November 1997, 92–93.

21. Benson, in *Woman*, 1.

22. Hinckley, "Our Responsibility to Our Young Women," *Ensign*, September 1988, 11.

23. Packer, "The Circle of Sisters," *Ensign*, November 1980, 111.

24. Hunter, *Teachings of Howard W. Hunter*, 139.

25. Ibid., 150.

26. Scott, "The Joy of Living the Great Plan of Happiness," *Ensign*, November 1996, 75.

27. Faust, "Womanhood: The Highest Place of Honor," *Ensign*, May 2000, 96.

28. Nadauld, "The Joy of Womanhood," *Ensign*, November 2000, 15.

29. Widtsoe, *Priesthood and Church Government*, 84.

30. Packer, "For Time and All Eternity," *Ensign*, November 1993, 22.

31. Lee, *Teachings of Harold B. Lee*, 291.

32. Lee, in Conference Report, October 1942, 12.

33. Packer, "For Time and All Eternity," *Ensign*, November 1993, 23.

34. Benson, in *Woman*, 70.

8

SEXUAL DIFFERENCES:
joys and cautions

Husbands and wives are commanded to be "one flesh" (see Genesis 2:24), but that does not mean that we perceive or experience sexual relations the same. We are at least as different in this facet of our relationships as in other dimensions. Once again, therefore, we will find plenty of opportunity to explore those differences as well as our own purity of motive and depth of love. These differences are yet another example of difference being good, but they must be recognized, and adjustments made accordingly. The sexual relationship is meant to be a binding celebration.

First, we must recognize that sexuality differs from gender and is very new to us. Although our gender differences preceded mortality, our sexuality did not fully blossom until the mortal experience of going through puberty and the subsequent hormonal cycles. At birth, it was obvious that we were male or female, but it was not until those exciting and confusing teen years that sexual differences became far more powerful and confusing. Having never before experienced these mortal things, we should not be surprised that we are somewhat confused by it all, and may even make mistakes requiring repentance. "Clearly," said Elder Neal A.

Maxwell, "whatever degree of spiritual progress we have achieved in the first estate, certain experiences are unique with the second estate. Some of the curriculum carries over, but certain 'courses' are offered for the first time here in mortality. Such experiences are largely those associated with learning to subject a mortal body to the things of the Spirit, such as in connection with the law of chastity."[1]

As if understanding one's own sexuality was not enough of a challenge, we then get married and discover that we know even less about the sexuality of our mate. Of those sexual differences, President Hugh B. Brown observed, "Thousands of young people come to the marriage altar almost illiterate insofar as this basic and fundamental function is concerned. . . . Some sound instruction in this area will help a man to realize the numberless, delicate differentiations and modifications in the life and reactions of the normal woman."[2] Notice, it is usually the young man who thinks he has sex all figured out, only to get married and discover he has no idea of what he once may have bragged about!

Author Victor B. Cline recommends that couples become informed. "Be a true expert on sex. Read whatever books or manuals you need on the topic. You would not bake bread without a recipe. And this is much more important. Knowledge is power. However," he adds the much-needed caution, "be discriminating in what you read, taking care that you find material compatible with your values. Some of these books contain considerable misinformation—written by 'quick-buck artists' rather than genuine experts and are essentially replacing old myths with new ones."[3]

Having been educated in the philosophies of men as a marriage therapist, I have had some exposure to what is commonly taught by sophists in the classroom. Much of this does not actually work in a marriage relationship. For example, I remember one professor extolling the virtues of commitment to spouse. I found this to be quite refreshing compared to the philosophy he normally advocated. However, the second half of the lecture focused on the possible benefit to "spicing up" a marital relationship with an occasional extramarital affair.

Being easily confused with the logic of the world, I raised my hand and suggested that the two halves of his lecture seemed incongruent with each other. He responded, "Young man, you have misunderstood what I meant by commitment. By commitment, I mean that you tell your wife when you are having an affair. That's commitment!" Apparently his wife also had trouble understanding what he meant by commitment, for this marriage professor was no longer married.

There are some insights from science and the study of the human body that can be helpful to a couple whose goal is to understand and serve each other and the Lord. First, it is crucial to recognize that males and females differ in how readily their interest in sexual things compares over time. Another way of saying this: both males and females oscillate in how easily their minds and bodies can be turned to things sexual. This is in response to hormonal fluctuations.

The male oscillation is frequent, every two to three days, and the oscillation is not very pronounced. In fact, from the female's perspective, the male seems pretty much always "straight line" on the graph, with no apparent fluctuation. Perhaps that can be explained by the fact that the male is typically so much higher on the sexual interest scale than the female that the small oscillations he experiences are comparatively insignificant.

The female, on the other hand, has a major oscillation correlated to her menstrual cycle. Her sexual interest peaks with the monthly ovulation and usually strongly declines when conception is less likely. On a scale of zero to 100 charting sexual interest, men hover at about 95, say their wives. Women, in contrast, oscillate somewhere between 20 and perhaps 60, according to their confused and frustrated husbands. In comparing testosterone levels in men and women, the male actually has about 200 times more units than the female—little wonder that we males and females are different!

Although young men typically begin the puberty experience a few years later than young women, they rise to the top of the sexual interest chart quickly and peak at about age 19. In comparison, the female sexual interest is usually not as high as the male, and her interest in sexual relations typically peaks in the mid-30s.

The point is, by divine design we are biologically different. How we interpret and adjust to those differences is one of the secrets to a good sexual relationship. Remember, different is good, but only if we recognize the differences, both move toward the other's paradigm, and celebrate the common goal of two becoming "one flesh" (see Genesis 2:24).

Although the sexual relationship will be experienced somewhat differently by husband and wife, it must be a mutually enjoyable and edifying facet of their union. This requires intimate awareness of our partner's perceptions and an attitude of love and service for each other.

Assuming that we are designed with differences for divine purposes, it may be beneficial for us to consider some possible interpretations of the way our bodies are hard wired. First, let us again take a look at the fact that most men are near the top of the chart, and at a comparatively early age. Many obvious complications come with these powerful drives in one still developing spiritual strength and self discipline. But could there be advantage in this design?

Consider these statements by President Boyd K. Packer: "This power must be strong, for most men by nature seek adventure. Except for the compelling persuasion of these feelings, men would be reluctant to accept the responsibility of sustaining a home and a family. This power must be constant, too, for it becomes a binding tie in family life."[4]

President Packer also noted that "the desire to mate in human kind is constant and very strong. Our happiness in mortal life, our joy and exaltation, are dependent upon how we respond to these persistent, compelling physical desires."[5]

Therefore, we can see that men are at the top of the chart because sexual desire is a powerful motivator to get married and accept the otherwise overburdening responsibilities of presiding, providing, and protecting a wife and children.

Of course, the Lord's designs are always for our benefit. The young single man often has worldly goals that may be quite self-centered. Yet the drive to get married places him in a family setting where he can mature and discover that the greatest happiness in this life is experienced only within that family setting. As young men, we are simply unaware of what is best for us, so we are designed to be brought to that awareness. The strong male sex drive encourages us to enroll in that needed tutorial experience of marriage and family.

Persuading the male to marry might take an additional push, as in admonitions from our prophets. For example, President Harold B. Lee said, "All women have a desire for companionship. They want to be wives; they want to be mothers; and when men refuse to assume their responsibility of marriage, for no good reason, they are unable to consummate marriage. Brethren, we are not doing our duty as holders of the priesthood when we go beyond the marriageable age and withhold ourselves from an honorable marriage to these lovely women, who are seeking the fulfillment of a woman's greatest desire to have a husband, a family, and a home."[6]

President Spencer W. Kimball counseled that "marriage should come when we are reasonably young, to procreate and bear children, to have the patience to teach and train them and to grow up with them."[7]

Elder Marvin J. Ashton gave this warning to single, marriageable men:

> I call [you] unto repentance. Do not procrastinate the day of your repentance. Believe us when we tell you there is someone for you and God will help you find her. I have little patience for a marriageable, mature man who hasn't found "Miss Perfect." I believe some men think of themselves as "Mr. Perfect." I suggest that any of these men who sincerely desire a happy, fulfilling, worthy life view single women and themselves more realistically. Don't be afraid to seek out

persons of the opposite sex who would be pleased to share dating and courtship time with someone who is worthy, sincere, and truly lovable. There may be excuses and a failure to make the commitment to a worthy lady, but frankly it is hard to find reasons for indefinite delay and an unwillingness to adapt, adjust, and grow by participating in an eternal partnership.[8]

Notice that this stronger sex drive is associated with words and phrases such as "accept responsibility," "sustaining a home and family," "binding tie," "duty," "grow up," "commitment," and "adapt, adjust, and grow." Most men are in serious need of developing these character traits but would be less likely to enter into the tutorial experience of marriage, or remain thus enrolled, if it were not for the scholarship benefits that are part of the education. This may give understanding to a wife who wonders why her spouse seems to have a stronger need for sexual relations than she.

As for the woman, she begins puberty earlier than the man but typically does not experience the need for full sexual relations with the same intensity as her husband. Yet, if the marriage relationship is kind, comfortable, and accepting, her interest in actual sexual relations often increases to peak in the mid-30s. What would be the design of having her increase in sexual desire, peaking almost two decades after her husband?

It would appear that this would enhance the likelihood of the sexual relationship and marriage progressively getting better and better. After all, the intent is to create a marriage that will last for a very long time. Of course, there is much more to a marriage than the sexual relationship, but those other aspects are more likely to blossom in the fertile soil of mutually enhancing, intimate relations.

"Remember," said Victor B. Cline, "that each time you have mutually satisfying sex in your marriage, you powerfully reinforce the pair-bonding in your relationship, which enhances and encourages fidelity and trust. What is the moral? Frequent good

sex cements and protects your marriage and overall relationship."[9]

One final observation about the differences reflected in this
chart: if the male peaks at about 19, that means his interest in sex
begins to diminish from that point on. Granted, the decrease in
interest is usually not dramatic or terminal. But if the husband
is on the steady decline, and the wife is increasing, they might
possibly meet joyfully in the middle. In fact, at the peak of her
monthly cycle, her interest may exceed his! Those differences,
which were once so prominent, may lose their significance as they
two become one flesh. Perhaps this is to remind us that all of our
differences can begin to fade away as we mature and, through
love and service, become of "one heart and one mind" (see Moses
7:18).

In addition to husbands and wives differing in sexual interest, they also differ in what stimulates that interest. That which
is sexually stimulating can usually be placed within one of three
categories; visual, physical touch, and emotional. If these three
categories are placed on a horizontal spectrum, we can again
chart differences between men and women.

Men respond to visual and physical sexual stimulations. Of
course, they also respond to the emotional but not with the same
response time or intensity. Women, on the other hand, are on the
opposite end of the spectrum. They generally require emotional
conditions to be just right for arousal to occur. Touch certainly can
be arousing, but not as much as with the male. And though she
would prefer that her husband look appealing, physical appearance is not as sexually stimulating to a woman as it is to a man.
Apparently this design factor takes into account the way most of
us men look!

Let's look at each of these factors in a little more detail. First,
the visual. Simply seeing a female is pleasant to a male. What
part of her is most pleasant? Well, pretty much all of her! The
hair, the hands, the ankles, the skin, the eyes, the smile, and the
general female curves, everything that makes her feminine. These
elements can be noticed and appreciated by all males, without

inappropriate sexual arousal.

However, seeing sexual body parts *is* sexually stimulating. That is one reason that these sacred body parts should never be exposed except within the sacred and totally private setting of marriage. Such exposure is sexual stimulation and is designed to lead to further sexual activity. Exposure, therefore, should never be used in a flirtatious manner beyond the bounds of marriage with one's mate.

Now, since this book is written mostly for a married audience, I will resist the temptation to spend a lot of time on why young women should be modest. However, I will say that a young woman's ignorance of how appealing and exciting her exposed body is to the male is a major factor in premarital sexual sins. Young women do not realize that their very beings have a powerful influence on young men, who can easily misinterpret the visual cues that are observed. The result is often tragedy. Recently in general conference Elder Dallin H. Oaks pleaded, "Young women, please understand that if you dress immodestly, you are magnifying this problem by becoming pornography to some of the men who see you."[10]

By divine design, men's bodies respond to these visual stimulants. The Savior recognized the challenges associated with this and warned, "Whosoever looketh on a woman, to lust after her, hath committed adultery already in his heart. Behold, I give unto you a commandment, that ye suffer none of these things to enter into your heart; For it is better that ye should deny yourselves of these things wherein ye will take up your cross, than that ye should be cast into hell" (3 Nephi 12:28–30).

A righteous man will do all that he can to avoid any inappropriate visual stimulation. To the extent that that is not always possible in the immodest world of today, he will strive for self-mastery, and even seek divine help, to prevent those unwanted exposures from entering into his heart.

Now, back to the marriage setting. Many, if not most, wives will never comprehend how visually exciting they are to their husbands. Since the wife does not experience the same reaction when viewing him, it seems to make no sense that he reacts so strongly and easily to seeing her. However, this response is very much a part of his sexual experience. Within the confines of marriage and mutual respect, it should be a mutually enjoyed part of the couple's shared experience.

However, husbands must recognize and respect their wives' modest and perhaps timid nature. Patience and respect should always control our sexual behaviors. Every facet of the sexual experience should be given, never taken. A good rule of thumb for the husband is to never take the sexual experience to a higher level of intimacy without being invited by the wife to do so.

The man also responds more quickly and easily to physical contact, intentional or otherwise. Therefore the dress modestly talks to young women usually include additional cautions about immodest contact as well. Once again, there is a gender difference, which almost all males struggle with. Physical contacts of sexual body parts is a stimulant to the male, even if it is not intended to be so from the young woman's perspective.

To her, contact may be nothing more than being close or just cuddling, but to the male it enhances stimulation and a desire for increased levels of stimulation. She means little, or nothing, by the contact. But it is difficult, if not impossible, for the male to not respond with arousal. Again, young men must learn that the contact young women may initiate is usually not meant to be sexually stimulating. And young women must learn that physical contact should be very limited and guarded—they can be very easily misunderstood.

Even in marriage, a husband and wife usually respond differently to physical contact. It takes very little to get him interested or ready for more contact. Although the wife may enjoy contact, her level of interest, intensity, and ultimate pleasure usually do not match that of the husband

In your mind's eye, visualize two different control panels that represent what it takes to turn on the man or the woman. His panel is quite simple, perhaps with just an on-off switch. But she may have several interrelated switches and dozens of knobs for the fine tuning and constant adjustments that must be made. What worked last time does not necessarily work this time. It's easier being a male unless, of course, you are married to a female!

The wife may prefer cuddling and have no need to progress to full intercourse. The husband, on the other hand, usually desires full consummation. However, over time, in a safe, comfortable marriage, the wife usually develops increased interest and pleasure in the physical aspect of the sexual relationship. Again, we start out being quite different, but we can work together as complementary opposites to become more like each other. As we learn from our partner, our sexual relationship should only get better.

What the husband has a harder time comprehending are the emotional, psychological, and relationship aspects of the sexual experience. Again, he can enjoy these elements, but usually not as intensely as she. What is essential for her may, at first, be only nice for him (at least, when compared with the visual and touch). Since he so readily responds to visual and touch stimulation, he may assume that she simply needs more of those. However, it is more likely that she needs talking, sharing, and caring—she wants to be loved and appreciated. Her ability, or even desire, to respond sexually is far more dependent upon the total relationship. But, over time, he too can develop more fully those emotional and romantic attributes that are critical to a mature, mutually enjoyable, sexual relationship.

The following generalizations about gender differences in physical intimacy may be close enough to the truth to spawn a worthwhile dialogue between a husband and wife. Either could validate these statements, clarify them, or refute them. In any case, that these things are talked about and shared is extremely beneficial. Because everyone is different, our primary source of sex education must be our spouse.

- To husbands, intimacy encourages a relationship.
- To wives, a relationship encourages intimacy.
- To husbands, the sexual experience is first physical and then emotional.

- To wives, the sexual experience is first emotional, then physical.
- Husbands are like a microwave.
- Wives are like a Crock-Pot.
- Husbands focus on the body.
- Wives focus on emotions.
- Husbands are stimulated by seeing and touching.
- Wives are stimulated by talking and touching.
- Husbands are spontaneous.
- Wives have to think about it.
- With husbands, full sexual intimacy is a physical necessity.
- With wives, full sexual intimacy may be nice but is not necessary.
- Husbands want wives to enjoy the sexual experience.
- Wives want to accommodate their husbands sexually. (She is often more successful than he.)
- Husbands consider the wife's refusal as rejection.
- Wives consider the husband's refusal as honesty.

Both the husband and the wife must become experts in understanding their own sexuality and becoming a compassionate observer of their spouse. As the husband and wife strive to serve each other, that attitude will be reflected in their intimate relationship. He will demonstrate he can love on an emotional level by not demanding sexual relations. She will demonstrate her desire to give pleasure by being more visual and physical. Their attitude of giving, and pleasing, will enhance the physical as well as the non-physical aspects of intimacy.

In a sense, sexual things are usually much easier for the husband. However, since sexual response is typically not as easy for the wife, the husband has a special responsibility to provide for her physical needs. Husbands, consider this counsel from two LDS authors, Doug Brinley and Stephen Lamb:

> You have an opportunity to make sexual relations
> a good experience for your wife. This is as much a part

of your stewardship as her spouse and companion as it is to provide for her spiritual, financial, and emotional well-being. It is a responsibility that you must approach with care and humility. Your wife has sexual feelings and needs that may be different from your own, something you will come to understand. For example, men are not as likely to separate love and sex as do women. Husbands don't just want to settle for a hug, a kiss, a cuddle on the couch, or to just hold a wife in tender embrace. They want to be sexually intimate. For wives, however, expressing love doesn't always mean sexual relations. Sometimes it just means being held, being close physically, being touched affectionately, or being understood. We hear some sad comments from unhappy wives: "I think that sex is the only reason he married me." "As long as he can have sex, he treats me nicely." "When he can't have sex he is very difficult to live with. He keeps asking, "How many more days do we have to wait?"...

There will be many times in your marriage when you will need to exercise self-restraint. If there is a plea we make to husbands, it is this: If you genuinely love your wife for her spiritual and emotional attributes as well as her physical endowments, demonstrate your love for her on occasions by sacrificing your own desires to be intimate.[11]

Here are a few additional reminders from LDS therapist, Victor B. Cline:

A major love need in most men is sexual acceptance. It is critical to a man's self-esteem, to valuing and accepting himself as a male, a father, and a husband. If he does not feel loved here, he will not feel loved at all. The loving wife helps her husband feel good about his male sexual nature, his virility, his organs, and his strong physical attraction and need for her. She is not afraid to caress or touch any part of his body or give herself completely to him in the act of physical love. . . .

Some wives need to be reminded that sex is not a spectator sport. It requires participation by both parties. Having an active and exciting sexual life together reinforces the commitment of both partners. . . .

I find that the primary love need of most wives is to be wanted, talked to, and accepted as a person—to be cherished, respected, and appreciated. And above all to be treated with kindness, consideration, and affection. If the wife isn't loved in these areas and treated appropriately, she won't feel loved at all—no matter how sexy or ardent her husband is later at night in his physical advances. . . .

What I am suggesting is that in a great sexual relationship you give to get. But you give different things to get back different things. Your partner will have unique needs. Ask. Find out. Identify them and fill them. . . .

In summary, sex should be a celebration. It comes from God. He created our sexual appetites and nature. He has ordained us to make love both physically and spiritually. He is pleased when He sees us bonded together sexually, in love, for this is the plan of creation. And this plan permits the husband and wife to jointly participate in creating new life and, in a sense, perpetuate part of themselves into eternity through their children. The sexual embrace should never be a chore or duty, but a loving part of a larger relationship; of giving to our partner, of cherishing, respecting, protecting each other. It won't always be easy. But the rewards can be incredibly great if we choose to make them so.[12]

If sexual relations are that important, we need to become knowledgeable and skilled in this facet of our being. We need to learn about the unique male and female physiology, contrasting arousal patterns, and the intricacies of orgasm. But what can we read that isn't tainted with the philosophies of the world? Like the deadly anthrax bacteria, ungodly sexual practices can destroy what could have been a healthy and enjoyable sexual relationship.

Most sex manuals encourage masturbation, oral sex, adultery, and even homosexual alternative lifestyles. This should not surprise us too much because most manuals are written from an evolutionary paradigm in which mankind is not descended from God and has no spiritual nature. If mankind were nothing more than glands and hormones, then we would not have to be so selective in reading material.

"Our sexuality has been animalized," noted Jeffrey R. Holland, "stripped of the intricacy of feeling with which human beings have endowed it, leaving us to contemplate only the act, and to fear our impotence in it. It is this animalization from which the sexual manuals cannot escape, even when they try to do so, because they are reflections of it. They might [as well] be textbooks for veterinarians."[13]

Since Latter-day Saints know that the Spirit should not be excluded from the sexual experience, what can a couple read that is appropriate? For decades, we have relied upon several books that are informative, yet moral. These books are usually written by good Christian husband-and-wife teams that explain human sexuality within the context of Christian principles found in the Bible. The most widely read book is titled *The Act of Marriage—The Beauty of Sexual Love,* written by Tim and Beverly LaHaye. I recommend this book, with the observation that their theology, based on Augustinian philosophy wherein the woman should submit to the man, taints some of their counsel. The LDS perspective that husbands and wives are equal partners has some definite sexual applications.

More reading of this type of book is probably not necessary and may even be detrimental. Consider this rule of thumb: The quality of your sexual relationship is inversely proportional to the number of sex manuals you read! Beyond some basic sexual knowledge, your most important source of information should be your spouse. As Cline noted, "What makes great sex really work is love, far more than technique. And mature love is *other*-centered. Sex must serve love, not vice versa."[14]

However, you probably cannot read too many marriage books that focus on the impact of the entire marital relationship on the sexual act. If your relationship with each other and the Lord is what it ought to be, you can discover together the physiological details. Kevin Leman's book *Sex Begins in the Kitchen* does a good job of introducing birth order, family style, and games couples play. Wendy Watson has published *Purity and Passion*, which focuses on bonding, passion, and a deeply spiritual marital sexual relationship. Stephen E. Lamb and Douglas E. Brinley recently wrote *Between Husband and Wife—Gospel Perspectives on Marital Intimacy.* This book is a must for all engaged and married couples.

Now, another reality about our bodies needs to be mentioned—hormones. Just as the woman's libido fluctuates with the monthly menstrual cycle, it can be inhibited, or almost eliminated, by pregnancy, various forms of birth control, or a hysterectomy. In addition, the hormonal systems of either the woman or the man can be negatively affected by poor nutrition, dieting, medications, menopause, age, and any number of medical conditions.

Until those problems are corrected, no amount of emotional bonding or sexual techniques can create sexual interest or responsiveness. Our sexuality is dependent upon a well-balanced hormonal system. Like any system in our bodies, the hormonal system sometimes malfunctions and requires intervention procedures. Women may talk more openly about these conditions, but men seem to be buying a lot of Viagra lately.

Why this much emphasis and focus? Because understanding is that important! Our understanding of our anatomy and that of our spouse is usually inadequate. Knowledge is power, in this case, the power to serve.

Another reason to study and learn these things is to refute false philosophies that have been introduced by Satan. In addition to wanting us to misuse and pervert our sexual powers outside of marriage, Satan also wants to prevent its edifying potential within marriage. After almost four hundred years of post-New Testament apostasy, a once unbridled and confused philosopher named Augustine concluded that sex, even in marriage, is evil. This philosophy, mingled with a few scriptures, has been used by Satan to twist, distort, and cheapen that which is intended to be beautiful and sacred. Apostate concepts such as original sin, total depravity, celibacy, asceticism, and the supposed sinfulness of newborn babes are all reflections of Satan's subtle lies.

Unfortunately, these philosophies, mingled with scripture, are very much a part of our Hellenized western culture. To some degree, many of us believe that sex is bad and that a truly good person would not do such a thing or, at least, would not enjoy doing such a thing. Too often, even some of our youth standards night speakers may convey the idea that the youth should not be involved in sex because sex is bad. Misunderstanding, a young lady might be motivated to avoid premarital sexual relations. However, she may later discover that after her temple marriage to a worthy returned missionary, she still has an aversion to sexual relations. Legally, she knows it is okay, but emotionally she may still consider it to be disgusting and even somehow immoral. To defeat Satan's attempts to impede our progress, we must resist all sexual activity outside of marriage. But we must also celebrate the edifying, sacred relationship within the marriage. It is therefore important that we teach chastity without destroying appropriate intimacy.

"Men . . . have no true conception of the sacredness of the most marvelous power with which God has endowed mortal men—the power of creation," taught Melvin J. Ballard. "Even though that power may be abused and may become a mere harp of pleasure to the wicked, nevertheless it is the most sacred and holy and divine function with which God has endowed man."[15]

Elder Bruce C. Hafen wrote, "Properly understood, the scriptures and the prophets counsel us to be virtuous not because romantic love is bad, but precisely because romantic love is so good. It is not only good, it is pure, precious, even sacred and holy."[16]

And President Packer said, "The eternal laws of the gospel of Jesus Christ do not prohibit our responding to inborn, God-given mating instincts. Alma admonished his son Shiblon, 'See that ye bridle all your passions, that ye may be filled with love' (Alma 38:12). A bridle is used to guide, to direct. Our passion is to be controlled—but not controlled by extermination as with a plague of insects; not controlled by eradication as with disease; but controlled as electricity is controlled, to generate power and life. When lawfully used the power of procreation will bless and sanctify."[17]

Elder Jeffrey R. Holland has written, "It is as if men and women are given, as part of their next step in development along the path to godhood, raw physical and spiritual ingredients— 'natural' resources, if you will. Those resources are not to run rampant but are to be harnessed and focused so that their power and potential (as is sometimes done with a 'natural' river or a 'natural' waterfall) can be channeled and thereby made even more productive and beneficial."[18]

And on another occasion, Elder Holland said this:

> This highest of all physical gratifications we were designed and created to enjoy. It is as natural as it is appealing. It is given of God to make us like God. And Satan has certainly capitalized on a divinely ordained appeal. But it is not yours without price. Not instantly. Not conveniently. Not with cozy corruption of eternal powers. It is to be earned over time and with discipline. It, like every good thing, is God's right to bestow, not Satan's. When faced with that inherent appetite, a disciple of Christ must be willing to say, "yes, but not this way." In time, with love, after marriage. The right and proper and sanctified physical relationship of a man and a woman is as much a part—indeed more a part of God's plan for us than is

the eating of our daily bread. . . . Salvation comes only through discipline and sacrifice. . . .

I plead with you not to yield to what one has called the "glandular stench of our times."

In your hours of temptations and vulnerability I ask you not, in your case, to submit to Satan's plan. Care more. I ask you to say of this highest, most intimate, most sacred physical expression, "Yes, but not this way." I ask you to be inconvenienced until you've earned the right and paid the divine prices to know the body and soul of the one you love.[19]

Certainly we must teach chastity, but not in such a way that we create frigidity and unnecessary marital problems. Recently, a bride just back from her honeymoon came to me with troubling concerns. Prior to her marriage, several so-called friends had warned her that she wouldn't like *it*, but *it* should be endured for the sake of her husband. She was prepared for *it* to be just awful. However, she found that *it* was actually quite enjoyable for herself, as well as her husband. "What is wrong with me?" she asked. "Am I evil or something?"

I reassured her that she was blessed rather than evil and expressed sympathy for her unfortunate friends. Now, those friends and their husbands probably lacked knowledge, relationship skills, and the patience and wisdom that will develop with time. However, they also were victims of Satanic deceptions that sex, in any setting, is nasty. Satan, who can never have sexual powers, tries to get us to misuse ours. Those who will not yield to extramarital temptation, he tries to hinder from appreciating that which is meant to be a celebration within marriage.

Because Satan has spread widely his philosophy of men and mingled scripture that sex is bad, it has become necessary for the Church to counter that falsehood. Recently the First Presidency and Quorum of the Twelve proclaimed, "We declare the means by which mortal life is created to be divinely appointed."[20] Church members are counseled by their priesthood leaders that marital intimacy is not only for procreation but also for expression of love and strengthening the marriage, both emotionally and spiritually.

Individual apostles and prophets have taught similar truths. "Our natural affections are planted in us by the Spirit of God, for a wise purpose," said Elder Parley P. Pratt. "And they are the very mainsprings of life and happiness—they are the cement of all virtuous and heavenly society—they are the essence of charity, or love; . . . There is not a more pure and holy principle in existence than the affection which glows in the bosom of a virtuous man for his companion; . . . The fact is, God made man, male and female; he planted in their bosoms those affections which are calculated to promote their happiness and union."[21]

President Joseph F. Smith wrote, "The lawful association of the sexes is ordained of God, not only as the sole means of race perpetuation, but for the development of the higher faculties and nobler traits of human nature, which the love-inspired companionship of man and woman alone can insure."[22]

Note that a proper sexual relationship will develop higher faculties and nobler traits. President Brown observed that "the sex instinct is not something which we need to fear or be ashamed of. It is God-given and has a high and holy purpose."[23]

President Spencer W. Kimball taught often about the devastating consequences of immorality. He once said, "Sexual encounters outside of legalized marriage render the individual a thing to be used, a thing to be exploited, and make him or her exchangeable, exploitable, expendable. . . . Pure sex life in proper marriage is approved. There is a time and an appropriateness for all things that have value."[24]

On another occasion, President Kimball taught, "It is the destiny of men and women to join together to make eternal family units. In the context of lawful marriage, the intimacy of sexual relations is right and divinely approved. There is nothing unholy or degrading about sexuality in itself, for by that means men and women join in a process of creation and in an expression of love."[25]

Adding the spiritual dimension to marital intimacy upgrades

what otherwise would only be a biological function to a sexual relationship. This does not detract from the experience; in fact, it greatly enhances it. Elder Parley P. Pratt noted:

> An intelligent being, in the image of God, possesses every organ, attribute, sense, sympathy, affection that is possessed by God himself. . . .
>
> But these are possessed by man, in his rudimental state, in a subordinate sense of the word. Or, in other words, these attributes are in embryo and are to be gradually developed. They resemble a bud, a germ, which gradually develops into bloom, and then, by progress, produces the mature fruit after its own kind. . . .
>
> The gift of the Holy Ghost adapts itself to all these organs or attributes. It quickens all the intellectual faculties, increases, enlarges, expands and purifies all the natural passions and affections, and adapts them by the gift of wisdom, to their lawful use. It inspires, develops, cultivates, and matures all the fine-toned sympathies, joys, tastes, kindred feelings, and affections of our nature. It inspires virtue, kindness, goodness, tenderness, gentleness, and charity. It develops beauty of person, form, and features. It tends to health, vigor, animation, and social feeling. It invigorates all the faculties of the physical and intellectual man. It strengthens and gives tone to the nerves. In short, it is, as it were, marrow to the bone, joy to the heart, light to the eyes, music to the ears, and life to the whole being.[26]

Everything, especially the sexual relationship, is enhanced by having the Holy Ghost in your life and marriage. Another husband-and-wife writing team, Les and Leslie Parrott, have written:

> Sociologist Andrew Greeley surveyed married people and found that the happiest couples were

those who pray together. Couples who frequently pray together are twice as likely as those who pray less often to describe their marriages as being highly romantic. They also report considerably higher sexual satisfaction and more sexual ecstasy! . . .

There is an old story about a young couple who decided to start their honeymoon by kneeling beside their bed to pray. The bride giggled when she heard her new husband's prayer: "For what we are about to receive may the Lord make us truly thankful." . . .

As strange as it may sound, there is a strong link in marriage between prayer and sex. For one thing, frequency of prayer is a more powerful predictor of marital satisfaction than frequency of sexual intimacy. But get this: Married couples who pray together are ninety percent more likely to report higher satisfaction with their sex life than couples who do not pray together. Also, women who pray with their partner tend to be more orgasmic. That does not sound right, does it? After all, married churchgoers are painted by the media as prudes who think sex is dirty. Well, let the media say what they want, but prayerful couples know better.[27]

While serving as president of Brigham Young University, Jeffrey R. Holland spoke to the student body about purity and "why we should be clean." In doing so, he did a masterful job of painting a word picture of the appropriate sexual relationship in marriage. His talk, "Of Souls, Symbols, and Sacraments," gives three major reasons for purity before and during marriage. Excerpts from his talk follow:

> One of the "plain and precious" truths restored to this dispensation is that "the spirit and the body are the soul of man" (D&C 88:15). . . .
>
> May I quote a 1913 sermon by Elder James E. Talmage on this doctrinal point:
>
> "We have been taught . . . to look upon these bodies

of ours as gifts from God. We Latter-day Saints do not regard the body as something to be condemned, something to be abhorred. . . . We regard [the body] as a sign of our royal birthright. . . . We recognize . . . that those who kept not their first estate . . . were denied that inestimable blessing. . . . We believe that these bodies . . . may be made, in very truth, the temple of the Holy Ghost. . . .

"It is peculiar to the theology of the Latter-day Saints that we regard the body as an essential part of the soul. Read your dictionaries, the lexicons, and encyclopedias, and you will find that nowhere [in Christianity], outside of the Church of Jesus Christ, is the solemn and eternal truth taught that the soul of man is the body and the spirit combined." [CR, October 1913, p. 117] . . .

Perhaps here Paul's warning to the Corinthians takes on newer, higher meaning: "Now the body is not for fornication, but for the Lord; and the Lord for the body. . . . Know ye not that your bodies are the members of Christ? Shall I then take the members of Christ, and make them the members of an harlot? God forbid. . . . Flee fornication. . . . He that committeth fornication sinneth against his own body. . . . Know ye not that your body is the temple of the Holy Ghost which is in you, which ye have of God, and ye are not your own? For ye are bought with a price: therefore glorify God in your body, and in your spirit, which are God's" [1 Corinthians 6:13–20]. . . .

Christ restored the very seeds of eternal lives (see D&C 132:19, 24), and we desecrate them at our peril. The first key reason for personal purity? Our very souls are involved and at stake.

Second, human intimacy, that sacred, physical union ordained of God for a married couple, deals with a symbol that demands special sanctity.

Such an act of love between a man and a woman is—or certainly was ordained to be—a symbol of total union: union of their hearts, their hopes, their lives, their love, their family, their future, their everything. . . .

And the external symbol of that union, the physical manifestation of what is a far deeper spiritual and metaphysical bonding, is the physical blending that is part of—indeed, a most beautiful and gratifying expression of—that larger, more complete union of eternal purpose and promise. . . .

It is in that act of ultimate physical intimacy we most nearly fulfill the commandment of the Lord given to Adam and Eve, living symbols for all married couples, when he invited them to cleave unto one another only, and thus become "one flesh" [Genesis 2:24]. . . .

You must wait until you can give everything, and you cannot give everything until you are at least legally and, for Latter-day Saint purposes, eternally pronounced as one. To give illicitly that which is not yours to give (remember, "you are not your own") and to give only part of that which cannot be followed with the gift of your whole heart and your whole life and your whole self is its own form of emotional Russian roulette. . . .

Sexual intimacy is not only a symbolic union between a man and a woman—the uniting of their very souls—but it is also symbolic of a union between mortals and deity, between otherwise ordinary and fallible humans uniting for a rare and special moment with God himself and all the powers by which he gives life in this wide universe of ours. . . .

And I submit that we will never be more like God at any other time in this life than when we are expressing that particular power . . .

Souls. Symbols. Sacraments. Do these words suggest why human intimacy is such a serious matter? Why it is so right and rewarding, so stunningly beautiful when it is within marriage and approved of God (not just "good" but "very good"), and so blasphemously wrong—like unto murder—when it is outside such a covenant?[28]

Now, since sexual relations are intended to be sacred and part of the purification process for godhood, we are not surprised to note that Satan does all that he can to disrupt and distort. "Show me one principle that has originated by the power of the devil," said President Brigham Young. "You cannot do it. I call evil inverted good, or a correct principle made an evil use of."[29] Satan has been very successful at perverting sex and thus hindering the progress of those so seduced. It is therefore necessary to give some cautions regarding sexual matters, even to those who are legally and lawfully married.

The First Presidency and Quorum of the Twelve have proclaimed, "We further declare that God has commanded that the sacred powers of procreation are to be employed only between man and woman, lawfully wedded as husband and wife."[30] Outside of those parameters, whether single or married, any sexual activity leads one away from eternal marriage and godhood.

"All sex activity outside of marriage" said President Spencer W. Kimball, "is sin. The early apostles and prophets mention numerous sins that were reprehensible to them. Many of them were sexual sins—adultery, being without natural affection, lustfulness, infidelity, incontinence, filthy communications, impurity, inordinate affection, fornication. They included all sexual relations outside marriage—petting, sex perversion, masturbation, and preoccupation with sex in one's thoughts and talking. Included are every hidden and secret sin and all unholy and impure thoughts and practices. One of the worst of these is incest."[31]

Of the ideal marriage relationship, President George Q. Cannon said:

> That union shall be perpetuated throughout eternity, and there shall be an increase of that love and of that union and an increase also of that power, because

the power of procreation is promised—the greatest power that man possesses on earth. That is promised unto those who are faithful. . . . Therefore, it can be said of us as it was said of our Lord and Savior, "to the increase of His kingdom there shall be no end." Why: Because of this principle that I spoke of—the principle of procreation. By it, and through that principle the worlds are peopled. The planetary orbs which stud our heavens so gloriously are peopled by that principle— the principle of procreation. God possesses it, and we as His children inherit the power. If we do what is right He promises to bestow it upon us.[32]

Only those who do what is right, and are resurrected as exalted beings, husbands and wives, will enjoy these sexual powers. President Brigham Young said, "Will we all become Gods, and be crowned kings? No, my brethren, there will be millions, even the greater part of the celestial world, who will not be capable of the fulness of that glory, immortality, eternal lives and a continuation of them, yet they will go into the celestial kingdom."[33]

Elder Merrill J. Bateman taught, "The sacred power of creation is given to us for a relatively short time—for only a few decades—and then removed. We are given laws and tested to see if we will respect this power, protect its use, and respect the body. If we are obedient, the power of life returns in the Resurrection. If we abuse the power and do not repent, the natural capacity to create never returns, and we live singly in the eternities (see D&C 131:1–4)."[34]

But what of those sexual powers once held by those who inherit only the telestial or terrestrial kingdoms? Joseph Fielding Smith explained:

Some will gain celestial bodies with all the powers of exaltation and eternal increase. These bodies will shine like the sun as our Savior's does, as described by John. Those who enter the terrestrial kingdom will have terrestrial bodies, and they will not shine like the sun, but they will be more glorious than the bodies of those who receive the telestial glory. . . . In both of these kingdoms there will be changes in the bodies and limitations. They will not have the power of increase, neither the power or nature to live as husbands and wives, for this will be denied them and they cannot increase. . . . Those who receive the exaltation in the celestial kingdom will have the 'continuation of the seeds forever.' They will live in the family relationship. In the terrestrial and in the telestial kingdoms there will be no marriage. Those who enter there will remain "separately and singly" forever. . . . Some of the functions in the celestial body will not appear in the terrestrial body, neither in the telestial body, and the power of procreation will be removed.[35]

It is a sobering thought to realize that those sexual powers and thoughts that are so much a part of our adult mortal existence are given to us only on a probationary status. If we prove trustworthy of those powers, and all other covenants, we will retain our sexuality in the resurrection. Otherwise, we will live eternally in a neutered condition appropriate for one of the lower kingdoms. Sexual powers, procreation, and eternal lives are reserved for the gods. Therefore, our approach to sexuality, even (or especially) in marriage, must continue to be godly.

The First Presidency has stated, "Sexual relations are proper only between husband and wife appropriately expressed within the bonds of marriage."[36] And President Brown observed that "many marriages have been wrecked on the dangerous rocks of ignorant and debased sex behavior, both before and after marriage. Gross ignorance on the part of newlyweds on the subject of the proper place and functioning of sex results in much unhappiness and many broken homes."[37]

Just because a married couple can have sex, it does not mean it is good sex. Even within marriage, sexual intimacies should be appropriately expressed and not debased sex behavior.

A respected psychologist, Rollo May, noted:

In an amazingly short period following World War I, we shifted from acting as though sex did not exist at all to being obsessed with it. We now place more emphasis on sex than any society since that of ancient Rome, and some scholars believe we are more preoccupied with sex than any other people in all of history. . . .

Partly as a result of this radical shift, many therapists today rarely see patients who exhibit repression of sex in the manner of Freud's pre-World War I hysterical patients. In fact, we find in the people who come for help just the opposite: a great deal of talk about sex, a great deal of sexual activity, practically no one complaining of cultural prohibitions over going to bed as often or with as many partners as one wishes. But what our patients do complain of is lack of feeling and passion. The curious thing about this ferment of discussion is how little anyone seems to be enjoying emancipation. So much sex and so little meaning or even fun in it! . . .

Our "dogmatic enlightenment" is self-defeating: it ends up destroying the very sexual passion it set out to protect.[38]

I would suggest that even within the marriage setting, if the sexual relationship is not a soul, symbol, and sacrament experience, it too will lose meaning, fun, and passion.

Should sexual satisfaction be sought outside of the marriage, even greater losses occur. "Take away regard for the seventh commandment," warned Elder Maxwell, "and behold the current celebration of sex, the secular religion with its own liturgy of lust and supporting music. Its theology focuses on 'self.' Its hereafter is 'now.' Its chief ritual is 'sensation'—though, ironically, it finally desensitizes its obsessed adherents, who become 'past feeling' (Ephesians 4:19; Moroni 9:20)."[39]

Elder Maxwell also noted this contrast, "The greater our sensitivity to the Spirit, the greater our response to beauty, grace, and truth in all their forms as these exist about us. Our righteousness opens us up like a blossoming flower to both detail and immensity. Sin, on the other hand, closes us down; it scalds the taste buds of the soul."[40] Holy-Ghost-worthy sex, where the relationship and bodies are enlivened by the Spirit, is the only truly good sex.

Therefore, the Brethren have on occasion expressed cautions to married couples regarding their sexual behavior. President David O. McKay wrote:

> Let us instruct young people who come to us, to know that a woman should be queen of her own body. The marriage covenant does not give the man the right to enslave her or to abuse her or to use her merely for the gratification of his passion. Your marriage ceremony does not give you that right.
>
> Second, let them remember that gentleness and consideration after the ceremony [are] just as appropriate and necessary and beautiful as gentleness and consideration before the wedding.
>
> Third, let us realize that manhood is not undermined by the practicing of continence, notwithstanding what some psychiatrists claim. Chastity is the crown of beautiful womanhood, and self-control is the source of true manhood, if you will know it, not indulgence. . . .
>
> Let us teach our young men to enter into matrimony with the idea that each will be just as courteous and considerate of a wife after the ceremony as during courtship.[41]

Much was said about such things by President Kimball. Here are a few examples:

> Even though sex can be an important and satisfactory part of married life, we must remember that life is not designed just for sex. Even marriage does not make proper certain extremes in sexual indulgence. To the Ephesian saints Paul begged for propriety in

marriage: "So ought men to love their wives as their own bodies. He that loveth his wife loveth himself" (Ephesians 5:28). And perhaps the Lord's condemnation included secret sexual sins in marriage, when he said: "... And those who are not pure and have said they were pure, shall be destroyed, saith the Lord God" (D&C 132:52).[42]

President Kimball provided this guideline in helping determine what was appropriate. "If it is unnatural," he wrote, "you just don't do it. That is all, and all the family life should be kept clean and worthy and on a very high plane. There are some people who have said that behind the bedroom doors anything goes. That is not true and the Lord would not condone it."[43]

And again, he wrote, "We urge, with Peter, '... Abstain from fleshly lusts, which war against the soul' (1 Peter 2:11). No indecent exposure or pornography or other aberrations to defile the mind and spirit. No fondling of bodies, one's own or that of others, and no sex between persons except in proper marriage relationships. This is positively prohibited by our Creator in all places, at all times, and we reaffirm it. Even in marriage there can be some excesses and distortions. No amount of rationalization to the contrary can satisfy a disappointed Father in heaven."[44]

In a general priesthood meeting, President N. Eldon Tanner expressed this concern:

> Brethren, we who lead the Church are responsible to see that you are taught in plainness. I, therefore, must make reference to a matter that otherwise I would not present in a meeting such as this. There are evil and degrading practices which, in the world, are not only condoned but encouraged. Sometimes married couples in their intimate expression of love to one another are drawn into practices that are unholy, unworthy, and unnatural. We receive letters from time to time asking for a definition of "unnatural" or "unworthy." Brethren, you know the answer to that. If in doubt at all,

do not do it. Surely no holder of the priesthood would feel worthy to accept advancement in the priesthood or sign his temple recommend if any impure practice were a part of his life. If perchance, one of you has been drawn into any degrading conduct, cast it away from you so that when you are subject to a worthiness interview you can answer to yourself, and to the Lord, and to the interviewing priesthood officer that you are worthy.[45]

President Hunter also provided this counsel to husbands:

> Keep yourselves above any domineering or unworthy behavior in the tender, intimate relationship between husband and wife. Because marriage is ordained of God, the intimate relationship between husbands and wives is good and honorable in the eyes of God. He has commanded that they be one flesh and that they multiply and replenish the earth (see Moses 2:28; 3:24). You are to love your wife as Christ loved the Church and gave himself for it (see Ephesians 5:25–31). . . . Tenderness and respect—never selfishness—must be the guiding principles in the intimate relationship between husband and wife. Each partner must be considerate and sensitive to the other's needs and desires. Any domineering, indecent, or uncontrolled behavior in the intimate relationship between husband and wife is condemned by the Lord.[46]

Similarly, President Packer cautioned, "A married couple may be tempted to introduce things into [their] relationship which are unworthy. Do not, as the scriptures warn, 'change the natural use into that which is against nature' (Romans 1:26). If you do, the tempter will drive a wedge between you. If something unworthy has become part of your relationship, don't ever do it again! Now, what exactly do I mean by that? You know what I mean by that."[47]

The Brethren do not provide Church members with an

exhaustive list of all the possible ways to be impure, indecent, unnatural, and unworthy. However, the counsel is sufficiently clear for those couples that sincerely want to include the Holy Ghost in their relationship, even their intimate relationship. Such couples not only want to meet the minimum criteria for temple recommends but also to please Heavenly Father. A good rule for a dating couple is "keep your expressions of feelings to those that are comfortable in the presence of your parents."[48] Similarly, a good rule for married couples is keep your expressions of sexual intimacy to those that are comfortable in the presence of your Heavenly Parents.

For those who are striving to be worthy of exaltation, the principles taught by the Brethren are adequate and appreciated. After all, this learning and testing experience of mortality is designed to determine who can be trusted in the resurrection with the greatest power of all, the power to procreate, the power of the gods!

Let's conclude this discussion of cautions regarding sexual sins by asking a very basic question: What is sin?

One might answer that sin is doing something that God told you not to do, breaking a commandment.

Well, yes, but why did God say not to do it? Is it a sin because God said not to do it, or did God say not to do it because the behavior automatically carries with it negative consequences? Is God making up commandments to see if we will be obedient, or is He showing us what is beneficial or detrimental to our happiness? To answer these questions, it may be helpful to stand back and look at the big picture.

Joseph Smith, the Prophet, invited us to expand our vision with this statement:

> God himself, finding he was in the midst of spirits and glory, because he was more intelligent, saw proper to institute laws whereby the rest could have a privilege to advance like himself. The relationship we have with God places us in a situation to advance in knowledge. He has power to institute laws to instruct the weaker

intelligences, that they may be exalted with himself, so that they might have one glory upon another, and all that knowledge, power, glory, and intelligence, which is requisite in order to save them.[49]

Since God instituted laws to help us advance, forbidden behaviors are those behaviors that would hinder our advancement, happiness, and potential godhood. "Whoever else suffers," said President Kimball, "every sin is against God, for it tends to frustrate the program and purposes of the Almighty. Likewise, every sin is committed against the sinner, for it limits his progress and curtails his development."[50]

We should keep the commandments because there is no other way to be happy and achieve our full potential.

It seems that it is easier to keep the commandments when we recognize that they are "for our good" (Deuteronomy 6:24). John the Beloved concluded, "For this is the love of God, that we keep his commandments: and his commandments are not grievous" (1 John 5:3). Because the Lord's "work and . . . glory [is] to bring to pass the immortality and eternal life of man" (Moses 1:39), He only asks of us that which will bless our lives.

The Lord said, "And again, I say unto you, I give unto you a new commandment, that you may understand my will concerning you; Or, in other words, I give unto you directions how you may act before me, that it may turn to you for your salvation" (D&C 82:8–9). To those who recognize commandments as blessings and faithfully and diligently obey, the Lord has promised, "And they shall also be crowned with blessings from above, yea, and with commandments not a few, and with revelations in their time" (D&C 59:3–4).

Notes

1. Maxwell, *We Will Prove Them Herewith*, 47.
2. Brown, *You and Your Marriage*, 73–74.
3. Cline, *How to Make a Good Marriage Great*, 35–36.
4. Packer, "Why Stay Morally Clean," *Ensign*, July 1972, 111–12.

5. Packer, *Things of the Soul*, 106.

6. Lee, "President Harold B. Lee's General Priesthood Address," *Ensign*, January 1974, 100.

7. Kimball, "Marriage Is Honorable," in *Brigham Young University Speeches of the Year, 1974*, 262.

8. Ashton, "Be A Quality Person," *Ensign*, February 1993, 67.

9. Cline, *How to Make a Good Marriage Great*, 29.

10. Oaks, "Pornography," *Ensign*, May 2005, 90.

11. Brinley and Lamb, *Between Husband and Wife*, 146–47.

12. Cline, *How to Make a Good Marriage Great*, 34–35.

13. Fairlie, *Seven Deadly Sins Today*, 182.

14. Cline, *How to Make a Good Marriage Great*, 28.

15. Ballard, *Sermons and Missionary Service of Melvin J. Ballard*, 167.

16. Hafen, "The Gospel and Romantic Love," *Ensign*, October 1982, 66.

17. Packer, *Things of the Soul*, 109.

18. Holland, *Christ and the New Covenant*, 408.

19. Holland, *However Long and Hard the Road*, 38.

20. The First Presidency and Council of the Twelve Apostles, "The Family—A Proclamation to the World," *Ensign*, November 1995, 102.

21. Pratt, *The Essential Parley P. Pratt*, 124.

22. Smith, "Unchastity—The Dominant Evil of the Age," *Improvement Era*, June 1917.

23. Brown, *Abundant Life*, 70.

24. Kimball, *Faith Precedes the Miracle*, 155.

25. Kimball, *The Teachings of Spencer W. Kimball*, 311.

26. Pratt, *Key to the Science of Theology*, 101–2.

27. Parrott and Parrott, *Saving Your Marriage before It Starts*, 145.

28. Holland, *Souls, Symbols, and Sacraments*, 11–13, 15, 17–18, 20, 27, 31, 34.

29. Young, in *Journal of Discourses*, 3: 157.

30. The First Presidency and Council of the Twelve Apostles, "The Family—A Proclamation to the World," 102.

31. Kimball, *Teachings of Spencer W. Kimball*, 264.

32. Cannon, in Conference Report, April 1899, 20.

33. Young, in *Journal of Discourses*, 4:271–72.

34. Bateman, "Lay Hold upon Every Good Thing," in *Brigham Young University 2001-2002 Devotional and Fireside Speeches*, 97.

35. Smith, *Doctrines of Salvation* 2:287–88.

36. First Presidency letter, 4 November 1991.

37. Brown, *You and Your Marriage*, 73–74.

38. May, *Love and Will*, 39, 42.

39. Maxwell, "Put Off the Natural Man, and Come Off Conqueror," *Ensign*, November 1990, 15–16.

40. Maxwell, "The Message: Creativity," *New Era*, August 1982, 7.

41. McKay, *Gospel Ideals*, 471–72.

42. Kimball, *Miracle of Forgiveness*, 73.

43. Kimball, *Teachings of Spencer W. Kimball*, 312.

44. Kimball, in Conference Report, April 1974, 8–9.

45. Tanner, "The Blessing of Church Interviews," *Ensign*, November 1978, 42.

46. Hunter, "Being a Righteous Husband and Father," *Ensign*, November 1994, 51.

47. Packer, *Fountain of Life*, 8.

48. Scott, "Making the Right Choices," *Ensign*, November 1994, 38.

49. Smith, *Teachings of the Prophet Joseph Smith*, 354.

50. Kimball, *Miracle of Forgiveness*, 26.

9

MULTIPLY AND
replenish

President Spencer W. Kimball spoke at Brigham Young University when I was an undergraduate student and not yet married. It was interesting to observe some couples squirm with discomfort as he chastised those who delayed or postponed marriage or the responsibilities of parenthood for educational purposes.[1]

President Kimball touched frequently on this topic:

> I have told many groups of young people that they should not postpone their marriage until they have acquired all of their education ambitions. I have told tens of thousands of young folks that when they marry they should not wait for children until they have finished their schooling and financial desires. Marriage is basically for the family, and when people have found their proper companions there should be no long delay. They should live together normally and let the children come . . . Young wives should be occupied in bearing and rearing their children. I know of no scriptures where an authorization is given to young wives to withhold their families and to go to work to put their

husbands through school. There are thousands of husbands who have worked their own way through school and have reared families at the same time. Though it is more difficult, young people can make their way through their educational programs.[2]

In his well-known book *The Miracle of Forgiveness,* President Kimball writes, "Degrees and letters and titles become idols. Young married couples who postpone parenthood until their degrees are attained might be shocked if their expressed preference were labeled idolatry."[3]

And again. "In a properly charted Latter-day Saint marriage," he counseled, "one must be conscious of the need to forget self and love one's companion more than self. There will not be postponement of parenthood, but a desire for children as the Lord intended, and without limiting the family as the world does. The children will be wanted and loved."[4]

And this counsel, which President Kimball shared at an area conference.

> Supreme happiness in marriage is governed considerably by a primary factor—that of the bearing and rearing of children. Too many young people today marry with a selfish motive—they are interested first in themselves. The more important purposes of marriage are ignored for the less important. Family life is made secondary. The college degrees, the occupation, the comforts, the convenience of the contracting parties is considered first. To many there seems to be a total forgetfulness of the purpose of marriage and its responsibilities and opportunities. And many young people set their minds, determining they will not marry or have children until they are more secure, until the military service period is over, until the debts are paid, or until it is more convenient. They have forgotten that the first commandment is to "be fruitful and multiply and replenish the earth and subdue it" (Genesis 1:28). And so, brides continue their employ-

ment and husbands encourage it, and contraceptives are used to prevent conception . . . but the excuses are many, mostly weak. . . . The Church cannot approve nor condone the measures which so greatly limit the family. Could it justify the employment of women who would use that as an excuse for postponing their responsibilities?

How do you suppose that the Lord would look upon a man and woman whose marriage seems to be largely for the purpose of living together and sex gratification without the responsibilities of marriage? How do you think that the Lord looks upon those who use the contraceptives because in their selfish life it is not the convenient moment to bear children? How do you feel the Lord looks upon those who would trade flesh and blood children for pianos or television or furniture or an automobile, and is this not actually the case when people will buy these luxuries and yet cannot afford to have their children?[5]

President Kimball wasn't the only prophet to espouse such teachings. President Ezra Taft Benson gave similar counsel:

Young mothers and fathers, with all my heart I counsel you not to postpone having your children, being co-creators with our Father in Heaven. Do not use the reasoning of the world, such as, "We'll wait until we can better afford having children, until we are more secure, until John has completed his education, until he has a better-paying job, until we have a larger home, until we've obtained a few of the material conveniences," and on and on. This is the reasoning of the world, and is not pleasing in the sight of God. Mothers who enjoy good health, have your children and have them early. And, husbands, always be considerate of your wives in the bearing of children. Do not curtail the number of your children for personal or selfish reasons. Material possessions, social convenience, and so-called professional advantages are nothing compared to a righteous posterity. In the eternal perspective, children—not possessions, not position, not prestige—are our greatest jewels.[6]

These are strongly worded quotes from President Kimball and President Benson. I chose to begin this chapter with such quotes, not to shock or arouse interest but to establish the importance prophets have placed on this topic.

To put this in perspective, let us go in our scriptures to the first recorded commandment. "So God created man in his own image, in the image of God created he him; male and female created he them. And God blessed them, and God said unto them, be fruitful, and multiply, and replenish the earth" (Genesis 1:27–28).

More recent, in 1995, the First Presidency reiterated this commandment:

> The first commandment that God gave to Adam and Eve pertained to their potential for parenthood as husband and wife. We declare that God's commandment for his children to multiply and replenish the Earth remains in force. We further declare that God has commanded that the sacred powers of procreation are to be employed only between man and woman, lawfully wedded as husband and wife.
>
> We declare the means by which mortal life is created to be divinely appointed. We affirm the sanctity of life and of its importance in God's eternal plan.
>
> Husband and wife have a solemn responsibility to love and care for each other and for their children. Children are an heritage of the Lord (see Psalm 127:3). Parents have a sacred duty to rear their children in love and righteousness, to provide for their physical and spiritual needs, to teach them to love and serve one another, to observe the commandments of God and to be law-abiding citizens wherever they live. Husbands and wives—mothers and fathers—will be

held accountable before God for the discharge of these obligations.[7]

An earlier (1942) First Presidency declared this:

> By virtue of the authority in us vested as the First Presidency of the Church, we warn our people. Amongst His earliest commands to Adam and Eve, the Lord said: "Multiply and replenish the earth." He has repeated that command in our day. He has again revealed in this, the last dispensation, the principle of the eternity of the marriage covenant.
>
> The Lord has told us that it is the duty of every husband and wife to obey the command given to Adam to multiply and replenish the earth, so that the legions of choice spirits waiting for their tabernacles of flesh may come here and move forward under God's great design to become perfect souls, for without these fleshy tabernacles they cannot progress to their God-planned destiny. Thus, every husband and wife should become a father and mother in Israel to children born under the holy, eternal covenant . . .
>
> No parent can escape that obligation and that responsibility, and for the proper meeting thereof, the Lord will hold us to a strict accountability. No loftier duty than this can be assumed by mortals.[8]

In 1993 Elder Boyd K. Packer quoted this 1942 First Presidency warning and then added, "That message and warning from the First Presidency is needed more, not less, today than when it was given. And no voice from any organization of the Church on any level of administration equals that of the First Presidency."[9]

Perhaps the most often quoted comment on this subject comes from President Brigham Young, who said: "There are multitudes of pure and holy spirits waiting to take tabernacles, now what is our duty? To prepare tabernacles for them; to take a course that will not tend to drive those spirits into the families of the wicked, where they will be trained in wickedness, debauchery, and every species of crime. It is the duty of every righteous man and woman to prepare tabernacles for all the spirits they can."[10]

Later prophets continued to emphasize this first commandment. For example, President Harold B. Lee said, "We declare it is a grievous sin before God to adopt restrictive measures in disobedience to God's divine command from the beginning of time to 'multiply and replenish the earth.' Surely those who project such measure to prevent life or to destroy life before or after birth will reap the whirlwind of God's retribution, for God will not be mocked."[11]

And President Benson said:

> The world teaches birth control. Tragically, many of our sisters subscribe to its pills and practices when they could easily provide earthly tabernacles for more of our Father's children. We know that every spirit assigned to this earth will come, whether through us or someone else. There are couples in the Church who think they are getting along just fine with their limited families but who will someday suffer the pains of remorse when they meet the spirits that might have been part of their posterity. The first commandment given to man was to multiply and replenish the earth with children. That commandment has never been altered, modified, or cancelled. The Lord did not say to multiply and replenish the earth if it is convenient, or if you are wealthy, or after you have gotten your schooling, or when there is peace on earth, or until you have four children. The Bible says, "Lo, children are an heritage of the Lord: . . . Happy is the man that hath his quiver full of them . . ." (Psalm 127:3, 5). We believe God is glorified by having numerous children and a program of perfection for them. So also will God glorify that husband and wife who have a large posterity and who have tried to raise them up in righteousness.[12]

The above comments were given to the church membership in general conference. Only a few days later, official correspondence from the First Presidency was sent to local priesthood leaders. In part, the letter stated:

> We seriously regret that there should exist a sentiment or feeling among any members of the Church to curtail the birth of their children. We have been commanded to multiply and replenish the earth that we may have joy and rejoicing in our posterity. Where husband and wife enjoy health and vigor and are free from impurities that would be entailed upon their posterity, it is contrary to the teachings of the Church artificially to curtail or prevent the birth of children. We believe that those who practice birth control will reap disappointment by and by.
>
> However, we feel that men must be considerate of their wives who bear the greater responsibility not only of bearing children, but of caring for them through childhood. To this end the mother's health and strength should be conserved and the husband's consideration for his wife is his first duty, and self-control a dominant factor in all their relationships.[13]

Thus the commandment has been given and repeatedly emphasized. Now Latter-day Saints who receive "the oath and covenant which belongeth to the priesthood" (D&C 84:39) must accept and keep this challenging commandment. To such, the Lord added, "And I now give unto you a commandment to beware concerning yourselves, to give diligent heed to the words of eternal life. For you shall live by every word that proceedeth forth from the mouth of God" (D&C 84:43–44).

Many couples are not aware that the Church has policies on many moral issues related to the sexual relationship. Couples struggling to achieve conception may want to seek counsel from their bishops regarding Church policies on artificial insemination and *in vitro* fertilization. Couples striving to prevent conception would want to know that the Church strongly discourages surgical sterilization, including vasectomy, as an elective form of birth control. Couples could receive more details and counsel from their bishops.

Although this counsel is appreciated and heeded, it still leaves the couple with responsibility and the necessity of discussion, decision, prayer, and confirmation. When I hear that the birth control method of choice among many young married couples is vasectomy, I wonder if these young couples are aware of the Church policy and have thought through the consequences of such a drastic procedure.

President Gordon B. Hinckley has said, "As far as I am concerned, whether it is a commandment or counsel, that which the Lord counsels becomes a commandment to Gordon B. Hinckley. I hope it does to you."[14]

Current Church policy reiterates that couples should consider parenthood as a privilege and responsibility. However, the Church does not dictate how many children to have, or when to have them. Couples are encouraged to make this a matter of discussion and consultation with the Lord. The policy statement seems to emphasize the obligation of the couple to make inspired decisions regarding their parenting responsibilities.

Every young couple, however, soon discovers that there are myriad interpretations of the "first commandment." Many are eager to counsel the new couple, even though that counsel may differ with what the Brethren have said. Add to that confusion the inexperience and selfishness of the "natural man" (see Mosiah 3:19), and most young couples are genuinely uninformed or perplexed with seemingly conflicting ideas, fears, and expectations. In frustration, one young bride proposed this solution to the apparent dilemma, "I guess it's up to us!" I wholeheartedly agree, if we expand the declaration to, "It's up to us—to live the principle and receive revelations as to how to do that!"

What is meant by the word *principle*? "That word *principle* in the revelation is a very important one," noted President Packer. "A *principle* is an enduring truth, a law, a rule you can adopt to guide you in making decisions. Generally, principles are not spelled out in detail. That leaves you free to find your way with an enduring truth, a principle as your anchor."[15]

Elder Richard G. Scott counseled, "As you seek spiritual knowledge, search for principles. Carefully separate them from the detail used to explain them. Principles are consecrated truth, packaged for application to a wide variety of circumstances. A true principle makes decisions clear even under the most confusing and compelling circumstances. It is worth great effort to organize the truth we gather to simple statements of principle."[16]

The principle involved in the first commandment is clear: we should have children. Beyond that, the details must be worked out between the Lord and the couple. "I teach them correct principles," declared the Prophet Joseph Smith, about his followers, "and let them govern themselves."[17]

More recently, Elder Dallin H. Oaks stated, "When we understand the plan of salvation, we also understand the purpose and effect of the commandments God has given his children. He teaches us correct principles and invites us to govern ourselves."[18]

Keeping an eternal perspective so that righteous decisions are made is one of the great challenges faced by all couples. President Boyd K. Packer observed:

> *Never* has a generation been so surrounded with those who speak irreverently of life. *Never* has there been such persuasion to avoid the responsibilities of parenthood. Never has it been so convenient to block that frail footpath of life across which new spirits enter mortality. . . .
>
> Several years ago, while representing the Church at the University of Montana, I found myself on a panel with representatives from several churches. The moderator asked each of us to respond to the question, "Do you believe in planned parenthood?" My answer was a resounding "yes!" with this explanation: we *plan* to have families. . . .
>
> Often when young couples come, they ask the

specific question, "How many children should we plan to have?" This I cannot answer, for it is not within my province to know. With some persons there are no restrictions of health, and perhaps a number of children will be born into the family. Some good parents who would have large families are blessed with but one or two children. And, occasionally, couples who make wonderful parents are not able to have natural offspring and enjoy the marvelous experience of fostering children born to others. Planned parenthood involves a good deal more than just the begetting of children. Nothing in our lives deserves more planning than our responsibilities in parenthood.[19]

Certainly we are given agency, but this does not mean that our decisions are of no consequence. In fact, the decisions we make and the process we go through in making those decisions may be the very factors used to determine if we will enjoy the highest degree of the celestial kingdom (see D&C 131:1–2) as eternal couples or live as separate, single, servants (see D&C 132:16–17) in a lower kingdom. In question is our determination to become like Heavenly Father and Heavenly Mother. No others will be married in the eternities.

Of the eternal marriage relationship, President George Q. Cannon said:

> That union shall be perpetuated throughout eternity, and there shall be an increase of that love and of that union and an increase also of that power, because the power of procreation is promised—the greatest power that man possesses on earth. That is promised unto those who are faithful . . . Therefore, it can be said of us as it was said of our Lord and Savior, "to the increase of His kingdom there shall be no end." Why? Because of this principle that I spoke of—the principle of procreation. By it, and through that principle the worlds are peopled. The planetary orbs which stud our heavens so gloriously are peopled by that principle—

the principle of procreation. God possesses it, and we as His children inherit the power. If we do what is right He promises to bestow it upon us.[20]

The fullness of priesthood includes more than just being married in the temple. The conditions explained in that ceremony must also be met before a couple will actually be married in the eternities. President Cannon also stated:

> When men go forward and attend to other ordinances, such as receiving their endowments, their washings, their anointings, receiving the promises connected therewith, these promises will be fulfilled to the very letter in time and in eternity—that is, if they themselves are true to the conditions upon which the blessings are promised. And it is when persons go to the altar and are married for time and eternity. . . . Just as sure as that promise is made, and the persons united (to whom the promise is made) conform with the conditions thereof, just so sure will it be fulfilled.[21]

But what of those sexual powers once held by those who will inherit only the telestial or terrestrial kingdoms? Joseph Fielding Smith explained:

> Some will gain celestial bodies with all the powers of exaltation and eternal increase. These bodies will shine like the sun as our Savior's does, as described by John. Those who enter the terrestrial kingdom will have terrestrial bodies, and they will not shine like the sun, but they will be more glorious than the bodies of those who receive the telestial glory. . . . In both of these kingdoms there will be changes in the bodies and limitations. They will not have the power of increase, neither the power or nature to live as husbands and wives, for this will be denied them and they cannot increase. Those who receive the exaltation in

the celestial kingdom will have the "continuation of the seeds forever." They will live in the family relationship. In the terrestrial and in the telestial kingdoms there will be no marriage. Those who enter there will remain "separately and singly" forever. Some of the functions in the celestial body will not appear in the terrestrial body, neither in the telestial body, and the power of procreation will be removed. I take it that men and women will, in these kingdoms, be just what the so-called Christian world expects us all to be—neither man nor woman, merely immortal beings having received the resurrection.[22]

In fact even the greater part of those in the celestial kingdom will be separate, single servants (see D&C 132:16–17) in contrast to the gods who shall be exalted to a status of "a fulness and a continuation of the seeds forever and ever" (D&C 132:19–20). Said President Brigham Young, "Will we all become Gods, and be crowned kings? No, my brethren, there will be million on millions, even the greater part of the celestial world, who will not be capable of the fulness of that glory, immortality, eternal lives and a continuation of them, yet they will go into the celestial kingdom."[23]

President Benson reminded us that "exaltation is eternal fatherhood and motherhood."[24] Keeping that eternal view in mind helps us focus on what is genuinely important as we strive to keep the first commandment. Someone has said, "The miracle of life is not that adults create children, it's that children create adults."

We need to have children, not just for their sake but also for our growth. Alma observed that "God gave unto them commandments, after having made known unto them the plan of redemption" (Alma 12:32). The more we ponder upon the plan, the better position we will be in to make decisions about our sexual relations and parenting responsibilities.

We must be extremely cautious that we do not approach this subject from a perspective of selfishness. "In most cases the desire not to have children has its birth in vanity, passion, and selfishness," wrote President David O. McKay. "Such feelings are the seeds sown in early married life that produce a harvest of discord, suspicion, estrangement, and divorce. All such efforts too often tend to put the marriage on a level with the panderer and the courtesan. They befoul the pure fountains of life with the slime of indulgence and sensuality. Such misguided couples are ever seeking but never finding the reality for which the heart is yearning."[25]

Similarly, President George Albert Smith taught that "children are an heritage from the Lord, and those who refuse the responsibility of bringing them into the world and caring for them are usually prompted by selfish motives, and the result is that they suffer the penalty of selfishness throughout eternity. There is no excuse for members of our Church adopting the custom of the world . . . we have been better taught than they."[26]

President Hugh B. Brown also spoke out boldly against birth control. He said:

> The Church has always advised against birth control and that is the only position the Church can take in view of our beliefs with respect to the eternity of the marriage covenant and the purpose of this divine relationship. There are, of course, circumstances under which people are justified in regulating the size of their families. . . . Where the health of the mother is concerned, and where the welfare of other children would be adversely affected, parents sometimes, under the advice of their physicians, deem it wisdom to take precautionary measures . . . The Church cannot give a blanket or over-all answer to the question which would be applicable to all situations. Seeking divine guidance and searching your own souls is recommended, but in a long lifetime of counseling on these matters, the General Authorities of the Church are united in recommending generally against birth control.[27]

More recently, Elder Dallin H. Oaks gave this counsel to Latter-day Saints:

> President Kimball said, "It is an act of extreme selfishness for a married couple to refuse to have children when they are able to do so" (*Ensign,* May 1979, p. 6). When married couples postpone childbearing until after they have satisfied their material goals, the mere passage of time assures that they seriously reduce their potential to participate in furthering our Heavenly Father's plan for all of his spirit children. Faithful Latter-day Saints cannot afford to look upon children as an interference with what the world calls "self-fulfillment." Our covenants with God and the ultimate purpose of life are tied up in those little ones who reach for our time, our love, and our sacrifices. . . .
>
> How many children should a couple have? All they can care for! Of course, to care for children means more than simply giving them life. Children must be loved, nurtured, taught, fed, clothed, housed and well started in their capacities to be good parents themselves. Exercising faith in God's promises to bless them when they are keeping his commandments, many LDS parents have large families. Others seek but are not blessed with children or with the number of children they desire. In a matter as intimate as this, we should not judge one another.[28]

Although a couple may be obedient to the first commandment to multiply and replenish the earth, they still must decide how many children to have and when to have them. President Hinckley explained:

> The Lord has told us to multiply and replenish the earth that we might have joy in our posterity, and there is no greater joy than the joy that comes of happy children in good families. But he did not designate the number, nor has the Church. That is a sacred matter

left to the couple and the Lord. The official statement of the Church includes this language: "Husbands must be considerate of their wives, who have the greater responsibility not only of bearing children but of caring for them through childhood, and should help them conserve their health and strength. Married couples should exercise self-control in all of their relationships. They should seek inspiration from the Lord in meeting their marital challenges and rearing their children according to the teachings of the gospel."[29]

President Gordon B. Hinckley has also said, "I like to think of the positive side of the equation, of the meaning and sanctity of life, of the purpose of this estate in our eternal journey, of the need for the experiences of mortal life under the great plan of God our Father, of the joy that is to be found only where there are children in the home, of the blessings that come of good posterity. When I think of these values and see them taught and observed, then I am willing to leave the question of numbers to the man and the woman and the Lord."[30]

So what began as questions such as "Should we have children?" and "How many children should we have?" actually comes down to more serious questions about our understanding of the plan of salvation and our commitment. Perhaps only after we have answered questions about ourselves, our testimonies, our faith, and our expectations can we focus on birth control questions.

When we see things as God sees them and are obedient because it has become our very nature, we will be in a position to answer the difficult questions about how to multiply and replenish the earth. When we understand the principles, live worthily, enjoy the Spirit in our lives, and have an eternal perspective, we will make right decisions.

Couples face many opportunities to exercise their agency and shoulder the subsequent responsibility for their choices. These opportunities are not easy, black-and-white, you're-faithful-or-you're-not issues. Couples are expected to struggle and grow as a result of dealing with these sensitive challenges.

Responding to direction from President Kimball, Dr. Homer S. Ellsworth was asked to address family planning questions. The response was printed with approval in the *Ensign*, and a condensed version was later included in the *Encyclopedia of Mormonism*. Both are quoted below. Note how the same principles are again stated, but the emphasis is on agency and personal responsibility. While at first the reader may think these thoughts seem permissive compared to earlier prophetic statements, a closer examination will reveal that we are now expected to accept more personal responsibility for our decisions and the consequent results.

I Have A Question

Dr. Homer Ellsworth

Is it our understanding that we are to propagate children as long and as frequently as the human body will permit? Is there not any kind of "gospel family-planning," for lack of a better way to say it?

I hear this type of question frequently from active and committed Latter-day Saints who often ask questions that are outside my professional responsibilities. Here are some of the principles and attitudes I believe apply to this fundamental question, a question most couples ask themselves many times during their childbearing years.

I rejoice in our basic understanding of the plan of salvation, which teaches us that we come to earth for growth and maturity, and for testing. In that process we marry and provide temporal bodies for our Heavenly Father's spirit children. That's basic, it seems to me. In contemplating this truth, I also take great delight in the Church's affirmative position that it is our blessing and joy, and our spiritual obligation, to bear children and to have a family. It impresses me that the positive is stressed as our goal.

I rejoice in our understanding that one of the most fundamental principles in the plan of salvation is free agency. The opportunity to make free agency choices is so important that our Heavenly Father was willing to withhold additional opportunities from a third of his children rather than deprive them of their right of choice. This principle of free agency is vital to the success of our probation. Many of the decisions we make involve the application of principles where precise yes-and-no answers are just not available in Church handbooks, meetings, or even in the scriptures.

Our growth process, then, results from weighing the alternatives, studying the matter carefully, and seeking inspiration from the Lord. This, it seems to me, is at the heart of the gospel plan. It has always given me great joy and confidence to observe that in their administration of God's teachings, our inspired prophets do not seek to violate this general plan of individual agency, but operate within broad guidelines that provide considerable individual flexibility.

I recall a president of the Church, now deceased, who visited his daughter in the hospital following a miscarriage. She was the mother of eight children and was in her early forties. She asked, "Father, may I quit now?" His response was, "Don't ask me. That decision is between you, your husband, and your Father in Heaven. If you two can face him with a good conscience and can say you have done the best you could, that you have really tried, then you may quit. But, that is between you and him. I have enough problems of my own to talk over with him when we meet!" So it is clear to me that the decisions regarding our children, when we have them, their number, and all related matters and questions can only be made after real discussion between the marriage partners and after prayer.

In this process of learning what is right for you

at any particular time, I have always found it helpful to use a basic measuring stick: Is it selfish? I have concluded that most of our sins are really sins of selfishness. If you don't pay tithing, selfishness is at the heart of it. If you commit adultery, selfishness is at the heart of it. If you are dishonest, selfishness is at the heart of it. I have noted that many times in the scriptures we observe the Lord chastising people because of their selfishness. Thus, on the family questions, if we limit our families because we are self-centered or materialistic, we will surely develop a character based on selfishness. As the scriptures make clear, that is not a description of a celestial character. I have found that we really have to analyze ourselves to discover our motives. Sometimes superficial motivations and excuses show up when we do that.

But, on the other hand, we need not be afraid of studying the question from important angles—the physical or mental health of the mother and father, the parents' capacity to provide basic necessities, and so on. If for certain personal reasons a couple prayerfully decides that having another child immediately is unwise, the method of spacing children—discounting possible medical or physical effects—makes little difference. Abstinence, of course, is also a form of contraception, and like any other method it has side effects, some of which are harmful to the marriage relationship.

As a physician I am often required to treat social-emotional symptoms related to various aspects of living. In doing so I have always been impressed that our prophets past and present have never stipulated that bearing children was the sole function of the marriage relationship. Prophets have taught that physical intimacy is a strong force in strengthening the love bond in marriage, enhancing and reinforcing marital unity. Indeed, it is the rightful gift of God to the married. As the Apostle Paul says, "The wife hath not power of her own body, but the husband; and likewise also the husband hath not power of his own body, but the wife." Paul continues, "Depart ye not one from the other, except it be with consent for a time, that ye may give yourselves to fasting and prayer, and come together again, that Satan tempt you not for your incontinency" (JST, 1 Corinthians 7:4–5).

Abstinence in marriage, Paul says, can cause unnecessary temptations and tensions, which are certainly harmful side effects.

So, as to the number and spacing of children, and other related questions on this subject, such decisions are to be made by husband and wife righteously and empathetically communicating together and seeking the inspiration of the Lord. I believe that the prophets have given wise counsel when they advise couples to be considerate and plan carefully so that the mother's health will not be impaired. When this recommendation of the First Presidency is ignored or unknown or misinterpreted, heartache can result.

I know a couple who had seven children. The wife, who was afflicted with high blood pressure, had been advised by her physician that additional pregnancy was fraught with grave danger and should not be attempted. But the couple interpreted the teachings of their local priesthood leaders to mean that they should consider no contraceptive measures under any circumstances. She died from a stroke during the delivery of her eighth child.

As I meet other people and learn of their circumstances, I am continually inspired by the counsel of the First Presidency in the *General Handbook of Instructions* that the health of the mother and the well-being of the family should be considered. Thirty-four years as a practicing gynecologist and as an observer of Latter-day Saint families have taught me that not only the physical well-being but the emotional well-being must also be considered. Some parents are less subject to mood swings and depression and can more easily cope with the pressures of many children. Some parents have more help from their families and friends. Some are more effective parents than others, even when their desire and motivation are the same. In addition, parents do owe their children the necessities of life. The desire for luxuries, of course, would not be an appropriate determinant of family size; luxuries are just not a legitimate consideration. I think every inspired human heart can quickly determine what is luxury and what is not.

In summary, it is clear to me that couples should not let the things that matter most be at the mercy of those that matter least. In searching for what is most important, I believe that we are accountable not only for what we do but for why we do it. Thus, regarding family size, spacing of children, and attendant questions, we should desire to multiply and replenish the earth as the Lord commands us. In that process, Heavenly Father intends that we use the free agency he has given in charting a wise course for ourselves and our families. We gain the wisdom to chart that wise course through study, prayer, and listening to the still small voice within us."[31]

And in the *Encyclopedia of Mormonism*, we read the following:

The *General Handbook of Instructions* for Church leaders has the following instructions concerning birth control: "Husbands must be considerate of their wives, who have a great responsibility not only for bearing children but also for caring for them through childhood . . . Married couples should seek inspiration from the Lord in meeting their marital challenges and rearing their children according to the teachings of the gospel" (*General Handbook*, 11–4).

Interpretation of these general instructions is left to the agency of Church members. One of the basic teachings of the Church, however, is that spirit children of God come to earth to obtain a physical body, to grow, and to be tested. In that process, adults should marry and provide temporal bodies for those spirit children. For Latter-day Saints, it is a blessing, a joy, and also an obligation to bear children and to raise a family.

One of the cornerstones of the gospel is agency or choice. Latter-day Saints believe that everyone will be held responsible for the choices they make. Many decisions involve the application of principles where precise instructions are not given in the *General Handbook of Instructions* or in the scriptures. The exercise of individual agency is therefore required, and Latter-day Saints believe that personal growth results from weighing the alternatives, studying matters carefully, counseling with appropriate Church leaders, and then seeking inspiration from the Lord before making a decision.

Church members are taught to study the question of family planning, including such important aspects as the physical and mental health of the mother and father and their capacity to provide the basic necessities of life. If, for personal reasons, a couple prayerfully decides that having another child immediately is unwise, birth control may be appropriate. Abstinence, of course, is a form of contraception. Like any other method, however, it has its side effects, some of which may be harmful to the marriage relationship.

Prophets past and present have never stipulated that bearing children was the sole function of the marriage relationship. They have taught that physical intimacy is a strong force in expressing and strengthening the love bond in marriage, enhancing and reinforcing marital unity.

Decisions regarding the number and spacing of children are to be made by husband and wife together, in righteousness, and through empathetic communication, and with prayer for the Lord's inspiration.

Latter-day Saints believe that persons are accountable not only for what they do but for why they do it.
Thus, regarding family size and attendant questions,
members should desire to multiply and replenish the
earth as the Lord has commanded. In that process,
God intends that his children use the agency that he
has given them in charting a wise course for themselves and their families." (The Church of Jesus Christ
of Latter-day Saints. *General Handbook of Instructions,*
11–4. Salt Lake City, 1989.)[32]

We have been commanded to bring children into the world
and to properly care for them. A couple should do all that they
can to keep this commandment, along with all others. A genuine
commitment to keep this commandment will eliminate many of
the what-if questions.

However, there are still many details and decisions that must
be worked out between the couple and the Lord regarding this
issue. For example, the couple and the Lord must determine if
birth control is appropriate, and for how long. This means frequent discussion and prayer. If birth control is appropriate, the
couple must determine which method to use.

Because all birth control methods have weaknesses, the decision is difficult and must be revisited often. It is almost as if
everything about this commandment is supposed to be difficult.
Perhaps that is the point: a humble, dedicated couple will pray
sincerely and frequently over this issue. If approached properly,
this commandment is designed to bring a couple closer to God
and godhood.

Husbands and wives should study all that has been said on
the subject. Familiarity with only a few quotes could mislead or
be used to justify a wide variety of behaviors. I've included here
additional quotes of interest on this subject. Each couple must
determine the principles involved and make a plan and commitment to live the commandment. This process challenges couples
to rid themselves of selfishness and develop open channels of com-

munication between themselves and the Lord. After the many variables and motives have been explored, a couple must make decisions that not only define their relationship on earth but may also determine their relationship in the eternities.

None of the issues is easy, nor are appropriate decisions obvious. We find more than ample opportunity to exercise our agency and, therefore, we must do much soul-searching and seeking for revelation. In this, our first (and perhaps only) experience in procreation, we will repeatedly be forced to face our motives, depth of faith and character, and willingness to be led.

It is likely that this is not supposed to be easy, for the entire experience determines who will be married and have these powers in the eternities. Through the difficult process of pondering, searching (our motives and the teaching of the Brethren), communicating as a couple, and receiving personal revelation, the Lord is developing eternal marriages that will enjoy eternal increase.

In dealing with such difficult issues, which will determine if we receive the greatest happiness and blessings, Elder Richard G. Scott recommended these steps:

> Learn the doctrinal foundation of the great plan of happiness by studying the scriptures, pondering their content, and praying to understand them. Carefully study and use the proclamation of the First Presidency and the Twelve on the family. It was inspired of the Lord.
>
> Listen to the voice of current and past prophets. Their declarations are inspired. You may verify that counsel in your own mind and heart by praying about it as it applies to your special circumstances. Ask the Lord to confirm your choices, and accept accountability for them.
>
> Obey the inner feelings that come as promptings from the Holy Ghost. Those feelings are engendered by your determination to seek the will of the Lord and to live it.

When needed, seek counsel and guidance from parents and your priesthood leaders.[33]

Additional Quotes of Interest

Lillie Freeze reported hearing the Prophet Joseph Smith state that "the time would come when none but the women of the Latter-day Saints would be willing to bear children."[34]

"We have heard that many of the diabolical practices of the world have been introduced . . . among some who profess to be Latter-day Saints, to prevent the bearing of children. No sin, unless it be that of murder, will meet with greater condemnation from God than this evil of tampering with the fountains of life. Such sins will destroy the strength of any people that practices them, and the nation whose people yield to such vices is in great danger of destruction. No Saint can practice or encourage such corruption without incurring the displeasure of an offended God."[35]

"Think of the promises that are made to you in the beautiful and glorious ceremony that is used in the marriage covenant in the temple. When two Latter-day Saints are united together in marriage, promises are made to them concerning their offspring, that reach from eternity to eternity. They are promised that they shall have the power and the right to govern and control and administer salvation and exaltation and glory to their offspring worlds without end. And what offspring they do not have here, undoubtedly there will be opportunities to have them hereafter. What else could a man wish? A man and a woman in the other life, having celestial bodies, free from sickness and disease, glorified and beautified beyond description, standing in the midst of their posterity, governing and controlling them, administering life, exaltation, and glory, worlds without end."[36]

"Motherhood lies at the foundation of happiness in the home, and of prosperity in the nation. God has laid upon men and women very sacred obligations with respect to motherhood, and they are obligations that cannot be disregarded without invoking divine displeasure. In 1 Timothy 2:13–15, we are told that 'Adam was first formed, then Eve. And Adam was not deceived, but the woman being deceived was in the transgression. Notwithstanding she shall be saved in childbearing, if they continue in faith and charity and holiness with sobriety.' Can she be saved without child-bearing? She indeed takes an awful risk if she wilfully disregards what is a pronounced requirement of God. How shall she plead her innocence when she is not innocent? How shall she excuse her guilt when it is fastened upon her?

"The question of parental obligation in the matter of children is not generally denied. A failure to fulfill the obligation, however, is too frequently excused.

"'Children,' we are told, 'are a heritage of the Lord'; they are also, the Psalmist tells us, 'his reward.' If children are cut off from their birthright, how shall the Lord be rewarded? They are not a source of weakness and poverty to family life, for they bring with them certain divine blessings that make for the prosperity of the home and the nation. 'As arrows are in the hand of a mighty man; so are children of the youth. Happy is the man that hath his quiver full of them: they shall not be ashamed, but they shall speak with the enemies in the gate' (Psalm 127:4, 5).

"What answer shall men and women make in excuse of conduct which contravenes the commandments of God? Those whose hearts are in touch with God's most sacred laws will make great sacrifices honestly to fulfill them."[37]

"Those who have taken upon themselves the responsibility of wedded life should see to it that they do not abuse the course of nature; that they do not destroy the principle of life within them, nor violate any of the commandments of God. The command which he gave in the beginning to multiply and replenish the earth is still in force upon the children of men. Possibly no greater sin could be committed by the people who have embraced this gospel than to prevent or to destroy life in the manner indicated. We are born into the world that we may have life, and we live that we may have a fulness of joy, and if we will obtain a fulness of joy, we must obey the law of our creation and the law by which we may obtain the consummation of our righteous hopes and desires—life eternal."[38]

"I think it is a crying evil, that there should exist a sentiment or a feeling among any members of the church to curtail the birth of their children. I think that it is a crime wherever it occurs, where husband and wife are in possession of health and vigor and are free from impurities that would be entailed upon their posterity. I believe that where people undertake to curtail or prevent the birth of their children that they are going to reap disappointment by and by. I have no hesitancy in saying that I believe this is one of the greatest crimes of the world today, this evil practice."[39]

"Is it proper and right in the sight of God for parents intentionally to prevent, by any means whatever, the spirits, the sons and daughters of our Heavenly Father, from obtaining earthly tabernacles? I have, of course, only references to parents lawfully married, and specifically to Latter-day Saints. In a general way, and as a rule, the answer to this question is an emphatic negative. I do not hesitate to say that prevention is wrong. It brings in its train a host of social evils. It destroys the morals of a community and nation. It creates hatred and selfishness in the hearts of men and women, and perverts their natural qualities of love and service, changing them to hate and aversion. It causes death, decay, and degeneration instead of life, growth, and advancement. And finally, it disregards or annuls the great commandment of God to man, 'Multiply and replenish the earth.' I am now speaking of the normally healthy man and woman. But, that there are weak and sickly people who in wisdom, discretion and common sense should be counted as exceptions, only strengthens the general rule."[40]

"When young people marry and refuse to fulfill this commandment given in the beginning of the world, and just as much in force today, they rob themselves of the greatest eternal blessing. I think love of the world and the wicked practices of the world mean more to a man and woman than to keep the commandment of the Lord in this respect, then they are shutting themselves off from the eternal blessing of increase. Those who wilfully and maliciously design to break this important commandment shall be damned. They cannot have the Spirit of the Lord.

"Small families is the rule today. Husbands and wives refuse to take upon themselves the responsibilities of family life. Many of them do not care to be bothered with children. Yet this commandment given to Adam has never been abrogated or set aside. If we refuse to live by the covenants we make, especially in the house of the Lord, then we cannot receive the blessings of those covenants in eternity. If the responsibilities of parenthood are willfully avoided here, then how can the Lord bestow upon the guilty the blessings of eternal increase? It cannot be, and they shall be denied such blessings."[41]

"How will those feel who fail to obey that first great command when they stand in the presence of the creator, who says to them, as He said to those in olden times, 'Suffer little children to come unto me, and forbid them not, for of such is the kingdom of heaven.' How can they comply with that invitation if they have no children to take to the Father? They must remain childless throughout eternity. They have been blind to their rights and privileges. It is only by a proper understanding of the laws of God, and by compliance with the Gospel of Jesus Christ, only by doing what the Lord has said we should do, that we will enjoy the fulness of happiness that our Father in heaven has promised those who are faithful. I do not feel to censure, but with all my heart I pity the man and woman who grace their home with the lesser animals of God's creation, and keep away from their firesides those angels from His presence who might be theirs through time and through all eternity. I realize there are some men and women who are grieved because they are not fathers and mothers, they are not blessed of the Lord in that particular, they have no children of their own, and by no fault of their own. I believe the Lord will provide in such cases. If they will do their duty in keeping the other commandments, their reproach will be taken away.

"I raise my voice among the sons and daughters of Zion, and warn you that if you dry up the springs of life and abuse the power that God has blessed you with, there will come a time of chastening to you, that all the tears you may shed will never remove. Remember the first great commandment; fulfill that obligation."[42]

"I am thankful that healthy, vigorous, strong, sweet babies are the best crop of Utah, and I hope and pray earnestly that it will ever be so. I hope that the fashion which is a thousand times worse than are the fashions of dress, namely, that of drying up the fountains of life, will never become popular among the Latter-day Saints."[43]

"Love realizes his sweetest happiness and his most divine consummation in the home where the coming of children is not restricted, where they are made most welcome, and where the duties of parenthood are accepted as a co-partnership with the eternal Creator. In all this, however, the mother's health should be guarded. In the realm of wifehood, the woman should reign supreme."[44]

"The increasing tendency to look upon family life as a burden, and the ever-spreading practice of birth control, are ominous threats to the perpetuation of the United States. In the light of what the restored gospel teaches us regarding pre-existence, the eternal nature of the marriage covenant, and of family relationship, no healthy wife in the Church should shun the responsibilities of normal motherhood."[45]

"Some young couples enter into marriage and procrastinate the bringing of children into their homes. They are running a great risk. Marriage is for the purpose of rearing a family, and youth is the time to do it. I admire these young mothers with four or five children around them now, still young, happy."[46]

"I regret that so many young couples are thinking today more of successful contraceptives than of having a posterity. They will have to answer for their sin when the proper time comes and actually may be denied the glorious celestial kingdom.

"When, because of lack of education, the earning power of the husband is below average and is thought necessary for the wife to work, and, therefore, to postpone having a family, the couple should pause and seriously count the cost. Limiting families leads to many evils, physical, moral, and spiritual. How foolish is the couple who postpones or deprives themselves of life's choicest blessings in the name of economy while at the same time indulging selfish, expensive habits or buying luxuries which lose their glamour and their value before they're paid for.

"The young couple should remind themselves frequently that 'if we buy this we can't have that.' Let 'this' represent an automobile and 'that' a baby. Who would compare their value. The one depreciates and becomes worthless, but who can appraise the worth of a soul and especially if it is 'of his own soul, a part?'"[47]

"The covenant given to Adam to multiply was renewed after the flood with Noah and his children after him. The Lord said to Noah: 'And you, be ye fruitful, and multiply; bring forth abundantly in the earth, and multiply therein. And God spake unto Noah, and to his sons with him, saying, And I, behold, I establish my covenant with you, and with your seed after you.'

"This covenant is still binding, although mankind has departed from the way of eternal life and has rejected the covenant of marriage which the Lord revealed.

"Birth Control Is Wickedness. The abuse of this holy covenant has been the primary cause for the downfall of nations. When the sacred vows of marriage are broken and the real purpose of marriage abused, as we find it so prevalent in the world today, then destruction is inevitable.

"No nation can endure for any length of time, if the marriage covenants are abused and treated with contempt. The anger of the Almighty was kindled against ancient nations for their immorality. There is nothing that should be held in greater sacredness than this covenant by which the spirits of men are clothed with mortal tabernacles."[48]

"When a man and a woman are married and they agree, or covenant, to limit their offspring to two or three, and practice devices to accomplish this purpose, they are guilty of iniquity which eventually must be punished. Unfortunately this evil doctrine is being taught as a virtue by many people who consider themselves cultured and highly educated. It has even crept in among members of the Church and has been advocated in some of the classes within the Church.

"It should be understood definitely that this kind of doctrine is not only not advocated by the authorities of the Church, but also is condemned by them as a wickedness in the sight of the Lord."[49]

"It follows that those who practice birth control—the regulation of the number of births in a family by the employment of artificial means or contraceptives to prevent conception—are running counter to the foreordained plan of the Almighty. They are in rebellion against God and are guilty of gross wickedness."[50]

"In family life, men must and should be considerate of their wives, not only in the bearing of children, but in caring for them through childhood. The mother's health must be conserved, and the husband's consideration for his wife is his first duty, and self-control a dominant factor in all their relationships."[51]

"As we look about us, we see many forces at work bent on the destruction of the family . . . abortion bids well to become a national scandal and is a very grave sin. Another erosion of the family is unwarranted and selfish birth control."⁵²

"Thus we see that in marriage, a husband and wife enter into an order of the priesthood called the new and everlasting covenant of marriage. This covenant includes a willingness to have children and to teach them the gospel. Many problems of the world today are brought about when parents do not accept the responsibilities of this covenant. It is contradictory to this covenant to prevent the birth of children if the parents are in good health.

"Thirty-five years ago when I first started practicing medicine, it was a rare thing for a married woman to seek advice about how she could keep from having babies. When I finished practicing medicine, it was a rare thing, except for some faithful Latter-day Saint women, for a married woman to want to have more than one or two children, and some did not want any children. We in the Church must not be caught up in the false doctrines of the world that would cause us to break sacred temple covenants."⁵³

Notes

1. Kimball, "In the World but Not of It," in *Brigham Young University Speeches of the Year*, 14 May 1968.

2. Kimball, "Marriage Is Honorable," in *Brigham Young University Speeches of the Year, 1973*, 263.

3. Kimball, *Miracle of Forgiveness*, 40–41.

4. Ibid., 250.

5. Kimball, *Teachings of Spencer W. Kimball*, 328.

6. Benson, *To the Mothers in Zion*, 3–4.

7. The First Presidency and Council of the Twelve Apostles, "The Family—A Proclamation to the World," *Ensign*, November 1995, 102.

8. First Presidency (Heber J. Grant, J. Reuben Clark Jr., David O. McKay), in Conference Report, October 1942, 12.

9. Boyd K. Packer, "For Time and All Eternity," *Ensign*, November 1993, 23.

10. Young, *Discourses of Brigham Young*, 197.

11. Lee, in Conference Report, October 1972, 63.

12. Benson, in Conference Report, April 1969, 12.

13. Letter from the First Presidency, 14 April 1969, to stake presidents,

bishops, and mission presidents.

14. Hinckley, *Teachings of Gordon B. Hinckley,* 703.

15. Packer, "The Word of Wisdom: The Principle and the Promises," *Ensign,* May 1996, 17.

16. Scott, "Acquiring Spiritual Knowledge," *Ensign,* November 1993, 86.

17. Smith, *Millennial Star,* 13: 339.

18. Oaks, "'The Great Plan of Happiness,'" *Ensign,* November 1993, 73.

19. Packer, in Conference Report, October 1966, 132.

20. Cannon, in Conference Report, April 1899, 20.

21. Cannon, in *Journal of Discourses* 26:249.

22. Smith, *Doctrines of Salvation,* 2:287–88.

23. Young, in *Journal of Discourses,* 4:271–72.

24. Benson, *Teachings of Ezra Taft Benson,* 548.

25. McKay, *Gospel Ideals,* 468.

26. Smith, "Birth Control," *Relief Society Magazine,* February 1917, 72.

27. In Petersen, *The Way of the Master,* 114–15.

28. Oaks, "'The Great Plan of Happiness,'" *Ensign,* November 1993, 75.

29. Hinckley, *Cornerstones of a Happy Home,* 15–16.

30. Hinckley, *Teachings of Gordon B. Hinckley,* 35–36.

31. Ellsworth, "I Have a Question," *Ensign,* August 1979, 23–24.

32. *Encyclopedia of Mormonism,* s.v. "Birth Control."

33. Scott, "The Joy of Living the Great Plan of Happiness," *Ensign,* November 1996, 75.

34. Smith, *Young Woman's Journal,* 2 November 1890, 81.

35. Cannon, *Juvenile Instructor,* 15 July 1895, 451.

36. Snow, *Teachings of Lorenzo Snow,* 138.

37. Smith, *Gospel Doctrine,* 288–89.

38. Ibid., 276–77.

39. Smith, *Relief Society Magazine* 4: 314; see also *Gospel Doctrine,* 349.

40. Smith, "A Vital Question," *Improvement Era,* October 1908, 259–60.

41. Smith, *Doctrines of Salvation,* 2:89.

42. George Albert Smith, Conference Report, October 1907, 38.

43. Grant, Conference Report, October 1913, 89.

44. McKay, *Gospel Ideals,* 469.

45. McKay, *Treasures of Life,* 57.

46. McKay, *Gospel Ideals,* 466.

47. Brown, *You and Your Marriage,* 152.

48. Smith, *Doctrines of Salvation,* 2:86–87.

49. Ibid., 2:87.

50. McConkie, *Mormon Doctrine,* 81.

51. Kimball, "A Report and a Challenge," *Ensign,* November 1976, 6–7.

52. Kimball, "We Need a Listening Ear," *Ensign*, November 1979, 5.
53. Washburn, "The Temple Is a Family Affair," *Ensign*, May 1995, 12.

10

FATHERS PROVIDE SO
mothers can nurture

Recently, the First Presidency proclaimed to members of the Church—and the world—that "by divine design, fathers are to preside over their families in love and righteousness and are responsible to *provide* the necessities of life and protection for their families. Mothers are primarily responsible for the *nurture* of their children. In these sacred responsibilities, fathers and mothers are obligated to help one another as equal partners. Disability, death, or other circumstances may necessitate individual adaptation. Extended families should lend support when needed."[1]

To the degree that we apply these principles in our family life, we will experience greater happiness. Since the world is generally following another path, a path devastating to family solidarity and happiness, we would expect to find those who are obedient to the prophets to stand in contrast to the world. However, those in the Church who are following the ways of the world on this subject can expect the same devastation to family happiness that the world is experiencing. President Ezra Taft Benson has warned members that "our beloved prophet Spencer W. Kimball had much to say about the role of mothers in the home and their callings and responsibilities. . . . I fear that much of his counsel has gone unheeded, and families have suffered because of it."[2]

Elder Henry B. Eyring has noted that several prophets have spoken on this subject. He said:

> In our own time, we have been warned with counsel on where to find safety from sin and from sorrow. One of the keys to recognizing those warnings is that they are repeated. For instance, more than once in these general conferences, you have heard our prophet say that he would quote a preceding prophet and would therefore be a second witness and sometimes even a third. Each of us who has listened has heard President Kimball give counsel on the importance of a mother in the home and then heard President Benson quote him, and we have heard President Hinckley quote them both. The Apostle Paul wrote that "in the mouth of two or three witnesses shall every word be established" (2 Corinthians 13:1). One of the ways we may know that the warning is from the Lord is that the law of witnesses, authorized witnesses, has been invoked. When the words of prophets seem repetitive, that should rivet our attention and fill our hearts with gratitude to live in such a blessed time. Looking for the path to safety in the counsel of prophets makes sense to those with strong faith.[3]

Since the law of witnesses is that numerous prophets declare the same truths, we will study this subject by reviewing what several prophets have said on the same topic. However, before reviewing what the Brethren have said on this issue, let us keep in mind the following questions:

1. What can a mother do for her children that others cannot?

2. Under what circumstances would mothers working outside of the home be justified?

3. What circumstances would not justify mothers working outside of the home?

4. What are some of the possible negative consequences of mothers working outside of the home?

5. What help is available only for those mothers who must work outside of the home?

6. What counsel is given to husbands about their wives working outside of the home?

President Gordon B. Hinckley

President Gordon B. Hinckley has said much about this subject. For example:

> Sisters, guard your children. They live in a world of evil. The forces are all about them. I am proud of so many of your sons and daughters who are living good lives. But I am deeply concerned about many others who are gradually taking on the ways of the world. Nothing is more precious to you as mothers, absolutely nothing. Your children are the most valuable thing you will have in time or all eternity. You will be fortunate indeed if, as you grow old and look at those you brought into the world, you find in them uprightness of life, virtue in living, and integrity in their behavior.
>
> I think the nurture and upbringing of children is more than a part-time responsibility. I recognize that some women must work, but I fear that there are far too many who do so only to get the means for a little more luxury and a few fancier toys.
>
> If you must work, you have an increased load to bear. You cannot afford to neglect your children. They need your supervision in studying, in working inside and outside the home, in the nurturing that only you can adequately give—the love, the blessing, the

encouragement, and the closeness of a mother.

Families are being torn asunder everywhere. Family relationships are strained as women try to keep up with the rigors of two full-time jobs.

I have many opportunities to speak with leaders who decry what is going on—gangs on the streets of our cities, children killing children, spending their time in practices that can only lead to prison or to death. We face a great overwhelming tide of children born to mothers without husbands. The futures of such children are almost inevitably blighted from the day they are born. Every home needs a good father and a good mother. We cannot build prisons fast enough in this country to accommodate the need.

I do not hesitate to say that you who are mothers can do more than any other group to change this situation. All of these problems find their root in the homes of the people. It is broken homes that lead to a breakup in society.

And so tonight, my beloved sisters, my message to you, my challenge to you, my prayer is that you will rededicate yourselves to the strengthening of your homes.[4]

Because the ideal must be taught, even if we live in a less than ideal world, President Hinckley counseled that "it will be better if the husband becomes the provider and the wife does not work when the children come. The situation may be necessary in some cases, but if you choose wisely now, it is not likely to become a requirement."[5]

President Hinckley provided the following advice to women who are employed outside of the home:

Some years ago President Benson delivered a message to the women of the Church. He encouraged them to leave their employment and give their individual time to their children. I sustain the position which he took.

Nevertheless, I recognize, as he recognizes, that there are some women (it has become very many, in fact) who have to work to provide for the needs of their families. To you I say, do the very best you can. I hope that if you are employed full-time you are doing it to ensure that basic needs are met and not simply to indulge a taste for an elaborate home, fancy cars, and other luxuries. The greatest job that any mother will ever do will be in nurturing, teaching, lifting, encouraging, and rearing her children in righteousness and truth. None other can adequately take her place.

It is well-nigh impossible to be a full-time homemaker and a full-time employee. I know how some of you struggle with decisions concerning this matter. I repeat, do the very best you can. You know your circumstances, and I know that you are deeply concerned for the welfare of your children. Each of you has a bishop who will counsel with you and assist you. If you feel you need to speak with an understanding woman, do not hesitate to get in touch with your Relief Society president.

To the mothers of this Church, every mother who is here today, I want to say that as the years pass, you will become increasingly grateful for that which you did in molding the lives of your children in the direction of righteousness and goodness, integrity and faith. That is most likely to happen if you can spend adequate time with them.[6]

To those mothers who feel they must work outside of the home, President Hinckley offers this caution:

To you women who find it necessary to work when you would rather be at home, may I speak briefly. I know that there are many of you who find yourselves in this situation. Some of you have been abandoned and are divorced, with children to care for. Some of you are widows with dependent families. I honor you and respect you for your integrity and spirit of self-reliance. I pray that the Lord will bless you with strength and great capacity, for you need both. You have the responsibilities of both breadwinner and homemaker. I know that it is difficult. I know that it is discouraging. I pray that the Lord will bless you with a special wisdom and the remarkable talent needed to provide your children with time and companionship and love and with that special direction which only a mother can give. I pray also that he will bless you with help, unstintingly given, from family, friends, and the Church, which will lift some of the burden from your shoulders and help you in your times of extremity.

We sense, at least in some small degree, the loneliness you must occasionally feel and the frustrations you must experience as you try to cope with problems that sometimes seem beyond your capacity to handle. Sometimes you need food for your tables, and we trust that bishops will be there to supply food and other goods and services under the great program which the Lord has provided in his Church. But we know that more often your greater need is for understanding and appreciation and companionship. We shall try a little harder to cultivate these virtues, and I urge you sisters who are in a position to do so to reach out with greater concern to those who find themselves in these less fortunate circumstances.[7]

To those mothers who work outside the home when it is not necessary, he added:

> Now to others who work when it is not necessary and who, while doing so, leave children to the care of those who often are only poor substitutes, I offer a word of caution. Do not follow a practice which will bring you later regret. If the purpose of your daily employment is simply to get money for a boat or a fancy automobile or some other desirable but unnecessary thing,

and in the process you lose the companionship of your children and the opportunity to rear them, you may find that you have lost the substance while grasping at the shadow.[8]

President Howard W. Hunter

To the husbands of working mothers, President Howard W. Hunter gave this serious caution:

> We urge you to do all in your power to allow your wife to remain in the home, caring for the children while you provide for the family the best you can. . . . You who hold the priesthood have the responsibility, unless disabled, to provide temporal support for your wife and children. No man can shift the burden of responsibility to another, not even to his wife. The Lord has commanded that women and children have claim on their husbands and fathers for their maintenance (see D&C 83; 1 Timothy 5:8). President Ezra Taft Benson has stated that when a husband encourages or insists that his wife work out of the home for their convenience, "not only will the family suffer in such instances, . . . but [his] own spiritual growth and progression will be hampered."[9]

To what level of effort should the father go to be the sole provider for his family? To answer this question we can look at the example of President Hunter. He shared his story:

> In a personal way, I recall the experiences my dear wife and I went through after deciding the course I should take for my life's work. I had taken some courses in pharmacy with the plan in mind of converting to a career in medicine. As many of us do, I changed my mind and engaged in another business, banking. We were blessed with steady employment, but I felt attracted toward the profession of law. This

was a serious decision because I was married and had a family to support but after fasting and prayer and obtaining the facts as to the best way to proceed, I completed my undergraduate work and entered law school. I took classes at night because it was necessary to be employed during the daytime. These were not easy years for us, but desires are usually accomplished if we are willing to make a determined effort. Needless to say, I had the help and support of my wife. She remained a homemaker and cared for our children. What she gave in love, encouragement, frugality, and companionship was far in excess of any material contribution she might have made by taking employment.

Our wives deserve great credit for the heavy work load they carry day in and day out within our homes. No one expends more energy than a devoted mother and wife. In the usual arrangement of things, however, it is the man to whom the Lord has assigned the breadwinner's role.

There are impelling reasons for our sisters to plan toward employment also. We want them to obtain all the education and vocational training possible before marriage. If they become widowed or divorced and need to work, we want them to have dignified and rewarding employment. If a sister does not marry, she has every right to engage in a profession that allows her to magnify her talents and gifts.

Brothers and Sisters, we need to do everything necessary to adequately prepare ourselves for employment or careers. We owe it to ourselves to do our best, and we owe our best in providing for our families.[10]

President Ezra Taft Benson

In 1987, President Ezra Taft Benson spoke at a fireside for parents; this talk was also distributed as a church pamphlet. In this address, President Benson said:

Now, my dear mothers, knowing of your divine role to bear and rear children and bring them back to Him, how will you accomplish this in the Lord's way? I say the "Lord's way," because it is different from the world's way. The Lord clearly defined the roles of mothers and fathers in providing for and rearing a righteous posterity. In the beginning, Adam—not Eve—was instructed to earn the bread by the sweat of his brow. Contrary to conventional wisdom, a mother's calling is in the home, not in the marketplace.

Again, in the Doctrine and Covenants, we read: "Women have claim on their husbands for their maintenance, until their husbands are taken" (D&C 83:2). This is the divine right of a wife and mother. She cares for and nourishes her children at home. Her husband earns the living for the family, which makes this nourishing possible. With that claim on their husbands for their financial support, the counsel of the Church has always been for mothers to spend their full time in the home in rearing and caring for their children.

We realize also that some of our choice sisters are widowed and divorced and that others find themselves in unusual circumstances where, out of necessity, they are required to work for a period of time. But these instances are the exception, not the rule.

In a home where there is an able-bodied husband, he is expected to be the breadwinner. Sometimes we hear of husbands who, because of economic conditions, have lost their jobs and expect their wives to go out of the home and work even though the husband is still capable of providing for his family. In these cases, we urge the husband to do all in his power to allow his wife to remain in the home caring for the children while he continues to provide for his family the best he can, even though the job he is able to secure may not be ideal and family budgeting will have to be tighter.

Our beloved prophet Spencer W. Kimball had much to say about the role of mothers in the home and their callings and responsibilities. I am impressed tonight to share with you some of his inspired pronouncements. I fear that much of his counsel has gone unheeded, and families have suffered because of it. But I stand this evening as a second witness to the truthfulness of what President Spencer W. Kimball said. He spoke as a true prophet of God.

President Kimball declared: "Women are to take care of the family—the Lord has so stated—to be an assistant to the husband, to work with him, but not to earn the living, except in unusual circumstances. Men ought to be men indeed and earn the living under normal circumstances" (*The Teachings of Spencer W. Kimball,* p. 318).

President Kimball continues: "Too many mothers work away from home to furnish sweaters and music lessons and trips and fun for their children. Too many women spend their time in socializing, in politicking, in public services when they should be home to teach and train and receive and love their children into security" (*The Teachings of Spencer W. Kimball,* p. 319).

Remember the counsel of President Kimball to John and Mary: "Mary, you are to become a career woman in the greatest career on earth—that of homemaker, wife, and mother. It was never intended by the Lord that married women should compete with men in employment. They have a far greater and more important service to render" (*Faith Precedes the Miracle* [Salt Lake City: Deseret Book Co., 1975], p. 128).

Again President Kimball speaks: "The husband is expected to support his family and only in an emergency should a wife secure outside employment. Her place is in the home, to build the home into a heaven of delight. Numerous divorces can be traced directly to the day when the wife left the home and went out into the world into employment. Two incomes raise the standard of living beyond its norm. Two spouses working prevent the complete and proper home life, break into the family prayers, create an independence which is not cooperative, causes distortion, limits the family, and frustrates the children already born" (fireside address, San Antonio, Texas, 3 Dec. 1977).

Finally, President Kimball counsels: "I beg of you, you who could and should be bearing and rearing a family: wives, come home from the typewriter, the laundry, the nursing, come home from the factory, the café. No career approaches in importance that of wife, homemaker, mother—cooking meals, washing dishes, making beds for one's precious husband and children. Come home, wives, to your husbands. Make home a heaven for them. Come home, wives, to your children, born and unborn. Wrap the motherly cloak about you and, unembarrassed, help in a major role to create the bodies for the immortal souls who anxiously await. When you have fully complemented your husband in home life and borne the children, growing up full of faith, integrity, responsibility, and goodness, then you have achieved your accomplishment supreme, without peer, and you will be the envy [of all] through time and eternity" (fireside address, San Antonio, Texas).

President Kimball spoke the truth. His words are prophetic. Mothers, this kind of heavenly, motherly teaching takes time—lots of time. It cannot be done effectively part-time. It must be done all the time in order to save and exalt your children. This is your divine calling.[11]

In 1987, President Benson also spoke to the fathers in Israel. To them he said:

> First, you have a sacred responsibility to provide for the material needs of your family. The Lord clearly defined the roles of providing for and rearing a righteous posterity. In the beginning, Adam, not Eve, was instructed to earn the bread by the sweat of his brow. The Apostle Paul counsels husbands and fathers, "But

if any provide not for his own, and specially for those of his own house, he hath denied the faith, and is worse than an infidel" (1 Timothy 5:8).

Early in the history of the restored Church, the Lord specifically charged men with the obligation to provide for their wives and family. In January of 1832, He said, "Verily I say unto you, that every man who is obliged to provide for his own family, let him provide, and he shall in nowise lose his crown" (D&C 75:28). Three months later the Lord said again, "Women have claim on their husbands for their maintenance, until their husbands are taken" (D&C 83:2). This is the divine right of a wife and mother. While she cares for and nourishes her children at home, her husband earns the living for the family, which makes this nourishing possible.

In a home where there is an able-bodied husband, he is expected to be the breadwinner. Sometimes we hear of husbands who, because of economic conditions, have lost their jobs and expect the wives to go out of the home and work, even though the husband is still capable of providing for his family. In these cases, we urge the husband to do all in his power to allow his wife to remain in the home caring for the children while he continues to provide for his family the best he can, even though the job he is able to secure may not be ideal and family budgeting may have to be tighter.

Also, the need for education or material things does not justify the postponing of children in order to keep the wife working as the breadwinner of the family . . .

Brethren of the priesthood, I continue to emphasize the importance of mothers staying home to nurture, care for, and train their children in the principles of righteousness . . . I say to all of you, the Lord has charged men with the responsibility to provide for their families in such a way that the wife is allowed to fulfill her role as mother in the home.[12]

On another occasion, President Benson noted the following:

> There are voices in our midst which would attempt to convince you that these home-centered truths are not applicable to our present-day conditions. If you listen and heed, you will be lured away from your principal obligations. Beguiling voices in the world cry out for "alternative life-styles" for women. They maintain that some women are better suited for careers than for marriage and motherhood.
>
> These individuals spread their discontent by the propaganda that there are more exciting and self-fulfilling roles for women than homemaking. Some even have been bold to suggest that the Church move away from the "Mormon woman stereotype" of homemaking and rearing children. They also say it is wise to limit your family so you can have more time for personal goals and self-fulfillment.[13]

These voices should not be hearkened to, counseled President Benson, who taught that "the first priority for a woman is to prepare herself for her divine and eternal mission, whether she is married soon or late. It is folly to neglect that preparation for education in unrelated fields just to prepare temporarily to earn money. Women, when you are married it is the husband's role to provide, not yours. Do not sacrifice your preparation for an eternally ordained mission for the temporary expediency of money-making skills which you may or may not use."[14]

And yet again, we find President Benson teaching us that "it is time that the hearts of us fathers be turned to our children and the hearts of the children be turned to us fathers, or we shall both be cursed. The seeds of divorce are often sown and the blessings of children delayed by wives working outside the home. Working mothers should remember that their children usually need more of mother than of money."[15]

At general conference in 1981, President Benson noted, "It is a fundamental truth that the responsibilities of motherhood cannot be successfully delegated. No, not to day-care centers, not to schools, not to nurseries, not to baby-sitters. We become enamored with men's theories such as the idea of preschool training outside the home for young children. Not only does this put added pressure on the budget, but it places young children in an environment away from mother's influence. Too often the pressure for popularity, on children and teens, places economic burden on the income of the father, so mother feels she must go to work to satisfy her children's needs. That decision can be most shortsighted."[16]

Again, speaking to mothers in Zion, President Benson urged, "Your God-given roles are so vital to your own exaltation and to the salvation and exaltation of your family. A child needs a mother more than all the things money can buy. Spending time with your children is the greatest gift of all."[17]

Finally, President Benson declared:

> We need to arise and shine and to get the vision of this great work and to incorporate it into our lives and homes and families. If we do so the Lord will bless us because He loves us. We are His people. We have accepted His gospel. You have taken upon yourselves sacred covenants and he wants to bless you. He wants to pour out His blessings, the blessings of heaven, upon you and your families. In those homes where you live the gospel, where mother and father and children are skimping just a little more to make ends meet, He will bless you even more, much more than He will in those homes where we find so many mothers unnecessarily working outside the home in order to get better clothes, a new living room suite, a new rug on the floor. Working mothers contribute to increased divorce, to infidelity, to the weakening of homes.[18]

President Spencer W. Kimball

As previously noted, President Kimball had much to say about fathers providing for families and mothers working outside the home. He asked this defining question:

> How do you feel the Lord looks upon those who would trade flesh-and-blood children for pianos or television or furniture or an automobile, and is this not actually the case when people will buy these luxuries and yet cannot afford to have their children? . . .
>
> Parental care cannot be delegated. We have often said, 'This divine service of motherhood can be rendered only by mothers.' It may not be passed to others. Nurses cannot do it; public nurseries cannot do it. Only by mother, aided as much as may be by a loving father, brothers and sisters, and other relatives, can the full needed measure of watchful care be given.[19]

Again, President Kimball reiterated his message and counsel to both husbands and wives, fathers and mothers:

> Normally, the husband is the breadwinner. We believe that the place of the woman is in the home, as a general rule. We realize that some women may need to be employed when their children are grown, or when there have been problems in their home and the breadwinner has been taken from them. The most sacred privileges that a woman could have are in the home, to be a partner with God in the creation of children. . . .
>
> The Lord said women have claim upon their husbands for their maintenance until their husbands be taken (see D&C 83:2). Women are to take care of the family—the Lord has so stated—to be an assistant to the husband, to work with him, but not to earn the living, except in unusual circumstances. Men ought to be men indeed and earn the living under normal circumstances. . . .

When both spouses work, tensions result. Through both spouses working, competition rather than cooperation enters into the family. Two weary workers return home with taut nerves, individual pride, [and] increased independence, and then misunderstandings arise. Little frictions pyramid into monumental ones. Frequently spouses sinfully turn to new and old romances and finally the seeming inevitable break comes through divorce with its heartaches, bitterness, and disillusionment, and always ugly scars. . . .

From such homes come many conflicts, marital problems, and divorces, and delinquent children. Few people in trouble ever ascribe their marital conflicts to these first causes, but blame each other for the problems which were born and nurtured in strained environments. Certainly the harmonious relationship of father and mother and the emotional climate prevailing between parents gives soundness and security to children. . . .

Pursuit of luxury prejudices children. Too many mothers work away from home to furnish sweaters and music lessons and trips and fun for their children. Too many women spend their time in socializing, in politicking, in public services when they should be home to teach and train and receive and love their children into security. . . .

Rationalization can make convenience into necessity. Some women, because of circumstances beyond their control, must work. We understand that. We understand further that as families are raised, the talents God has given you and blessed you with can often be put to effective use in additional service to mankind. Do not, however, make the mistake of being drawn off into secondary tasks which will cause the neglect of your eternal assignments such as giving birth to and rearing the spirit children of our Father in Heaven. Pray carefully over all your decisions.[20]

Clearly, we see that President Kimball didn't shy away from asking difficult questions. Here is yet another:

> How can mothers justify their abandonment of home when they are needed so much by their off-spring? Rationalization must take over as they justify themselves in leaving home and children.
>
> Of course, there are *some* mothers who *must* work to support their children, and they are to be praised, not criticized, but let every working mother honestly weigh the matter and be sure the Lord approves before she rushes her babies off to the nursery, her children off to school, her husband off to work, and herself off to her employment. Let her be certain that she is not rationalizing herself away from her children merely to provide for them greater material things. Let her analyze well before she permits her precious ones to come home to an empty house where their plaintive cry, 'Mother,' finds no loving answer.[21]

Many other Church leaders have also spoken on this sensitive issue. Following is a small collection of their counsel.

J. Reuben Clark

In a general epistle of the First Presidency, President Clark noted that the "divine service of motherhood can be rendered only by mothers. It may not be passed to others. Nurses cannot do it; public nurseries cannot do it; hired help cannot do it—only mother, aided as much as may be by the loving hands of father, brothers, and sisters, can give the full needed measure of watchful care. . . . The mother who entrusts her child to the care of others, that she may do non-motherly work, whether for gold, for fame, or for civic service, should remember that 'a child left to himself bringeth his mother to shame' (Proverbs 29:15). In our day the Lord has said that unless parents teach their children the doctrines of the Church 'the sin be upon the heads of the parents' (D&C 68:25)."[22]

Boyd K. Packer

"During World War II, men were called away to fight. In the emergency, wives and mothers were drawn into the work force as never before. The most devastating effect of the war was on the family. It lingers to this generation.

"The First Presidency counseled that 'the mother who entrusts her child to the care of others, that she may do non-motherly work, whether for gold, for fame, or for civic service, should remember that "a child left to himself bringeth his mother to shame" (Proverbs 29:15). In our day the Lord has said that unless parents teach their children the doctrines of the Church "the sin be upon the heads of the parents" (D&C 68:25).' . . .

"That message and warning from the First Presidency is needed more, not less, today than when it was given. And no voice from any organization of the Church on any level of administration equals that of the First Presidency."[23]

Dallin H. Oaks

"Marriage is disdained by an increasing number of couples, and many who marry choose to forgo children or place severe limits on their number. In recent years strong economic pressures in many nations have altered the traditional assumption of a single breadwinner per family. Increases in the number of working mothers of young children inevitably signal a reduced commitment of parental time to nurturing the young. The effect of these reductions is evident in the rising numbers of abortions, divorces, child neglect, and juvenile crime."[24]

Richard G. Scott

"President Benson has taught that a mother with children should be in the home. He also said, 'We realize . . . that some of our choice sisters are widowed and divorced and that others find themselves in unusual circumstances where, out of necessity, they are required to work for a period of time. But these instances are the exception, not the rule' (Ezra Taft Benson, *To the Mothers in*

Zion [pamphlet, 1987], 5–6). You in these unusual circumstances qualify for additional inspiration and strength from the Lord. Those who leave the home for lesser reasons will not."[25]

"Beware of the subtle ways Satan employs to take you from the plan of God and true happiness. One of Satan's most effective approaches is to demean the role of wife and mother in the home. This is an attack at the very heart of God's plan to foster love between husband and wife and to nurture children in an atmosphere of understanding, peace, appreciation, and support. Much of the violence that is rampant in the world today is the harvest of weakened homes. Government and social plans will not effectively correct that, nor can the best efforts of schools and churches fully compensate for the absence of the tender care of a compassionate mother and wife in the home.

"This morning President Hinckley spoke of the importance of a mother in the home. Study his message. As a mother guided by the Lord, you weave a fabric of character in your children from threads of truth through careful instruction and worthy example. You imbue the traits of honesty, faith in God, duty, respect for others, kindness, self-confidence, and the desire to contribute, to learn, and to give in your trusting children's minds and hearts. No day-care center can do that. It is your sacred right and privilege.

"Of course, as a woman you can do exceptionally well in the workplace, but is that the best use of your divinely appointed talents and feminine traits? As a husband, don't encourage your wife to go to work to help your divinely appointed responsibility of providing resources for the family, if you can possibly avoid it. As the prophets have counseled, to the extent possible with the help of the Lord, as parents, work together to keep Mother in the home. Your presence there will strengthen the self-confidence of your children and decrease the chance of emotional challenges. Moreover, as you teach truth by word and example, those children will come to understand who they are and what they can obtain as divine children of Father in Heaven."[26]

Neal A. Maxwell

"Malfunctioning fathers are a much more common phenomenon in the Church than are malfunctioning mothers. Often the success-oriented male leaves untended some of his responsibilities to his wife and family. Even so, having one 'sentry' who has gone AWOL joined by another 'sentry,' the wife and mother, is no help."[27]

"Some mothers in today's world feel 'cumbered' by home duties and are thus attracted by other more 'romantic' challenges. Such women could make the same error of perspective that Martha made. The woman, for instance, who deserts the cradle in order to help defend civilization against the barbarians may well later meet, among the barbarians, her own neglected child."[28]

John H. Vandenberg

"There are further comments that advise us that economic factors indirectly play a part in the absence of parental discipline. Working mothers are not at home during most of the day, and they are unaware of what their children are doing before or after school hours or with whom they are associating. Usually when the working mother is at home, her waking hours are filled with the usual domestic chores of washing, ironing, and general household duties. The school, therefore, during five days of supervision each week, must play a serious part in teaching morality. Admittedly, this is a poor substitute for a mother's duty, and the evidence stares at us. . . .

"After discussing the subject at a recent stake conference, I received this letter from a working mother. The letter reads:

"'At our stake conference today, I could have stood up and cheered your comments about working mothers. I am thoroughly convinced that many of the nation's ills could be eliminated by mothers remaining at home and being good homemakers and wives. Husbands would respond to the dependence of being provider and head of the family; youngsters could contribute to their own miscellaneous needs for money by paper routes, etc., and not be contributing to delinquency. The whole family could definitely benefit and grow by working together in harmony and understanding to live within the wage that was brought into the home. Being a good wife and mother and sweetheart is career enough for any woman."

"For us, 25 years of ideal marriage (20 years of temple marriage) has evaporated in divorce and despair. . . . A goodly portion of the breakdown came from my going out of the home to work, and the chain reaction of minute events that grew like a cancer, quietly and deadly.'"[29]

Theodore Tuttle

"I would like to say a word about working mothers, brethren. I know I am not talking to working mothers. But I am talking to some fathers whose children have working mothers. You are the ones who cause, or at least permit, mothers to work. Brethren before you count the profit of such an endeavor, count the cost. In our affluent society many of us cannot distinguish between luxuries and necessities. Too often mothers work to pay for luxuries that are not worth the cost."[30]

Synopsis

It may prove helpful to the reader to again refer to our beginning questions and summarize some answers from the Brethren. A partial summary follows:

1. What can a mother do for her children that others cannot?

- Nurturing, teaching, lifting, encouraging, and rearing her children in righteousness and truth.
- Molding the lives of your children in the direction of righteousness and goodness, integrity and faith.
- She remained a homemaker and cared for our children. What she gave in love, encouragement, frugality, and companionship was far in excess of any material contribution she might have made by working.

- Her place is in the home, to build the home into a heaven of delight.
- Wrap the motherly cloak about you and, unembarrassed, help in a major role to create the bodies for the immortal souls, who anxiously await.
- Mothers, this kind of heavenly, motherly teaching takes time—lots of time. It cannot be done effectively part-time. It must be done all the time in order to save and exalt your children. This is your divine calling.
- The responsibilities of motherhood cannot be successfully delegated. No, not to day-care centers, not to schools, not to nurseries, not to baby-sitters.
- We become enamored with men's theories such as the idea of preschool training outside the home for young children. Not only does this put added pressure on the budget, but it places young children in an environment away from Mother's influence.
- Mothers in Zion, your God-given roles are so vital to your own exaltation.
- When you have fully complemented your husband in home life and borne the children, growing up full of faith, integrity, responsibility and goodness, then you have achieved your accomplishment supreme, without peer, and you will be the envy [of all] through time and eternity.
- This divine service of motherhood can be rendered only by mothers.
- The most sacred privileges that a woman could have are in the home, to be a partner with God in the creation of children.
- Mothers should be home to teach and train and receive and love their children into security.
- This divine service of motherhood can be rendered only by mothers. It may not be passed to others. Nurses cannot do it; public nurseries cannot do it; hired help cannot do it—only Mother.
- As a mother guided by the Lord, you weave a fabric

of character in your children from threads of truth through careful instruction and worthy example. You imbue the traits of honesty, faith in God, duty, respect for others, kindness, self-confidence, and the desire to contribute, to learn, and to give in your trusting children's minds and hearts.

- Your presence in the home will strengthen the self-confidence of your children and decrease the chance of emotional challenges. Moreover, as you teach truth by word and example, those children will come to understand who they are and what they can obtain as divine children of Father in Heaven.
- The whole family could definitely benefit and grow by working together in harmony and understanding to live within the wage that was brought into the home. Being a good wife and mother and sweetheart is career enough for any woman.

2. Under what circumstances would a mother working outside of the home be justified?

- Disability, death, or other circumstances may necessitate individual adaptation.
- Some women must work to provide for the needs of their families.
- If they become widowed or divorced and need to work.
- Some of our choice sisters are widowed and divorced; others find themselves in unusual circumstances where, out of necessity, they are required to work for a period of time. But these instances are the exception, not the rule.
- Only in an emergency should a wife secure outside employment.
- Some women may need to be employed when their children are grown, or when there have been problems in their home and the breadwinner has been taken from them.

- Some women, because of circumstances beyond their control, must work. We understand that.
- Some mothers must work to support their children, and they are to be praised, not criticized, but let every working mother honestly weigh the matter and be sure the Lord approves.

3. What circumstances would not justify mothers working outside of the home?

- I fear that there are far too many who do so only to get the means for a little more luxury and a few fancier toys.
- The situation may be necessary in some cases, but if you choose wisely now, it is not likely to become a requirement.
- Money for a boat or a fancy automobile or some other desirable but unnecessary things.
- Too many mothers work away from home to furnish sweaters and music lessons and trips and fun for their children.
- The need for education or material things does not justify the postponing of children in order to keep the wife working as the breadwinner of the family.
- Too often the pressure for popularity on children and teens places economic burden on the income of the father, so mother feels she must go to work to satisfy her children's needs. That decision can be most short-sighted.
- A child needs a mother more than all the things money can buy including better clothes, a new living room suite, a new rug on the floor.
- How do you feel the Lord looks upon those who would trade flesh-and-blood children for pianos or television or furniture or an automobile, and is this not actually the case when people will buy these luxuries and yet cannot afford to have their children?
- Rationalization can make convenience into neces-

sity.

- How can mothers justify their abandonment of home when they are needed so much by their offspring? Rationalization must take over as they justify themselves in leaving home and children.
- Let Mother be certain that she is not rationalizing herself away from her children merely to provide for them greater material things.
- For gold, for fame, or for civic service.

4. What are some of the possible negative consequences of mothers working outside of the home?

- We have been warned with counsel on where to find safety from sin and from sorrow.
- Do not follow a practice that will later bring you regret.
- In the process you lose the companionship of your children and the opportunity to rear them; you may also find that you have lost the substance while grasping at the shadow.
- Families have suffered because of it.
- Numerous divorces can be traced directly to the day when the wife left the home and went out into the world into employment. Two incomes raise the standard of living beyond its norm. But when both spouses work, they prevent the complete and proper home life, make it difficult to hold family prayer, create an independence that is not cooperative, limit the family, and frustrate the children already born.
- The seeds of divorce are often sown and the blessings of children delayed by wives working outside the home. Working mothers should remember that their children usually need more of mother than of money.
- Working mothers contribute to increased divorce, to infidelity, to the weakening of homes.
- If a few million of the working mothers who need not

work were to go home to their families, there might be employment for men now unemployed, and part and full-time work for youth who ought to help in family finances and who need occupation for their abundant energy.

- When both spouses work, tensions result. Through both spouses working, competition rather than cooperation enters into the family. Two weary workers return home with taut nerves, individual pride, [and] increased independence, and then misunderstandings arise. Little frictions pyramid into monumental ones. Frequently spouses sinfully turn to new and old romances and finally the seeming inevitable break comes through divorce with its heartaches, bitterness, and disillusionment, and always ugly scars.

- Pursuit of luxury prejudices children.

- Do not, however, make the mistake of being drawn off into secondary tasks, which will cause the neglect of your eternal assignments, such as giving birth to and rearing the spirit children of our Father in Heaven. Pray carefully over all your decisions.

- Let Mother analyze well before she permits her precious ones to come home to an empty house where their plaintive cry, 'Mother,' finds no loving answer.

- During World War II, men were called away to fight. In the emergency, wives and mothers were drawn into the work force as never before. The most devastating effect of the war was on the family. It lingers to this generation.

- Increases in the number of working mothers of young children inevitably signal a reduced commitment of parental time to nurturing the young. The effect of these reductions is evident in the rising numbers of abortions, divorces, child neglect, and juvenile crime.

- Those who leave the home for lesser reasons will not qualify for additional inspiration and strength from the Lord.

- Beware of the subtle ways Satan employs to take you from the plan of God and true happiness.
- Much of the violence that is rampant in the world today is the harvest of weakened homes.
- Unless parents teach their children the doctrines of the Church "the sin be upon the heads of the parent."
- The woman, for instance, who deserts the cradle in order to help defend civilization against the barbarians may well later meet, among the barbarians, her own neglected child.
- Working mothers are not at home during most of the day, and they are unaware of what their children are doing before or after school hours or with whom they are associating.
- Many of the nation's ills could be eliminated by mothers remaining at home and being good homemakers and wives.

5. What help is available only for those mothers who must work outside of the home?

- I pray that the Lord will bless you with strength and great capacity, for you need both. You have the responsibilities of both breadwinner and homemaker. I know that it is difficult. I know that it is discouraging. I pray that the Lord will bless you with a special wisdom and the remarkable talent needed to provide your children with time and companionship and love and with that special direction which only a mother can give. I pray also that he will bless you with help, unstintingly given, from family, friends, and the Church, which will lift some of the burden from your shoulders and help you in your times of extremity.
- Sometimes you need food for your tables, and we trust that bishops will be there to supply food and other goods and services under the great program that the Lord has provided in his Church. But we know that

more often your greater need is for understanding and appreciation and companionship.

- He will bless you even more, much more than He will in those homes where we find so many mothers unnecessarily working outside the home
- You in these unusual circumstances qualify for additional inspiration and strength from the Lord. Those who leave the home for lesser reasons will not.

6. What counsel is given to husbands about their wives working outside of the home?

- By divine design, fathers are to . . . provide the necessities of life.
- It will be better if the husband becomes the provider and the wife does not work when the children come.
- You who hold the priesthood have the responsibility, unless disabled, to provide temporal support for your wife and children. No man can shift the burden of responsibility to another, not even to his wife. The Lord has commanded that women and children have claim on their husbands and fathers for their maintenance (see D&C 83:1; 1 Timothy 5:8). President Ezra Taft Benson has stated that when a husband encourages or insists that his wife work out of the home for their convenience, "Not only will the family suffer in such instances, . . . but [his] own spiritual growth and progression will be hampered."
- We urge you to do all in your power to allow your wife to remain in the home, caring for the children, while you provide for the family the best you can.
- It is the man to whom the Lord has assigned the breadwinner's role.
- The Lord clearly defined the roles of mothers and fathers in providing for and rearing a righteous posterity. In the beginning, Adam—not Eve—was instructed to earn the bread by the sweat of his brow.

- Mother cares for and nourishes her children at home. Father earns the living for the family, which makes this nourishing possible.
- Early in the history of the restored Church, the Lord specifically charged men with the obligation to provide for their wives and family.
- In a home where there is an able-bodied husband, he is expected to be the breadwinner. Sometimes we hear of husbands who, because of economic conditions, have lost their jobs and expect the wives to go out of the home and work, even though the husband is still capable of providing for his family. In these cases, we urge the husband to do all in his power to allow his wife to remain in the home caring for the children while he continues to provide for his family the best he can, even though the job he is able to secure may not be ideal and family budgeting may have to be tighter.
- I say to all of you, the Lord has charged men with the responsibility to provide for their families in such a way that the wife is allowed to fulfill her role as mother in the home.
- It is time that the hearts of us fathers be turned to our children and the hearts of the children be turned to us fathers, or we shall both be cursed.
- The husband is expected to support his family, and only in an emergency should a wife secure outside employment.
- Men ought to be men indeed and earn the living under normal circumstances.
- As a husband, don't encourage your wife to go to work to help your divinely appointed responsibility of providing resources for the family, if you can possibly avoid it.
- I am thoroughly convinced that many of the nation's ills could be eliminated by mothers remaining at home and being good homemakers and wives. Husbands would respond to the dependence of being

provider and head of the family.

- I am talking to some fathers whose children have working mothers. You are the ones who cause or at least permit, mothers to work. Brethren, before you count the profit of such an endeavor, count the cost.

We began this chapter with a quote from the Proclamation on the Family, to which I would like to return: "By divine design, fathers are to preside over their families in love and righteousness and are responsible to *provide* the necessities of life and protection for their families. Mothers are primarily responsible for the *nurture* of their children. In these sacred responsibilities, fathers and mothers are obligated to help one another as equal partners. Disability, death, or other circumstances may necessitate individual adaptation. Extended families should lend support when needed."[31]

This is not only the ideal, but also the only way to gain the greatest blessings. But, ironically, it is very difficult to live these principles in a time of such prosperity. Materialism is so much a part of our culture. We have more *things* than any other people, not only in the world, but in all of world history! However, since you can never get enough of what you don't need, we are constantly enticed to want even more. How can we be in the world of materialism, but not become enslaved to it? Since this seems to be the major justification for Mother leaving the home, to add to the family buying power, we wonder what we could do differently that would enable us to better live the principles of the Proclamation?

Elder Henry B. Eyring gave this counsel: "To begin with, we can decide to plan for success, not failure. Statistics are thrown at us every day to persuade us that a family composed of a loving father and mother with children loved, taught, and cared for in the way the proclamation enjoins is going the way of the dinosaurs, toward extinction. You have enough evidence in your own families that righteous people sometimes have their families ripped apart by circumstances beyond their control. It takes courage and faith to plan for what God holds before you as the ideal rather than what might be forced upon you by circumstances. . . . There are important ways in which planning for failure can make failure more likely and the ideal less so. Consider these twin commandments as an example: 'Fathers are to . . . provide the necessities of life . . . for their families' and 'mothers are primarily responsible for the nurture of their children.' Knowing how hard that might be, a young man might choose a career on the basis of how much money he could make, even if it meant he couldn't be home enough to be an equal partner. By doing that, he has already decided he cannot hope to do what would be best. A young woman might prepare for a career incompatible with being primarily responsible for the future of her children because of the possibilities of not marrying, of not having children, or of being left alone to provide for them herself. Or, she might fail to focus her education on the gospel and the knowledge of the world that nurturing a family would require, not realizing that the highest and best use she could make of her talents and her education would be in her home. Because a young man and woman had planned to take care of the worst, they might make the best less likely."[32]

We would all do well to take the Proclamation more seriously. Elder Richard G. Scott asked this: "How can you receive the greatest happiness and blessings from this earth experience? Learn the doctrinal foundation of the great plan of happiness by studying the scriptures, pondering their content, and praying to understand them. Carefully study and use the proclamation of the First Presidency and the Twelve on the family. It was inspired of the Lord."[33]

All couples would benefit by identifying the principles taught in the Proclamation on the Family, making a plan to abide by those principles, and then sticking to that plan, even if it takes faith to do so.

Consider once more the words of President Ezra Taft Benson, "The first priority for a woman is to prepare herself for her divine and eternal mission, whether she is married soon or late. It is folly to neglect that preparation for education in unrelated fields just to prepare temporarily to earn money. Women, when you are married, it is the husband's role to provide, not yours. Do not sacrifice your preparation for an eternally ordained mission for the temporary expediency of money-making skills which you may or may not use."[34]

The most often cited reason for mothers working out of the home is to provide the family with more money. However, the actual increase in spendable income is far less than what might be expected. There are staggering expenses associated with working out of the home. Added expenses in food, clothing, transportation, taxes, and child care can eat away at the wages earned. Mothers working full time can easily lose 75 percent or more of their income through expenses! Remember, it's not what you make. It's how much you keep. Usually the actual increase in buying power is so minimal compared to the expense, and the sacrifice of non-tangibles is so horrific. It simply does not pay enough for what is lost.

It is not a question of whether or not the woman is capable of succeeding in the world of work. She has more than enough ability. But the question must be asked, "Of course you can do his job, but then who will do your job?" Neither the husband, nor any person or agency, can do the job of being a mother.

Children have needs that only a mother can meet. For example, no one but the mother seems to be motivated with the purity of love and nurturing ability to focus so much time upon the child. Time and involvement are essential to its full development. Recent research has indicated that even after birth, perhaps up to the age of four, the brain of the child is continuing to develop. The extent of brain development is dependent upon the amount of stimulation given to the infant and toddler. Nobody but a mother can give the amount of stimulation and love necessary to provide for the full development of her child's brain. The same can be said of language skills, social skills, and motor skills.

Nobody can replace Mother, certainly not Father, and not even Grandmother! Now, I say this with utmost admiration and respect to grandmothers. In fact, I am married to one! We have twenty-four very loved and wanted grandchildren. With only six of our thirteen children married, we have the potential of having many more grandchildren. We love them dearly, but not like their mothers do. There is something about the love and care of a mother that is sacred, an endowment from heaven. Nobody can take the place of a mother.

If grandmothers cannot take the place of Mother, how would a babysitter, a nanny, or a child-care center do? To even consider a serious comparison is insulting to the sacred role of mother. No matter how well motivated the hireling may be, a child needs a mother. A child-care center cannot meet children's needs for health, safety, warm relationships, learning, and the assurance that "Mother is here."

Now, before I say more about child-care centers, let me say that I assume that those who own and work at such businesses are probably some of the nicest people in the world. Some of those very nice, but frustrated, people have been my students. Frustrated because they see first hand that the enormous needs of children cannot be met under these artificial conditions. For example, one worker observed that there is a very obvious difference in behavior of those children who are regularly left for a full day compared to those children left only a few hours. Children left for extensive lengths of time typically develop poorer social skills and misbehave more.

One young male worker said that he was not allowed to touch the children beyond what was needed for changing diapers and feeding. This restraint was due to gender and concerns about lawsuits. Visualize that scenario: the child receives no more care than food and dry pants. Another worker said she would dearly love to do more, but with a child-to-worker ratio of 20-to-1, she didn't have time for doing any more than changing diapers and feeding. For a business to succeed, there are always cost-cutting measures that must be implemented. However, it appears that it is the child who pays the price.

One student reported that she didn't work at a child-care center, but her roommate did. One day she decided to tag along with her roommate at the center. She reported that while the workers were engaged in the essentials of their profession, she was free to observe the children. More important, the children observed that here was a caring adult who didn't have to rush off to another housekeeping chore.

Soon the children were literally clinging to this young woman's legs and begging for what they couldn't get from the workers—attention and affection. This young woman now regularly goes to this child-care center to donate what is needed so desperately, her unhurried time and affection.

The concern is not the motivation of the child-care provider but the almost insatiable needs of the child. Needs which only a mother, motivated by love and that gift of nurturing, is capable of giving. The nicest hireling cannot give the child the security that comes from uninterrupted time with Mother. Mothers provide affection and unhurried attention that cannot be duplicated. A child needs the foundation of a constant mother. There is security and identity in knowing that, of all the things Mother is capable of doing, she chooses to raise me.

Notes

1. The First Presidency and Council of the Twelve Apostles, "The Family—A Proclamation to the World," *Ensign*, November 1995, 102.

2. Benson, "To the Mothers in Zion," *Teachings of Ezra Taft Benson*, 514.

3. Eyring, "Finding Safety in Counsel," *Ensign*, May 1997, 25.

4. Hinckley, "Walking in the Light of the Lord," *Ensign*, November 1998, 99–100.

5. Hinckley, *Church News*, 1 November 1997, 4.

6. Hinckley, "Women of the Church," *Ensign*, November 1996, 69.

7. Hinckley, "Live Up to Your Inheritance," *Ensign*, November 1983, 83.

8. Ibid., 83.

9. Hunter, "Being a Righteous Husband and Father," *Ensign*, November 1994, 51.

10. Hunter, "Prepare for Honorable Employment," *Ensign*, November 1975, 123–24.

11. Benson, "To the Mothers in Zion," *Teachings of Ezra Taft Benson*, 515.

12. Benson, "To the Fathers in Israel," *Teachings of Ezra Taft Benson*, 505.

13. Benson, "The Honored Place of Women," *Ensign*, November 1981, 105.

14. Benson, *In His Steps*, 64.

15. Benson, in Conference Report, October 1970, 24.

16. Benson, "The Honored Place of Woman," *Ensign*, November 1981, 105.

17. Benson, *Teachings of Ezra Taft Benson*, 515.

18. Ibid., 526–27

19. Kimball, *Teachings of Spencer W. Kimball*, 329, 336.

20. Ibid., 318–19.

21. Kimball, *Faith Precedes the Miracle*, 116–17.

22. Clark, *Messages of the First Presidency*, 6: 170–85.

23. Packer, "For Time and All Eternity," *Ensign*, November 1993, 22–23.

24. Oaks, "'The Great Plan of Happiness,'" *Ensign*, November 1993, 74.

25. Scott, "The Power of Correct Principles," *Ensign*, May 1993, 34.

26. Scott, "The Joy of Living the Great Plan of Happiness," *Ensign*, November 1996, 74–75.

27. Maxwell, *Deposition of a Disciple*, 84.

28. Maxwell, *Wherefore, We Must Press Forward*, 101.

29. Vandenberg, in Conference Report, October 1967, 77–78.

30. Tuttle, in Conference Report, April 1967, 94.

31. The First Presidency and Council of the Twelve Apostles, "The Proclamation on the Family," *Ensign*, November 1995, 102.

32. Eyring, *To Draw Closer to God*, 166.

33. Scott, "The Joy of Living the Great Plan of Happiness," *Ensign*, November 1996, 73.

34. Benson, *Teachings of Ezra Taft Benson*, 64.

11

parenthood

Children are a great blessing and responsibility. In "The Family: A Proclamation to the World," we are reminded that "husband and wife have a solemn responsibility to love and care for each other and for their children. 'Children are an heritage of the Lord' (Psalm 127:3). Parents have a sacred duty to rear their children in love and righteousness, to provide for their physical and spiritual needs, to teach them to love and serve one another, to observe the commandments of God and to be law-abiding citizens wherever they live. Husbands and wives will be held accountable before God for the discharge of these obligations."[1]

Although we have a solemn responsibility as parents, that does not prohibit us from enjoying the experience. The Psalmist wrote, "Lo, children are an heritage of the Lord: and the fruit of the womb is his reward. As arrows are in the hand of a mighty man; so are children of the youth. Happy is the man that hath his quiver full of them" (Psalm 127:3–5). However, that promised happiness is contingent upon living certain principles.

The Proclamation on the Family further states that "happiness in family life is most likely to be achieved when founded upon the teachings of the Lord Jesus Christ. Successful marriages and families are established and maintained on principles of faith, prayer, repentance, forgiveness, respect, love, compassion, work, and wholesome recreational activities."[2]

Happy families are not only founded upon the teachings of the Lord Jesus Christ, they are also founded upon Him. "I have learned that there are many things that matter in maintaining a healthy marriage," observed Elder H. Burke Peterson. "However, there are only a few things that matter most. Not that other things are unimportant, but when a few basic elements are in place a tone and pattern are set which allow everything else to fall into line. After many years of observation and interviews I have come to understand that the quality of a marriage rests on the strength of each marriage partner's faith and testimony in the Savior and his mission."[3]

Parenthood is a noble calling, but one filled with challenge as well as joy. President Gordon B. Hinckley said, "Of all the joys of life, none other equals that of happy parenthood. Of all the responsibilities with which we struggle, none other is so serious. To rear children in an atmosphere of love, security, and faith is the most rewarding of all challenges. The good result from such efforts becomes life's most satisfying compensation. . . . I am satisfied that no other experiences of life draw us nearer to heaven than those that exist between happy parents and happy children."[4]

President James E. Faust made a similar statement:

> While few human challenges are greater than that of being good parents, few opportunities offer greater potential for joy. Surely no more important work is to be done in this world than preparing our children to be God-fearing, happy, honorable, and productive. Parents will find no more fulfilling happiness than to have their children honor them and their teachings. It is the glory of parenthood. John testified, "I have no greater joy than to hear that my children walk in truth" (3 John 1:4). In my opinion, the teaching, rearing, and training of children requires more intelligence, intui-

tive understanding, humility, strength, wisdom, spirituality, perseverance, and hard work than any other
challenge we might have in life.[5]

In my experience, those who think they know all about parenting are usually graduate students who have no children! Similarly,
those of us who are a little older and more experienced simply
smile at parents of toddlers who say they have already figured out
how to raise trouble-free, responsible teenagers. The realities are
that, just as marriage is designed to humble us and help us overcome selfishness, parenting is designed to complete the humbling
process so we can recognize our total dependence upon the Lord
and, thus, become more teachable. Though challenging, parenting can be successful and enjoyable, especially if we follow the
counsel of the Brethren.

Since we must have a vision of the ideal home, even if we all
have far to go before that ideal is achieved, consider this description by President Joseph F. Smith:

> What then is an ideal home-model home, such as
> it should be the ambition of the Latter-day Saints to
> build; such as a young man starting out in life should
> wish to erect for himself? And the answer came to me:
> It is one in which all worldly considerations are second-
> ary. One in which the father is devoted to the family
> with which God has blessed him, counting them of
> first importance, and in which they in turn permit him
> to live in their hearts. One in which there is confi-
> dence, union, love, sacred devotion between father and
> mother and children and parents. One in which the
> mother takes every pleasure in her children, supported
> by the father—all being moral, pure, God-fearing.
>
> As the tree is judged by its fruit, so also do we
> judge the home by the children. In the ideal home true
> parents rear loving, thoughtful children, loyal to the
> death, to father and mother and home! In it there is
> the religious spirit, for both parents and children have

faith in God, and their practices are in conformity with that faith; the members are free from the vices and contaminations of the world, are pure in morals, having upright hearts beyond bribes and temptations, ranging high in the exalted standards of manhood and womanhood.

Peace, order, and contentment reign in the hearts of the inmates—let them be rich or poor, in things material. There are no vain regrets; no expressions of discontent against father, from the boys and girls, in which they complain: "If we only had this or that, or were like this family or that, or could do like so and so!"—complaints that have caused fathers many uncertain steps, dim eyes, restless nights, and untold anxiety. In their place is the loving thoughtfulness to mother and father by which the boys and girls work with a will and a determination to carry some of the burden that the parents have staggered under these many years. There is the kiss for mother, the caress for father, the thought that they have sacrificed their own hopes and ambitions, their strength, even life itself to their children—there is gratitude in payment for all that has been given them![6]

For those of us who have yet to realize the ideal and are still waiting for that kiss for mother, the caress for father from appreciative, financially contributing children, we may need to learn what more we can do, as well as the necessity of patience and perhaps faith.

Elder Richard G. Scott has counseled us to strive for the ideal by doing the best we can. He said:

Throughout your life on earth, seek diligently to fulfill the fundamental purposes of this life through the ideal family. While you may not have yet reached that ideal, do all you can through obedience and faith in the Lord to consistently draw as close to it as you are able. Let nothing dissuade you from that objective. . . .

❧

Don't become overanxious. Do the best you can. . . . Are there so many fascinating, exciting things to do or so many challenges pressing down upon you that it is hard to keep focused on that which is essential? When things of the world crowd in, all too often the wrong things take highest priority. Then it is easy to forget the fundamental purpose of life.

Satan has a powerful tool to use against good people. It is distraction. He would have good people fill life with "good things" so there is no room for the essential ones. Have you unconsciously been caught in that trap? . . .

Why has your moral agency been given to you? Only to live a pleasurable life and to make choices to do the things you want to do? Or is there a more fundamental reason—to be able to make the choices that will lead you to fully implement your purpose for being here on earth and to establish priorities in your life that will assure the development and happiness the Lord wants you to receive. . . . While wholesome pleasure results from much we do that is good, it is not our prime purpose for being on earth. Seek to know and do the will of the Lord, not just what is convenient or what makes life easy. . . .

Find a retreat of peace and quiet where periodically you can ponder and let the Lord establish the direction of your life. Each of us needs to periodically check our bearings and confirm that we are on course. Sometime soon you may benefit from taking this personal inventory: What are my highest priorities to be accomplished on earth? How do I use my discretionary time? Is there anything I know I should not be doing? If so, I will repent and stop it now. . . . Put first things first. Do the best you can while on earth to have an ideal family.[7]

Although we can apply many commandments in the scriptures to parenting, one commandment is stated more than any other: parents are to teach their children. For example: "And again, inasmuch as parents have children in Zion, or in any of her stakes which are organized that teach them not to understand the doctrine of repentance, faith in Christ the Son of the living God, and of baptism and the gift of the Holy Ghost by the laying on of the hands, when eight years old, the sin be upon the heads of the parents.

"For this shall be a law unto the inhabitants of Zion, or in any of her stakes which are organized.

"And their children shall be baptized for the remission of their sins when eight years old, and receive the laying on of hands.

"And they shall also teach their children to pray, and to walk uprightly before the Lord" (D&C 68:25–28).

Elder A. Theodore Tuttle asked the rhetorical question: "Tell me, how much of the gospel would your children know, if all they knew is what they had been taught at home? Ponder that. I repeat, how much of the gospel would your children know if all they knew is what they had been taught at home? Remember, the Church exists to help the home. Parents, the divine charge to teach has never been changed. Do not abdicate your duty."[8]

President Heber J. Grant also taught the responsibility of parents teaching their children. He said:

> Some men and women argue, "Well, I am a Latter-day Saint, and we were married in the temple and were sealed over the altar by one having the Priesthood of God, according to the new and everlasting covenant, and our children are bound to grow up and be good Latter-day Saints, they cannot help it; it is born in them." I have learned the multiplication table, and so has my wife, but do you think I am a big enough fool to believe that our children will be born with a knowledge of the multiplication table?
>
> I may know that the gospel is true, and so may my wife; but I want to tell you that our children will not know that the gospel is true, unless they study it and gain a testimony for themselves. Parents are deceiv-

ing themselves in imagining that their children will be born with a knowledge of the gospel. Of course, they will have greater claim upon the blessings of God, being born under the new and everlasting covenant, and it will come natural for them to grow up and perform their duties; but the devil realizes this, and is therefore seeking all the harder to lead our children from the truth.[9]

President Ezra Taft Benson has given additional direction to parents. He said:

> Setting your home in order is keeping the commandments of God. This brings harmony and love in the home between you and your companion and between you and your children. It is daily family prayer. It is teaching your family to understand the gospel of Jesus Christ. It is each family member keeping the commandments of God. It is you and your companion being worthy to receive a temple recommend, all family members receiving the ordinances of exaltation, and your family being sealed together for eternity. It is being free from excessive debt, with family members paying honest tithes and offerings.[10]

President Benson also taught:

> Take time to pray with your children. Family prayers, under the direction of the father should be held morning and night. Have your children feel of your faith as you call down the blessings of heaven upon them. . . . Take time daily to read the scriptures together as a family. Individual scripture reading is important, but family scripture reading is vital. Reading the Book of Mormon together as a family will especially bring increased spirituality into your home and will give both parents and children the power to resist temptation and to have the Holy Ghost as their constant companion.[11]

The special blessings associated with reading the Book of Mormon as a family were thus emphasized by President Marion G. Romney, when he said:

> I feel certain that if, in our homes parents will read from the Book of Mormon prayerfully and regularly, both by themselves and with their children, the spirit of that great book will come to permeate our homes and all who dwell therein. The spirit of reverence will increase, mutual respect and consideration for each other will grow. The spirit of contention will depart. Parents will counsel their children in greater love and wisdom. Children will be more responsive and submissive to that counsel. Righteousness will increase. Faith, hope, and charity—the pure love of Christ—will abound in our homes and lives, bringing in their wake peace, joy, and happiness.[12]

Elder L. Tom Perry shared with us counsel as to what parents should teach in their homes. He recalled:

> At the time I was a new parent, President David O. McKay presided over the Church. His counsel was clear and direct regarding our responsibilities to our children. He taught us the most precious gift a man and woman can receive is a child of God, and that the raising of a child is basically, fundamentally, and most exclusively a spiritual process. . . . He directed us to basic principles we need to teach our children. The first and most important inner quality you can instill in a child is faith in God. The first and most important action a child can learn is obedience. And the most powerful tool you have with which to teach a child is love. (See *Instructor*, December 1949, 620)[13]

In addition to obedience, President Benson provided additional subject matter. "If our children and their children are taught well by us," he said, "[the] temple will have special significance. It will be an ever-present reminder that God intends the family to be eternal."[14] Of temples, he further taught, "Now let me say something to all who can worthily go to the house of the Lord. . . . Yes, there is a power associated with the ordinances of heaven—even the power of godliness—which can and will thwart the forces of evil if we will be worthy of those sacred blessings. This community will be protected, our children will be safeguarded as we live the gospel, visit the temple, and live close to the Lord."[15]

We must do all that we can to make our homes, like temples, places of refuge and instruction. We do this by "teach[ing] and train[ing] our children in the ways of the Lord," said Elder David B. Haight. "Children should not be left to their own devices in learning character and family values, or in listening to and watching unsupervised music or television or movies as a means of gaining knowledge and understanding as to how to live their lives!"[16]

The First Presidency taught that by teaching and rearing children in the principles of the gospel, parents can protect their families from corrosive elements. They further counseled parents and children "to give highest priority to family prayer, family home evening, gospel study and instruction, and wholesome family activities. However worthy and appropriate other demands or activities may be, they must not be permitted to displace the divinely-appointed duties that only parents and families can adequately perform."[17]

President Spencer W. Kimball has warned us that "the time will come when only those who believe deeply and actively in the family will be able to preserve their families in the midst of the gathering evil around us."[18]

That warning was given more than twenty years ago, and it appears that we have arrived at the time spoken of. Therefore, this added counsel from President Kimball may have additional relevance. He said, "In the past, having family prayer once a day may have been all right. But in the future it will not be enough if we are going to save our families."[19]

On another occasion, President Kimball said:

Spirituality enhances marriage. If two people love the Lord more than their own lives and then love each other more than their own lives, working together in total harmony with the gospel program as their basic structure, they are sure to have this great happiness. When a husband and wife go together frequently to the holy temple, kneel in prayer together in their home with their family, go hand in hand to their religious meetings, keep their lives wholly chaste, mentally and physically, so that their whole thoughts and desires and love are all centered in one being, their companion, and both are working together for the upbuilding of the kingdom of God, then happiness is at its pinnacle.[20]

Decades earlier, President Joseph F. Smith gave similar counsel:

The home is what needs reforming. Try today, and tomorrow, to make a change in your home by praying twice a day with your family. . . . Ask a blessing upon every meal you eat. Spend ten minutes . . . reading a chapter from the words of the Lord in the [scriptures]. . . . Let love, peace, and the Spirit of the Lord, kindness, charity, sacrifice for others, abound in your families. Banish harsh words . . . and let the Spirit of God take possession of your hearts. Teach to your children these things, in spirit and power. . . . Not one child in a hundred would go astray, if the home environment, example and training were in harmony with . . . the gospel of Christ.[21]

"Successful parents," said President Benson, "have found that it is not easy to rear children in an environment polluted with evil. Therefore, they take deliberate steps to provide the best of wholesome influences. Moral principles are taught. Good books are made available and read. Television watching is controlled. Good and uplifting music is provided. But most important, the scriptures are read and discussed as a means to help develop spiritual-mindedness."[22]

President Benson further said:

> It is time to awaken to the fact that there are deliberate efforts to restructure the family along the lines of humanistic values. Images of the family and of love as depicted in television and film often portray a philosophy contrary to the commandments of God.
>
> Innocent sounding phrases are now used to give approval to sinful practices. Thus, the term "alternative life-style" is used to justify adultery and homosexuality, "freedom of choice" to justify abortion, "meaningful relationship" and "self-fulfillment" to justify sex outside of marriage.
>
> Rearing happy, peaceful children is no easy challenge in today's world, but it can be done, and it is being done. Responsible parenthood is the key.
>
> Above all else, children need to know and feel they are loved, wanted, and appreciated. They need to be assured of that often. Obviously, this is a role parents should fill, and most often the mother can do it best.
>
> Children need to know who they are in the eternal sense of their identity. They need to know that they have an eternal Heavenly Father on whom they can rely, to whom they can pray, and from whom they can receive guidance. They need to know whence they came so that their lives will have meaning and purpose.
>
> Children must be taught to pray, to rely on the Lord for guidance, and to express appreciation for the blessings that are theirs. I recall kneeling at the bedsides of our young children, helping them with their prayers.
>
> Children must be taught right from wrong. They can and must learn the commandments of God. They must be taught that it is wrong to steal, lie, cheat, or covet what others have.
>
> Children must be taught to work at home. They should learn there that honest labor develops dignity

and self-respect. They should learn the pleasure of work, of doing a job well.

The leisure time of children must be constructively directed to wholesome, positive pursuits. Too much time viewing television can be destructive, and pornography in this medium should not be tolerated. It is estimated that growing children today watch television over twenty-five hours per week.

Communities have a responsibility to assist the family in promoting wholesome entertainment. What a community tolerates will become tomorrow's standard for today's youth.

Families must spend more time together in work and recreation. Family home evenings should be scheduled once a week as a time for recreation, work projects, skits, songs around the piano, games, special refreshments, and family prayers. Like iron links in a chain, this practice will bind a family together, in love, pride, tradition, strength and loyalty.

Family study of the scriptures should be the practice in our homes each Sabbath day. Daily devotionals are also a commendable practice, where scripture reading, singing of hymns, and family prayer are a part of our daily routine.[23]

Such homes will be places of refuge and spiritual strengthening. Elder Horacio A. Tenorio makes this comparison:

> In medieval times, great fortresses were built around castles or cities to protect them from enemy attacks. In the Book of Mormon, the Nephites built fortresses to defend their families against their enemies. We must make of our homes fortresses to protect our families against the constant attacks of the adversary.
>
> I am not suggesting that we isolate ourselves from the world by digging deep moats or constructing barriers several meters high around our homes, but rather that in our family councils, under the influence of

the Spirit, we establish the activities, entertainment, books, friendships, rules, and habits that will constitute our fortresses.

Our fortress consists of teaching our children the gospel through the scriptures, establishing the habit of reading them every day as a family, and basing a large part of our conversations on them. It means kneeling together daily to pray and to teach our children the importance of direct, personal communication with our Heavenly Father.

Our fortress is erected by showing our children, through our example, that the principles and teachings of the gospel are a way of life that helps us find peace and happiness on this earth and provides the strength necessary to withstand the trials and tribulations that come into our lives. We must teach our children to avoid compromising themselves with inappropriate fashions and negative practices of the world by simply saying no when confronted with them.

Creating a fortress requires the family to counsel together in weekly family home evenings, where they make decisions and agreements.[24]

Regarding the proper home environment, a few more suggestions may prove helpful. Elder Neal A. Maxwell cautioned, "Those who do too much *for* their children will soon find they can do nothing *with* their children. So many children have been so much *done for* they are almost *done in*."[25] And Elder L. Tom Perry noted:

I read recently an article in a magazine designed especially for Latter-day Saints about a study that was made of the benefits of reading to children. It stated that when a mother or a father consistently reads to a child, the child enters school at a much higher level and excels in reading during these early grades. If there is a direct correlation between the early training a child receives from parents and the rapidity with which a child learns, how important would it be, then, for us to spend time reading the gospel of Jesus Christ to our children, to imbue and instill in them, in their tender and early years, faith in the gospel of our Lord and Savior?[26]

Elder Perry also shared:

If I were cast again in the role of having a young family around me, I would be determined to give them more time. I would try to see that the special times the Church has encouraged me to spend with my family were now strictly followed and properly organized to be more productive. . . .

First, I would be certain that sufficient time was calendared each week for a family executive committee meeting to plan family strategy. The executive committee, composed of a husband and wife, would meet together to fully communicate, discuss, plan, and prepare for their leadership role in the family organization. . . . Second, I would make the family home evening times on Monday night a family council meeting where children were taught by parents how to prepare for their roles as family members and prospective parents.

Family home evening would begin with a family dinner together, followed by a council meeting, where such topics as the following would be discussed and training would be given: temple preparation, missionary preparation, home management, family finances, career development, education, community involvement, cultural improvement, acquisition and care of real and personal property, family planning calendars, use of leisure time, and work assignments. The evening could then be climaxed with a special dessert and time for parents to have individual meeting with each child. . . .

Third, Saturday would be a special activity day

divided into two parts: first, a time for teaching children the blessings of work, how to care for and improve the home, the yard, the garden, the field; second, a time for family activity, to build a family heritage of things you enjoy doing together. . . .

Fourth, Sunday would become the special day in each week. Careful preparation would precede the three-hour worship service time at the chapel. The family would arrive at church rested, relaxed, and spiritually prepared to enjoy the meetings together. The balance of the day would be spent in a climate of spiritual uplift. We would dress to fit the occasion—boys in something somewhat better than Levis and T-shirts, girls in comfortable, decent dresses, not in shorts or slacks. It would be a time for our family scripture study, genealogical research, personal journals, family histories, letter writing, missionary contacts, and visits to extended family, to friends, and to shut-ins.[27]

Obviously, there is much we can be doing to create the proper environment and thus invite happiness and the Spirit into our homes. However, even in the best of homes, it will sometimes be necessary to further love and teach through administering discipline. This presents a special challenge. Thankfully, we can again turn to the counsel of the Brethren for guidance.

President Joseph F. Smith said:

Fathers, (1) if you wish your children to be taught in the principles of the gospel, if you (2) wish them to love the truth and understand it, (3) if you wish them to be obedient to and united with you, love them! And prove to them that you do love them by your every word or act to them. For your own sake, for the love that should exist between you and your boys—however wayward they might be . . . when you speak or talk harshly to them, do it not in anger, do it not harshly, in a condemning spirit.

Speak to them kindly, get them down and weep with them if necessary and get them to shed tears with you if possible. Soften their hearts, get them to feel tenderly toward you. Approach them with reason, with persuasion and love unfeigned . . . get them to feel as you feel, have interest in the things in which you take interest, to love the gospel as you love it, to love one another as you love them; to love their parents as the parents love their children. You can't do it any other way.[28]

Frustrated parents, notice that it is not a question of who is at fault, or if they deserve your wrath, it is a question of what works! "You can't do it any other way" says a prophet of the Lord.

President George Q. Cannon said this:

Let us try to make our children all that we would like them to be, as far as our influence goes. I say to you parents who have children in the covenant, if you pray for them, God will feel after them, in the meantime doing all you can yourselves to have those promises fulfilled, so that there will be no neglect on your part. Your children may err, and do things that are sinful and are painful and sorrowful to you. But cling to them. Pray for them. Exercise faith in their behalf. Treat them with kindness; not, however, condoning their sins and their transgressions. But be full of charity, full of long-suffering, full of patience, and full of mercy to your children. Don't drive them away by your severity, or by being too strict. But be kind and merciful to them, correcting their faults when they need correcting, at the same time showing them that your corrections are not prompted by anything but love for them and for their happiness.[29]

It is essential to recognize that child rearing is individualistic. Every child is different and unique. What works with one may not work with another. I do not know who is wise enough to say what discipline is too harsh or what is too lenient except the parents of the children themselves, who love them most. It is a matter of prayerful discernment for the parents.

Certainly the overarching and undergirding principle is that the discipline of children must be motivated more by love than by punishment. President Brigham Young counseled, "If you are ever called upon to chasten a person, never chasten beyond the balm you have within you to bind up."[30]

Direction and discipline are, however, certainly an indispensable part of child rearing. If parents do not discipline their children, then the public will discipline them in a way the parents do not like. Without discipline, children will not respect either the rules of the home or of society. President James E. Faust said, "A principle purpose for discipline is to teach obedience."[31]

That the discipline must be tailor made for each individual, adult or child, is illustrated by President Brigham Young, who said, "You may, figuratively speaking, pound one Elder over the head with a club, and he does not know but what you have handed him a straw dipped in molasses to suck. There are others, if you speak a word to them, or take up a straw and chasten them, whose hearts are broken; they are as tender in their feelings as an infant, and will melt like wax before the flame. You must chasten according to the spirit that is in the person."[32]

And President Young offered more wisdom about teaching children. "Bring up your children," said President Brigham Young, "in the love and fear of the Lord; study their dispositions and their temperaments, and deal with them accordingly, never allowing yourself to correct them in the heat of passion; teach them to love you rather than to fear you."[33]

"Everyone," declared President Howard W. Hunter, "is different. Each of us is unique. Each child is unique. Just as each of us starts at a different point in the race of life, and just as each of us has different strengths and weaknesses and talents, so each child is blessed with his own special set of characteristics. We must not assume that the Lord will judge the success of one in precisely the same way as another. As parents we often assume that, if our child doesn't become an over-achiever in every way, we have failed. We should be careful in our judgments."[34]

Elder Rex D. Pinegar wrote:

> Brothers and sisters, we must not fail to do the simple and easy things that the gospel requires and thereby deny ourselves and our families the great blessings that the Lord has promised. . . .
>
> Charles Francis Adams, the grandson of the second president of the United States, was a successful lawyer, a member of the U.S. House of Representatives, and ambassador to the Britain. Amidst his responsibilities, he had little time to spare. He did, however, keep a diary. One day he wrote, "Went fishing with my son today—a day wasted!" On that same date, Charles's son, Brooke Adams, had printed in his own diary, "Went fishing with my father today—the most wonderful day of my life" . . .
>
> President Hunter has said, "Frequently it is the commonplace tasks that have the greatest positive effect on the lives of others" ("What Is True Greatness?" *BYU 1986–87 Devotionals and Fireside Speeches*, p. 115). I pray that we will heed the counsel of our prophet and have the faith to follow the Savior by doing the simple things His gospel requires.[35]

President Hinckley said this about parenting:

> Then there is the terrible, inexcusable, and evil phenomenon of physical and sexual abuse. It is unnecessary; it is unjustified; it is indefensible. In terms of physical abuse, I have never accepted the principle of "spare the rod and spoil the child." I will be forever grateful for a father who never laid a hand in anger upon his children. Somehow he had the wonderful talent to let them know what was expected of them and to give them encouragement in achieving it.
>
> I am persuaded that violent fathers produce vio-

❦

lent sons. I am satisfied that such punishment in most instances does more damage than good. Children don't need beating. They need love and encouragement. They need fathers to whom they can look with respect rather than fear. Above all they need example. I recently read a biography of George H. Brimhall, who at one time served as president of Brigham Young University. Concerning him someone said that, "He raised his boys with a rod—a fishing rod." That says it all.[36]

President Hinckley also observed:

As children grow through the years, their lives, in large measure, become an extension and a reflection of family teaching. If there is harshness, abuse, uncontrolled anger, disloyalty, the fruits will be certain and discernable, and in all likelihood they will be repeated in the generation that follows. If, on the other hand, there is forbearance, forgiveness, respect, consideration, kindness, mercy, and compassion, the fruits again will be discernable, and they will be eternally rewarding. They will be positive and sweet and wonderful. And as mercy is given and taught by parents, it will be repeated in the lives and actions of the next generation.

I speak to the fathers and mothers everywhere with a plea to put harshness behind us, to bridle our anger, to lower our voices, and to deal with mercy and love and respect one toward another in our homes.[37]

However, we must acknowledge that even if we do our very best to create a gospel-centered home, some of our children may chose to misuse their agency. President Kimball observed:

I have sometimes seen children of good families rebel, resist, stray, sin, and even actually fight God. In this they bring sorrow to their parents, who have done their best to set in movement a current and to teach and live as examples. But I have repeatedly seen many of these same children, after years of wandering, mellow, realize what they have been missing, repent, and make great contribution to the spiritual life of their community.

The reason I believe that this can take place is that, despite all the adverse winds to which these people have been subjected, they have been influenced still more, and much more than they realized, by the current of life in the homes in which they were reared. When, in later years, they feel a longing to recreate in their own families the same atmosphere they enjoyed as children, they are likely to turn to the faith that gave meaning to their parents' lives.[38]

Parents of struggling youth may take encouragement from thoughts like this expressed by President Hunter: "A successful parent is one who has loved, one who has sacrificed, and one who has cared for, taught, and ministered to the needs of a child. If you have done all these and your child is still wayward or troublesome or worldly, it could well be that you are, nevertheless, a successful parent. Perhaps there are children who have come into the world that would challenge any set of parents under any set of circumstances. Likewise, perhaps there are others who would bless the lives of, and be a joy to, almost any father or mother."[39]

President James E. Faust expressed similar encouragement. "Let parents who have been conscientious, loving, and concerned and who have lived the principles of righteousness as best they could be comforted in knowing that they are good parents despite the actions of some of their children. The children themselves have a responsibility to listen, obey, and, having been taught, to learn. Parents cannot always answer for all their children's misconduct because they cannot ensure the children's good behavior. Some few children could tax even Solomon's wisdom and Job's patience."[40]

"Some of you have children," said Elder Scott, "who do

not respond to you, choosing entirely different paths. Father in Heaven has repeatedly had that same experience. While some of His children have used His gift of agency to make choices against His counsel, He continues to love them. Yet, I am sure, He has never blamed Himself for their unwise choices."[41]

While we parents have never done as well or as much as our heavenly parents, we should not be overly critical of our efforts with our children if we have done our best, and continue to do our best, to love them. No family is beyond such challenges. Elder Jeffrey R. Holland noted that "even that beloved and wonderfully successful parent President Joseph F. Smith pled, 'Oh! God, let me not lose my own.' That is every parent's cry, and in it is something of every parent's fear. But no one has failed who keeps trying and keeps praying. You have every right to receive encouragement and to know in the end your children will call your name blessed."[42]

If the child is struggling and hurting, the parent is struggling and hurting. I hope the child will eventually choose to use his agency wisely. Similarly, the parents too will learn from life's parenting experiences and thus become better persons. Someone once said, "The miracle of life is not that adults create children, it's that children create adults."

In fact, it may be accurate to conclude that it is the parent who is doing most of the learning. Parenting is for the tutorial experience of the parent. Then, you might ask, "Who will raise our children?" Our grandchildren will take care of that! It is wonderful to see how teachable our children finally become, once our grandchildren get hold of them.

President Packer shared, "Most of what I know about how our Father in Heaven really feels about us, His children, I have learned from the way I feel about my wife and my children. This I have learned at home. I have learned it from my parents and from my wife's parents, from my beloved wife and from my children, and I can therefore testify of a loving Heavenly Father and of a redeeming Lord."[43]

Part of the learning experience for parents is learning to think in terms of what is best for the family, not just "What is in it for me?" Elder McConkie said:

> It follows that everything we have in the Church centers around celestial marriage, and that salvation is a family affair. . . . Every major decision should be made on the basis of the effect it will have on the family unit. Our courtship, schooling, and choice of friends; our employment, hobbies, and place of residence; our social life, the organizations we join, and the service we render mankind; and above all, our obedience or the lack of it to the standards of revealed truth—all these things should be decided on the basis of their effect on the family unit. . . . There is nothing in this world as important as the creation and perfection of family units of the kind contemplated in the gospel of Jesus Christ.[44]

Only in the family setting, and over time, do we grow into that focus on family, rather than self.

Parents must practice what they preach, pointed out President Faust when he said:

> When parents try to teach their children to avoid danger, it is no answer for parents to say to their children, "We are experienced and wise in the ways of the world and we can get closer to the edge of the cliff than you." Parental hypocrisy can make children cynical and unbelieving of what they are taught in the home. For instance, when parents attend movies they forbid their children to see, parental credibility is diminished. If children are expected to be honest, parents must be honest. If children are expected to be virtuous, parents must be virtuous. If you expect your children to be honorable, you must be honorable.[45]

Many parents have been blessed by having to set a good example for the children. Parenting also helps us to prioritize from an eternal perspective. Elder Maxwell taught:

> Obviously, family values mirror our personal priorities. Given the gravity of current conditions, would parents be willing to give up just one outside thing, giving that time and talent instead to the family? Parents and grandparents, please scrutinize your schedules and priorities in order to ensure that life's prime relationships get more prime time! Even consecrated and devoted Brigham Young was once told by the Lord, "Take especial care of your family" (D&C 126:3). Sometimes it is the most conscientious who need this message the most.[46]

One of the more essential, though painful, learning experiences of parenting is admitting that we are often the one in need of repentance. President Packer gave this counsel to parents:

> If you want to reclaim your son or daughter, why don't you leave off trying to alter your child just for a little while and concentrate on yourself. The changes must begin with you, not with your children. . . . You can't continue to do what you have been doing (even though you thought it was right) and expect to unproduce some behavior in your child, when your conduct was one of the things that produced it. . . .
>
> There! It's been said! After all the evading, all the concern for wayward children. After all the blaming of others, the care to be gentle with parents. It's out! . . . It's you, not the child, that needs immediate attention. . . . Now parents, there is substantial help for you if you will accept it. I add with emphasis that the help we propose is not easy, for the measures are equal to the seriousness of your problem. There is no patent medicine to effect an immediate cure. . . .
>
> And parents, if you seek for a cure that ignores faith and religious doctrine, you look for a cure where it never will be found. When we talk of religious prin-

ciples and doctrines and quote scripture, interesting, isn't it, how many don't feel comfortable with talk like that. But when we talk about your problems with your family and offer a solution, then your interest is intense. . . . Know that you can't talk about one without talking about the other, and expect to solve your problems. Once parents know that there is a God and that we are his children, they can face problems like this and win.

If you are helpless, he is not.
If you are lost, he is not.
If you don't know what to do next, he knows.
It would take a miracle you say?
Well, if it takes a miracle, why not.[47]

Now, if we as parents are still in process, if this parenting thing is a learning experience for us, if we need to learn patience with ourselves as we learn, then it naturally follows that we must also have patience with our parents. We may even need to forgive our parents for their inadequacies.

At the outset we must understand that conscientious parents try their best, yet nearly all have made mistakes. One does not launch into such a project as parenthood without soon realizing that there will be many errors along the way. Surely our Heavenly Father knows, when He entrusted His spirit children into the care of young and inexperienced parents, that there will be mistakes and errors in judgment.

For every set of parents there are many first-time experiences that help to build wisdom and understanding, but each such experience results from the plowing of new ground, with the possibility that errors might be made. With the arrival of the first child, the parents must make decisions about how to teach and train, how to correct and discipline. Soon there is the first day at school and the first bicycle. Then follows the first date of the first teenager, the first problem with school grades, and possibly, the first request to stay out late or the first request to buy a car.

"It is a rare father or mother indeed who travels the difficult path of parenting without making errors along the way," noted President Hunter, "especially at these first-time milestones when experience and understanding are somewhat lacking. Even after the parent has gained experience, the second-time and third-time occurrences of these milestones are sometimes not much easier to handle, nor do they come with much less chance of error."[48]

"Let us also learn," said President Benson, "to be forgiving of our parents, who, perhaps having made mistakes as they reared us, almost always did the best they knew how. May we ever forgive them as we would likewise wish to be forgiven by our own children for mistakes we make."[49]

We must do all that we can to help save our parents, ourselves, and our children. Our greatest joy in the eternities will be if there are no links missing in the chain of eternal family. "When you attend the temple," said President Benson, "and perform the ordinances that pertain to the house of the Lord, certain blessings will come to you: You will receive the spirit of Elijah, which will turn your hearts to your spouse, to your children, and to your forebearers. You will love your family with a deeper love than you have loved before. You will be endowed with power from on high as the Lord promised."[50]

President Faust expressed similar observations and promises:

> Perhaps we regard the power bestowed by Elijah as something associated only with formal ordinances performed in sacred places. But these ordinances become dynamic and productive of good only as they reveal themselves in our daily lives. Malachi said that the power of Elijah would turn the hearts of the fathers and the children to each other. The heart is the seat of the emotions and a conduit for revelation (see Malachi 4:5–6). This sealing power thus reveals itself in family relationships, in attributes and virtues developed in a nurturing environment, and in loving service. These are the cords that bind families together, and the priesthood advances their development. In imperceptible

but real ways, the "doctrine of the priesthood shall distill upon thy soul [and thy home] as the dews from heaven" (D&C 121:45).[51]

Notice that these promises are not guaranteed based only upon the completion of essential ordinances. The power and purpose behind the ordinances must permeate our souls. The spirit of Elijah must enter into our hearts and affect the way we feel, the depth of our love and commitment, the way we treat each other after we leave the temple.

Remember the words of Elder Washburn: "We go to the temple to make covenants, but we go home to keep the covenants that we have made. The home is the testing ground. The home is the place where we learn to be more Christlike. The home is the place where we learn to overcome selfishness and give ourselves in service to others."[52]

For those who participate fully in the ordinances of justification, and who then strive diligently to develop the Christlike character required for sanctification, there are wonderful promises that should give much-needed encouragement and hope. Joseph Smith, the Prophet, declared that, "When a seal is put upon the father and mother, it secures their posterity, so that they cannot be lost, but will be saved by virtue of the covenant of their father and mother."[53]

Elder Orson F. Whitney added:

> The Prophet Joseph Smith declared—and he never taught a more comforting doctrine—that the eternal sealings of faithful parents and the divine promises made to them for valiant service in the Cause of Truth, would save not only themselves, but likewise their posterity. Though some of the sheep may wander, the eye of the Shepherd is upon them, and sooner or later they will feel the tentacles of Divine Providence reaching out after them and drawing them back to the fold. They will have to pay their debt to justice; they will suffer for their sins; and may tread a thorny path;

but if it leads them at last, like the penitent Prodigal, to a loving and forgiving father's heart and home, the painful experience will not have been in vain. Pray for your careless and disobedient children; hold on to them with your faith. Hope on, trust on, till you see the salvation of God.[54]

Notice that being in the covenant does not negate responsibility for our actions. In fact, with covenants we have even greater responsibility. Obedience is always better than repentance, but thankfully, we do have that option. President Joseph F. Smith taught that a person can and will be forgiven if he repents: "The blood of Christ will make him free and will wash him clean, though his sins be as scarlet; but all this will not return to him any loss sustained, nor place him on an equal footing with his neighbor who has kept the commandments of the better law. Nor will it place him in a position where he would have been, had he not committed wrong."[55]

President Joseph Fielding Smith declared that "children born under the covenant, who drift away, are still the children of their parents and the parents have a claim upon them; and if the children have not sinned away all their rights, the parents may be able to bring them through repentance into the Celestial Kingdom, but not to receive the exaltation."[56]

Again, we are reminded how totally dependent we are, both as individuals and as parents, upon the Atonement of Jesus Christ. It is only "through the merits, and mercy, and grace of the Holy Messiah" (2 Nephi 2:8) that we or our children have any hope. But in Him, we have Hope, for He is gracious!

Elder Whitney also said:

> You parents of the willful and the wayward! Don't give them up. Don't cast them off. They are not utterly lost. The Shepherd will find his sheep. They were his before they were yours—long before he entrusted them to your care; and you cannot begin to love them as he loves them. They have but strayed in ignorance from

the Path of Right, and God is merciful to ignorance. Only the fullness of knowledge brings the fullness of accountability. Our Heavenly Father is far more merciful, infinitely more charitable, than even the best of his servants, and the Everlasting Gospel is mightier in power to save than our narrow finite minds can comprehend.[57]

In conclusion, consider this counsel from President Brigham Young:

> Let the father and mother, who are members of this Church and Kingdom, take a righteous course, and strive with all their might never to do a wrong, but to do good all their lives; if they have one child or one hundred children, if they conduct themselves toward them as they should, binding them to the Lord by their faith and prayers, I care not where those children go, they are bound up to their parents by an everlasting tie, and no power of earth or hell can separate them from their parents in eternity; they will return again to the fountain from whence they sprang.[58]

Notes

1. The First Presidency and Counsel of the Twelve Apostles, "The Family—A Proclamation to the World," *Ensign*, November 1995, 102.

2. Ibid.

3. In Brinley and Judd, ed., *Eternal Companions*, 2.

4. Hinckley, "Don't Drop the Ball," *Ensign*, November 1994, 54.

5. Faust, "The Greatest Challenge in the World: Good Parenting," *Ensign*, November 1990, 32–33.

6. Smith, *Gospel Doctrine*, 302.

7. Scott, "First Things First," Ensign, May 2001, 7.

8. Tuttle, in Conference Report, November 1979, 27–28.

9. Grant, in Conference Report, April 1902, 79–80.

10. Benson, "Great Things Required of Their Fathers," *Ensign*, May 1981, 36.

11. Benson, *Teachings of Ezra Taft Benson*, 517.

12. Romney, in Conference Report, April 1960, 110.

13. Perry, in Conference Report, April 1983, 106.

14. Benson, *Teachings of Ezra Taft Benson*, 252.

15. Benson, *Teachings of Ezra Taft Benson*, 254, 256.

16. Haight, in Conference Report, October 1992, 105.

17. Hales, in "Strengthening Our Families: Our Sacred Duty," *Ensign*, May 1999, 32.

18. Kimball, "Families Can Be Eternal," *Ensign*, November 1980, 4.

19. Kimball, in Faust, "The Greatest Challenge in the World—Good Parenting," *Ensign*, November 1990, 33.

20. Kimball, *The Teachings of Spencer W. Kimball*, 309.

21. Smith, *Gospel Doctrine*, 5th ed., 302.

22. Benson, in Conference Report, April 1984, 6–7.

23. Benson, in Conference Report, October 1982, 84–87.

24. Tenorio, in Conference Report, October 1994, 29.

25. Maxwell, in Conference Report, April 1975, 150; emphasis added.

26. Perry, in Conference Report, April 1983, 106.

27. Perry, "'For Whatsoever a Man Soweth, That Shall He also Reap,'" *Ensign*, November 1980, 6.

28. Smith, *Gospel Doctrine*, 316.

29. Cannon, in *The Latter-day Saints' Millennial Star* 53, no. 29 (20 July 1891): 452.

30. Young, in *Journal of Discourses*, 9:124–25.

31. Faust, in Conference Report, October 1990, 39–43.

32. Young, *Discourses of Brigham Young*, 150.

33. Young, in *Journal of Discourses*, 19:221.

34. Hunter, in Conference Report, October 1983, 91–94.

35. Pinegar, "The Simple Things," *Ensign*, November 1994, 82.

36. Hinckley, "Save the Children," *Ensign*, November 1994, 53.

37. Hinckley, "Blessed Are the Merciful," *Ensign*, May 1990, 70.

38. Kimball, in Conference Report, October 1974, 160.

39. Hunter, in Conference Report, October 1983, 91.

40. Faust, in Conference Report, October 1990, 42.

41. Scott, in Conference Report, April 1993, 43.

42. Holland, in Conference Report, April 1997, 48.

43. Packer, in Conference Report, April 1987, 14.

44. McConkie, in Conference Report, April 1970, 27.

45. Faust, in Conference Report, October, 1990, 39.

46. Maxwell, in Conference Report, April 1994, 118.

47. Packer, in Conference Report, October 1970, 119.

48. Hunter, in Conference Report, October 1983, 91.

49. Benson, "To the Elderly in the Church," *Ensign*, November, 1989, 92.

50. Benson, *Teachings of Ezra Taft Benson*, 254.

51. Faust, "Father, Come Home," *Ensign*, May 1993, 37.

52. Washburn, "The Temple Is a Family Affair," *Ensign*, May 1995, 12.

53. Smith, *Teachings of the Prophet Joseph Smith*, 321.

54. Whitney, in Conference Report, April 1929, 110.

55. Smith, *Gospel Doctrine*, 372; see also Kimball, *Miracle of Forgiveness*, 310–11.

56. Smith, *Doctrines of Salvation*, 2:91.

57. Whitney, in Conference Report, April 1929, 110.

58. Young, *Discourses of Brigham Young*, 208.

CONCLUSION:

have fervent charity

Although each of the previous chapters contain valuable principles that, if followed, will bless any marriage, what does this all add up to? What would be the cumulative result of following the counsel of God's prophets regarding celestial marriage?

The scriptures clearly answer this question. "And above all things, clothe yourselves with the bond of charity, as with a mantle, which is the bond of perfectness and peace" (D&C 88:125).

Peter also used the "above all things" phrase when he said, "And above all things have fervent charity among yourselves: for charity preventeth a multitude of sins" (JST, 1 Peter 4:8). And Paul said, "Though I speak with the tongues of men and of angels, and have not charity, I am become as sounding brass, or a tinkling cymbal" (1 Corinthians 13:1).

Elder Bruce R. McConkie made a similar observation. "Above all the attributes of godliness and perfection, charity is the one most devoutly to be desired," he declared. "Charity is more than love, far more; it is everlasting love, perfect love, the pure love of Christ which endureth forever. It is love so centered in righteousness that the possessor has no aim or desire except for the eternal welfare of his own soul and for the souls of those around him."[1]

An individual and a marriage partnership may have many wonderful qualities, but according to these scripture, if the individuals who make up the partnership lack charity, the partnership has not transformed into a celestial marriage. "None is acceptable before God, save the meek and lowly in heart; . . . he must needs have charity; for if he have not charity he is nothing; wherefore he must needs have charity" (Moroni 7:44).

Mormon added, "Charity is the pure love of Christ, and it endureth forever; and whoso is found possessed of it at the last day, it shall be well with him" (Moroni 7:47). He added, "Except men shall have charity they cannot inherit that place which thou hast prepared in the mansions of thy Father" (Ether 12:34).

Both Mormon, in Moroni 7, and Paul, in 1 Corinthians 13, have given us a comprehensive definition of charity. Enjoy this sweet translation of 1 Corinthians 13:4–8 from the Phillips Modern English Translation:

> This love of which I speak is slow to lose patience— it looks for a way of being constructive. It is not possessive: it is neither anxious to impress nor does it cherish inflated ideas of its own importance.
>
> Love has good manners and does not pursue selfish advantage. It is not touchy. It does not keep account of evil or gloat over the wickedness of other people. On the contrary, it is glad with all good men when truth prevails.
>
> Love knows no limit to its endurance, no end to its trust, no fading of its hope; it can outlast anything. It is, in fact, the one thing that still stands when all else has fallen.

Charity = Envieth not, is not puffed up

The scriptures teach that "Thou shalt love thy wife with all thy heart" (D&C 42:22). President Ezra Taft Benson had this to say about love: "What does it mean to love someone with all your heart? It means to love with all your emotional feelings and with all your devotion. Surely when you love your wife with all your heart, you cannot demean her, criticize her, find fault with her, or abuse her by words, sullen behavior, or actions."[2]

This pure, selfless love takes time to develop. For most of us, a lifetime of character building is required before we love as fully as we could—and should. President Joseph Fielding Smith wrote, "Marriage is a principle which, when entered, presents more serious problems than any other," wrote President Joseph Fielding Smith. "It should be received in the spirit of patience and love, even that greater love which comes through the power of the Holy Spirit. Nothing will prepare mankind for glory in the kingdom of God as readily as faithfulness to the marriage covenant."[3]

Overcoming weaknesses is a crucial part of the process of developing Christlike love. C. S. Lewis illustrated the painful process of recognizing one's present limitations when he wrote:

> When I come to my evening prayers and try to reckon up the sins of the day, nine times out of ten the most obvious one is some sin against charity; I have sulked or snapped or sneered or snubbed or stormed. And the excuse that immediately springs to my mind is that the provocation was so sudden and unexpected: I was caught off guard, I had not time to collect myself.
>
> Now that may be an extenuating circumstance as regards those particular acts: they would obviously be worse if they had been deliberate and premeditated. On the other hand, surely what a man does when he is taken off his guard is the best evidence for what sort of a man he is? Surely what pops out before the man has time to put on a disguise is the truth? If there are rats in a cellar you are most likely to see them if you go in very suddenly. But the suddenness does not create the rats: it only prevents them from hiding. In the same way the suddenness of the provocation does not make me an ill-tempered man: it only shows me what an ill-tempered man I am.[4]

This process of developing charity requires much self-discipline. Elder Marvin J. Ashton said:

> Real charity is not something you give away; it is something that you acquire and make a part of yourself. And when the virtue of charity becomes implanted in your heart, you are never the same again. It makes the thought of being [critical or verbally abusive] repulsive. . . . Charity is accepting someone's differences, weaknesses, and shortcomings; having patience with someone who has let us down; or resisting the impulse to become offended when someone doesn't handle something the way we might have hoped. Charity is refusing to take advantage of another's weakness and being willing to forgive someone who has hurt us.[5]

The commitment to upgrade our love to the level of charity is a commitment to hard work. President James E. Faust wrote:

> It is far more difficult to be of one heart and mind than to be physically one. This unity of heart and mind is manifest in sincere expressions of "I appreciate you" and "I am proud of you." Such domestic harmony results from forgiving and forgetting, essential elements of a maturing marriage relationship. Someone has said that we should keep our eyes wide open before marriage and half shut afterward. True charity ought to begin in marriage, for it is a relationship that must be rebuilt every day.[6]

Charity = Doth not behave itself unseemly

Within the pure love of Christ, there is safety. Each person in the partnership could say, "Because you love me with the pure love of Christ; I am safe in your love. When I stumble over my weaknesses, you are not critical. Your acceptance of me gives me the courage to grow and blossom into my full potential. In your love, I am safe."

The spirit of charity is offended by any form of unrighteous dominion. "We have heard of men," said President Spencer W. Kimball, "who have said to their wives, 'I hold the priesthood and you've got to do what I say.' Such a man should be tried for his membership. Certainly he should not be honored in his priesthood. We rule in love and understanding."[7]

Similarly, Orson Hyde wrote, "I will here venture the assertion that no man can be exalted to a celestial glory in the Kingdom of God whose wife rules over him; and as the man is not without the woman nor the woman without the man in the Lord, it follows as a matter of course, that the woman who rules over her husband thereby deprives herself of a celestial glory."[8]

Charity = Seeketh not her own

Many scriptures warn against being self-centered. For example, Paul said, "This know also, that in the last days perilous times shall come. For men shall be lovers of their own selves" (2 Timothy 3:1–2). And Alma records, "thus saith the Lord: Ye shall not esteem one flesh above another, or one man shall not think himself above another" (Mosiah 23:7).

President Ezra Taft Benson noted that, "The world today speaks a great deal about love, and it is sought for by many. But the pure love of Christ differs greatly from what the world thinks of love. Charity never seeks selfish gratification. The pure love of Christ seeks only the eternal growth and joy of others."[9]

In contrast, President Gordon B. Hinckley noted that, "Selfishness is the great destroyer of happy family life. I have this one suggestion to offer. If you will make your first concern the comfort, the well-being, and the happiness of your companion, sublimating any personal concern to that loftier goal, you will be happy, and your marriage will go on through eternity."[10]

We definitely need to become other-centered, beginning with our mate. "We need to be kinder with one another, more gentle and more forgiving," admonished President Howard W. Hunter. "We need to be slower to anger and more prompt to help. . . . In short, we need to love one another with the pure love of Christ, with genuine charity and compassion and, if necessary, shared suffering, for that is the way God loves us."[11]

Charity = Is not easily provoked, thinketh no evil

Elder Jeffrey R. Holland said, "Moroni 7:45 says that true charity—real love—'is not easily provoked, thinketh no evil, and rejoiceth not in iniquity.' Think of how many arguments could be avoided, how many hurt feelings could be spared, how many cold shoulders and silent treatments could be ended, and, in a worst-case scenario, how many breakups and divorces could be avoided if we were not so easily provoked, if we thought no evil of one another, and if we not only did not rejoice in iniquity but didn't rejoice even in little mistakes."[12]

Instead of being easily provoked by our mate, what if we assumed the best? Elder Marvin J. Ashton said, "Perhaps the greatest charity comes when we are kind to each other, when we don't judge or categorize someone else, when we simply give each other the benefit of the doubt or remain quiet. . . . Charity is expecting the best of each other."[13]

I was once giving a lecture to college-age young adults on the destructive nature of criticism in marriage. I was trying to show that criticism is extremely corrosive to a relationship and ought to be avoided. A young man, who was leaning against the back wall with his fiancée, suddenly blurted out, "If you can't criticize your wife, how are you supposed to let her know when she does something that you don't like?"

He said this with such harshness and venom that the entire class turned to look at this engaged couple. I don't know who the class was looking at, but I was looking at her, not him. In my mind, I was wondering, "Dear, did you hear the venom in your fiancé's voice? Are you sure you want to commit yourself to a life with this man?" I failed at softening his attitude, and he stormed out of the class; neither of them ever returned.

In contrast, another young man raised his hand and, when

called upon, said, "I have noticed in dealing with my fiancé that when I have charity, the little annoyances become endearing." What a marvelous insight! If we are motivated by charity, that determines how we react to the behaviors of our mate.

Charity = In all things

Elder Robert D. Hales shared this story:

> The principle of helping one in need is well expressed in the touching love story of Thomas Moore, a famous nineteenth century Irish poet, who, when he returned from a business trip found his wife had locked herself in her upstairs bedroom and had asked to see no one. Moore learned the terrible truth that his beautiful wife had contracted smallpox and her milky complexion was now pocked and scarred. She had looked at herself in the mirror and demanded that the shutters be drawn, and that she never see her husband again.
>
> Thomas Moore did not listen. He went upstairs to the darkened room and started to light the lamp. His wife pleaded with him to let her remain in darkness alone. She felt it best not to subject her husband to seeing his loved one with her beauty marred. She asked him to go.
>
> Moore did go. He went downstairs and spent the rest of the night in prayerful writing. He had never written a song before, but that night he wrote not only words but also composed music. As daylight broke, Moore returned to his wife's darkened room. "Are you awake?" he asked.
>
> "Yes," she said, "but you must not see me. Please don't press me, Thomas."
>
> "I'll sing to you then," he said. Thomas Moore sang to his wife the song that still lives today.
>
> *Believe me, if all those endearing young charms,*
> *Which I gaze on so fondly today,*
> *Were to change by tomorrow and fleet in my arms,*

Like fairy gifts fading away,
Thou wouldst still be adored as this moment thou art.

Moore heard a movement in the corner of the darkened room where his wife lay in loneliness. He continued:

Let thy loveliness fade as it will, And around the dear ruin each wish of my heart, Would entwine itself verdantly still. (Irish Melodies, "Believe Me, If All Those Endearing Young Charms," st.1; cited in Bartlett's Familiar Quotations, p. 542).

The song ended. As his voice faded, Moore heard his bride arise. She crossed the room to the window, reached up and slowly withdrew the shutters, opened the curtain, and let in the morning light.

I would like at this time to thank my wife for opening up the shutters and letting in her light and her life and sharing it with me. I would not be here today without her love and companionship.[14]

Charity = Relationship to Holy Ghost

Mormon taught that charity "Beareth all things, believeth all things, hopeth all things, endureth all things" (Moroni 7:45). This "all things" phrase was later used by Moroni when he wrote, "And by the power of the Holy Ghost ye may know the truth of all things" (Moroni 10:5). It would thus appear that charity and the gift of the Holy Ghost are synonymous.

In Moses 6:61, we read another description of the Holy Ghost: "the Comforter; the peaceable things of immortal glory; the truth of all things; that which quickeneth all things, which maketh alive all things; that which knoweth all things, and hath all power according to wisdom, mercy, truth, justice, and judgment."

That seems very similar to this description from Parley P. Pratt, who wrote that "the gift of the Holy Ghost . . . inspires, develops, cultivates and matures all the fine-toned sympathies, joys, tastes, kindred feelings and affections of our nature. It inspires virtue, kindness, goodness, tenderness, gentleness and charity."[15]

The reader will note that these are also descriptions of the attributes of charity. These charitable attributes are mentioned in the Book of Mormon as gifts of the Holy Spirit. For example, King Benjamin taught, "For the natural man is an enemy to God, and has been from the fall of Adam, and will be, forever and ever, unless he yields to the enticings of the Holy Spirit, and putteth off the natural man and becometh a saint through the atonement of Christ the Lord, and becometh as a child, submissive, meek, humble, patient, full of love, willing to submit to all things which the Lord seeth fit to inflict upon him, even as a child doth submit to his father" (Mosiah 3:19).

And Alma counseled all to "be led by the Holy Spirit, becoming humble, meek, submissive, patient, full of love and all long-suffering" (Alma 13:28).

Recognizing this correlation between charity and the gift of the Holy Ghost can be deeply empowering to a marriage. Those behaviors that bring the Holy Ghost into a marriage will also endow it with charity. Those activities that chase away the Spirit will make the marriage less loving. Elder Orson Pratt said:

> The more righteous a people become the more they are qualified for loving others and rendering them happy. A wicked man can have but little love for his wife; while a righteous man, being filled with the love of God, is sure to manifest this heavenly attribute in every thought and feeling of his heart, and in every word and deed. Love, joy, and innocence will radiate from his very countenance, and be expressed in every look. This will beget confidence in the wife of his bosom, and she will love him in return; for love begets love; happiness imparts happiness; and these heaven born emotions will continue to increase more and more, until they are perfected and glorified in all the fulness of eternal love itself.[16]

Charity = Relationship to Grace

Charity is closely related to the principle of grace. Hugh Nibley explained the correlation:

> You have to keep repenting and repent every day, unless you are perfect. When can you stop repenting? When you are like the Son, full of grace and truth. Then you can stop repenting; there won't be need for anything else. You will have all knowledge, all truth, and nothing but grace. That's to be well meaning and have no ulterior motives and nothing else but pure charity. Grace is what charity is. *Charis* and *grace* are the same thing. *Caritas* is cognate with the Greek *charis,* and that's our word *grace.* Anyway, when you are full of grace and truth, then you can stop any old time.[17]

Based on the similar meanings of *charity* and *grace,* we might paraphrase a familiar verse this way, "It is by the gift of charity that our marriages are saved, after all we can do" (see 2 Nephi 25:23).

Charity = Relationship to Conversion

Elder Dallin H. Oaks has said:

> We are challenged to move through a process of conversion toward that status and condition called eternal life. This is achieved not just by doing what is right, but by doing it for the right reason—for the pure love of Christ. The Apostle Paul illustrated this in his famous teaching about the importance of charity (see 1 Cor. 13). The reason charity never fails and the reason charity is greater than even the most significant acts of goodness he cited is that charity, "the pure love of Christ" (Moro. 7:47), is not an *act* but a *condition* or state of being. Charity is attained through a succession of acts that result in a conversion. Charity is something

one becomes. Thus, as Moroni declared, "except men *have* charity they cannot inherit" the place prepared for them in the mansions of the Father.[18]

Thus charity in marriage means a lifetime of doing numerous things for our spouse and of being converted to a more Christlike way of dealing with others. President Spencer W. Kimball worded it this way: "It is not enough to refrain from adultery. We need to make the marriage relationship sacred, to sacrifice and work to maintain the warmth and respect which we enjoyed during courtship. God intended marriage to be eternal, sealed by the power of the priesthood, to last beyond the grave. Daily acts of courtesy and kindness, conscientiously and lovingly carried out, are part of what the Lord expects."[19]

Charity = Relationship to Sacrifice/Service

The Christlike life is all about service, especially in marriage. President Harold B. Lee noted:

> If young people would resolve at the moment of their marriage that from that time forth they would do everything in their power to please each other in things that are right, even to the sacrifice of their own pleasures, their own appetites, their own desires, the problem of adjustment in married life would take care of itself, and their home would indeed be happy. Great love is built on great sacrifice, and that home where the principle of sacrifice for the welfare of each other is daily expressed is that home where there abides a great love.[20]

Such marriages are not created without monumental effort. President Spencer W. Kimball cautioned:

> Many people there are, though, who do not find divorce attorneys and who do not end their marriages, but who have permitted their marriages to grow stale

and weak and cheap. There are spouses who have fallen from the throne of adoration and worship and are in the low state of mere joint occupancy of the home, joint sitters at the table, joint possessors of certain things which cannot be easily divided. These people are on the path that leads to trouble. These people will do well to reevaluate, to renew their courting, to express their affection, to acknowledge kindnesses, and to increase their consideration so their marriage again can become beautiful, sweet, and growing.

Love is like a flower, and, like the body, it needs constant feeding. The mortal body would soon be emaciated and die if there were not frequent feedings. The tender flower would wither and die without food and water. And so love, also, cannot be expected to last forever unless it is continually fed with portions of love, the manifestation of esteem and admiration, the expressions of gratitude, and the consideration of unselfishness.

Total unselfishness is sure to accomplish another factor in successful marriage. If one is forever seeking the interests, comforts, and happiness of the other, the love found in courtship and cemented in marriage will grow into mighty proportions. Many couples permit their marriages to become stale and their love to grow cold like old bread or worn-out jokes or cold gravy. Certainly the foods most vital for love are consideration, kindness, thoughtfulness, concern, expressions of affection, embraces of appreciation, admiration, pride, companionship, confidence, faith, partnership, equality, and dependence.[21]

Other prophets have also used the garden analogy. Elder Russell M. Nelson noted that "keeping the garden of marriage well cultivated and free from weeds of neglect requires the time and commitment of love. It is not only a pleasant privilege, it is a scriptural requirement with promise of eternal glory."[22]

And President Gordon B. Hinckley warned, "I lift a warning

voice to our people. We have moved too far toward the mainstream of society in this matter. Now of course there are good families. There are good families everywhere. But there are too many who are in trouble. This is a malady with a cure. The prescription is simple and wonderfully effective. It is love. It is plain, simple, everyday love and respect. It is a tender plant that needs nurturing. But it is worth all of the effort we can put into it."[23]

A young couple I worked with discovered a priceless gem while refurbishing a house. Behind several layers of kitchen wallpaper they found this anonymous quote pasted to the wall: "Most people get married believing a myth—that marriage is a beautiful box full of things they have longed for; companionship, sexual fulfillment, intimacy, friendship. The truth is that marriage, at the start, is an empty box. You must put something in before you can take anything out. There is no love in marriage; love is in people, and people put it into marriage. There is no romance in marriage; people have to infuse it into their marriages. A couple must learn the art and form the habit of giving, loving, serving, praising—keeping the box full. If you take out more than you put in, the box will be empty."

Charity = Relationship to Prayer

How do we go about gaining this charity that we seek? An essential prerequisite is praying, begging, pleading for this gift. After giving a beautiful sermon on charity, Mormon counsels, "Wherefore, my beloved brethren, pray unto the Father with all the energy of heart, that ye may be filled with this love, which he hath bestowed upon all who are true followers of his Son, Jesus Christ; that ye may become the sons of God; that when he shall appear we shall be like him, for we shall see him as he is; that we may have this hope; that we may be purified even as he is pure" (Moroni 7:48).

Elder Joseph B. Wirthlin commented, "Note that charity is given only to those who seek it, only to those who earnestly pray for it, only to those who are disciples of Christ."[24]

"If any of us are imperfect," counseled President George Q. Cannon, "it is our duty to pray for the gift that will make us perfect. Have I imperfections? I am full of them. What is my duty? To pray to God to give to me the gifts that will correct these imperfections. If I am an angry man, it is my duty to pray for charity, which suffereth long and is kind. Am I am envious man? It is my duty to seek for charity, which envieth not. So with all the gifts of the Gospel. They are intended for this purpose."[25]

Almost one hundred years later, Elder Joe J. Christensen noted "Elder Kimball [once] shared this wise counsel: 'Well, don't just pray to marry the one you love. Instead, pray to love the one you marry.' We should pray to become more kind, courteous, humble, patient, forgiving, and, especially, less selfish."[26]

What marvelous counsel, pray to love the one you marry. If you feel your love is waning, pray to love the one you marry. If you catch yourself becoming critical, pray to love the one you marry. If you notice that you are slipping into pride or selfishness, pray to love the one you marry. If you would like your love for your spouse to increase and become the pure love of charity, then pray to love the one you marry.

President Hinckley strongly endorsed the practice of couple prayer. He said:

> I know of no single practice that will have a more salutary effect upon your lives than the practice of kneeling together as you begin and close each day. Somehow the little storms that seem to afflict every marriage are dissipated when, kneeling before the Lord, you thank him for one another, in the presence of one another, and then together invoke his blessings upon your lives, your home, your loved ones, and your dreams. God then will be your partner, and your daily conversations with him will bring peace into your hearts and a joy into your lives that can come from no other source. Your companionship will sweeten through the years; your love will strengthen. Your appreciation for one another will grow.[27]

Ultimately, Charity Is an Endowment

We all desire this perfect love, this charity. It is important that we do all we can to develop this pure love of Christ. But we can never do enough; ultimately, charity is an endowment. As Elder Bruce Hafen has written:

> We do not achieve perfection solely through our own efforts. Knowing just that much is a source of new perspective. Because we feel overwhelmed with the scriptural injunction to seek perfection, the idea that divine grace is the final source of our perfection may seem too good to be true. That is how Christ's grace appears to those carrying the burden of truly serious sins. Honest people called "Saints" may feel the same way as they stumble daily through the discouraging debris of their obvious imperfections. But the gospel has good news not only for the serious transgressor, but for all who long to be better than they are.
>
> Through the Holy Ghost, the Atonement makes possible certain spiritual endowments that actually purify our nature and enable us to live a more "eternal" or Godlike life. At that ultimate stage, we will eat the fruit of the tree of life and partake of God's divine nature. Then we will exhibit divine character not just because we think we should, but because that is the way we are.
>
> The gift of charity illustrates this process. . . . This love, the very "love which [the Lord hath] had for the children of men" (Ether 12:34), is not developed entirely by our own power, even though our faithfulness is a necessary qualification to receive it. Rather, charity is "bestowed upon" the "true followers" of Christ (Moro. 7:48). Its source, like all other blessings of the Atonement, is the grace of God. Said Moroni, "I prayed unto the Lord that he would give unto the Gentiles grace, that they might have charity" (Ether 12:36). . . .

The ultimate purpose is to transform his followers to become like him: "he hath bestowed [this love]
upon all who are true followers of his Son, . . . that
when he shall appear we shall be like him" (Moroni
7:48). "At-one-ment" thus seems to mean not only
being with God, but also being like God.[28]

As husband and wife, we must do all that we can to develop
charity in our marriage. Then we petition the Lord to endow our
marriage with that which we seek in all diligence. Like all aspects
of the Atonement, it will ultimately be a matter of grace. Only by
following this pattern can we truly celebrate a celestial marriage.

Notes

1. McConkie, *Mormon Doctrine,* 121.

2. Benson, "To the Fathers in Israel," *Ensign,* November 1987, 59.

3. Smith, *Doctrines of Salvation,* 2:58–59.

4. Lewis, *Mere Christianity,* 163–65.

5. Ashton, "The Tongue Can Be a Sharp Sword," *Ensign,* May 1992, 19.

6. Faust, *Finding Light in a Dark World,* 134.

7. Kimball, *Teachings of Spencer W. Kimball,* 316.

8. Hyde, in *Journal of Discourses,* 4:258.

9. Benson, "Godly Characteristics of the Master," *Ensign,* November
1986, 47.

10. Hinckley, *Teachings of Gordon B. Hinckley,* 328–29.

11. Hunter, *Teachings of Howard W. Hunter,* 173.

12. Holland, "How Do I Love Thee?" in *Brigham Young University 1999–
2000 Devotional and Fireside Speeches,* 158.

13. Ashton, "The Tongue Can Be a Sharp Sword," *Ensign,* May 1992,
19.

14. Hales, "We Can't Do It Alone," *Ensign,* November 1975, 90.

15. Pratt, *Key to the Science of Theology,* 101.

16. Pratt, *The Seer,* October 1853, 156.

17. Nibley, *Teachings of the Book of Mormon–Semester 1,* 81.

18. Oaks, "The Challenge to Become," *Ensign,* November 2000, 34.

19. Kimball, in Conference Report, October 1978, 7.

20. Lee, in Conference Report, April 1947, 45–50.

21. Kimball, "Marriage and Divorce," in *Brigham Young University 1975–
76 Devotional and Fireside Speeches,* 46–47.

22. Nelson, "Listen to Learn," *Ensign*, May 1991, 23.

23. Hinckley, "Look to the Future," *Ensign*, November 1997, 69.

24. Wirthlin, "Cultivating Divine Attributes: Faith, Hope, and Charity," *Ensign*, November 1998, 26.

25. Cannon, *Gospel Truth*, 155.

26. Christensen, "Marriage and the Great Plan of Happiness," *Ensign*, May 1995, 64.

27. Hinckley, "'Except the Lord Build the House,'" *Ensign*, June 1971, 72.

28. Hafen, "Beauty for Ashes," *Ensign*, April 1990, 12–13.

SOURCES

Andrus, Hyrum, and Helen Mae Andrus, comp. *They Knew the Prophet.* Salt Lake City: Bookcraft, 1974.

Ballard, Melvin J. *Sermons and Missionary Services of Melvin J. Ballard.* Edited by Bryant S. Hinckley. Salt Lake City: Deseret Book, 1949.

Barlow, Brent. *Twelve Traps in Today's Marriages and How to Avoid Them.* Salt Lake City: Deseret Book, 1986.

Benson, Ezra Taft. *Come, Listen to a Prophet's Voice.* Salt Lake City: Deseret Book, 1990.

———. *In His Steps.* Provo, Utah: Brigham Young University Publications, 1979.

———. *The Teachings of Ezra Taft Benson.* Salt Lake City: Bookcraft, 1988.

———. *To the Mothers in Zion.* Salt Lake City: The Church of Jesus Christ of Latter-day Saints, 1987.

Brinley, Douglas E., and Daniel K. Judd, ed. *Eternal Companions.* Salt Lake City: Bookcraft, 1995.

Brown, Hugh B. *The Abundant Life.* Salt Lake City: Bookcraft, 1965.

———. *You and Your Marriage.* Salt Lake City: Bookcraft, 1960.

Burton, Rulon T. *We Believe.* Salt Lake City: Bookcraft, 1994.

Cannon, George Q. *Gospel Truth: Discourses and Writings of President George Q. Cannon.* Edited by Jerreld L. Newquist. 2 vols. Salt Lake City: Deseret Book, 1974.

Charge to Religious Educators. 3d ed. Salt Lake City: The Church of Jesus Christ of Latter-day Saints, 1994.

Clark, James R. *Messages of the First Presidency of The Church of Jesus Christ of Latter-day Saints*. Salt Lake City: Bookcraft, 1970.

Cline, Victor B. *How to Make a Good Marriage Great: Insights from an LDS Psychologist*. Salt Lake City: Bookcraft, 1996.

Conference Reports of The Church of Jesus Christ of Latter-day Saints. Salt Lake City: The Church of Jesus Christ of Latter-day Saints, 1898 to present.

Cowley, Matthew. *Matthew Cowley Speaks*. Salt Lake City: Deseret Book, 1954.

Dew, Sheri L. *Go Forward with Faith: The Biography of Gordon B. Hinckley*. Salt Lake City: Deseret Book, 1996.

Ellis, Albert. *Humanistic Psychotherapy: Rational/Emotive Applications*. New York: Julian Press, 1973.

Encyclopedia of Mormonism. Edited by Daniel H. Ludlow. 4 vols. New York: Macmillan, 1992.

Eternal Marriage Student Manual. Salt Lake City: The Church of Jesus Christ of Latter-day Saints, 2001.

Eyring, Henry B. *To Draw Closer to God: A Collection of Discourses*. Salt Lake City: Deseret Book, 1997.

Fairlie, Henry. *The Seven Deadly Sins Today*. London: University of Notre Dame Press, 1979.

Faust, James E. *Finding Light in a Dark World*. Salt Lake City: Deseret Book, 1995.

The First Presidency and Quorum of the Twelve Apostles. *Hope*. Salt Lake City: Deseret Book, 1988.

———. *Woman*. Salt Lake City: Deseret Book, 1988.

Grant, Heber J. *Gospel Standards: Selections from the Sermons and Writings of Heber J. Grant*. Compiled by G. Homer Durham. Salt Lake City: Improvement Era, 1981.

Hafen, Bruce C. *The Broken Heart: Applying the Atonement to Life's Experiences*. Salt Lake City: Deseret Book, 1989.

Hinckley, Gordon B. *Cornerstones of a Happy Home*. Salt Lake City: The Church of Jesus Christ of Latter-day Saints, 1984.

———. *Teachings of Gordon B. Hinckley*. Salt Lake City: Deseret Book, 1997.

Holland, Jeffrey R. *Christ and the New Covenant: The Messianic Message of the Book of Mormon.* Salt Lake City: Deseret Book: 1997.

———. *However Long and Hard the Road.* Salt Lake City: Deseret Book, 1985.

———. *Souls, Symbols, and Sacraments.* Salt Lake City: Deseret Book, 2001.

Holland, Jeffrey R. and Patricia T. Holland. *On Earth As It Is in Heaven.* Salt Lake City: Deseret Book, 1989.

Hunter, Howard W. *The Teachings of Howard W. Hunter.* Edited by Clyde J. Williams. Salt Lake City: Bookcraft, 1997.

Journal of Discourses. 26 vols. London: Latter-day Saints' Book Depot, 1854–86.

Judd, Daniel K. "The Doctrines of Submission and Forgiveness." In *Doctrines for Exaltation: The 1989 Sperry Symposium on the Doctrine and Covenants.* Edited by H. Dean Garret and Rex C. Reeve Jr. Salt Lake City: Deseret Book, 1989.

Kimball, Spencer W. *Faith Precedes the Miracle.* Salt Lake City: Deseret Book, 1972.

———. *Marriage and Divorce.* Salt Lake City: Deseret Book, 1976.

———. *The Miracle of Forgiveness.* Salt Lake City: Bookcraft, 1969.

———. *The Teachings of Spencer W. Kimball.* Edited by Edward L. Kimball. Salt Lake City: Bookcraft, 1982.

Lamb, Stephen E., and Douglas E. Brinley. *Between Husband and Wife: Gospel Perspectives on Marital Intimacy.* American Fork: Covenant Communications, 2000.

Landis, Mary, and Judson Landis. *Building a Successful Marriage.* Englewood Cliffs, N.J.: Prentice Hall, 1958.

The Latter-day Saints' Millennial Star. Manchester, Liverpool, and London, England: The Church of Jesus Christ of Latter-day Saints, 1840–1970.

Lee, Harold B. *Ye Are the Light of the World: Selected Sermons and Writings of Harold B. Lee.* Salt Lake City: Deseret Book, 1974.

———. *The Teachings of Harold B. Lee.* Edited by Clyde J. Williams. Salt Lake City: Bookcraft, 1996.

Lewis, C. S. *Mere Christianity.* New York: Simon & Schuster, 1996.

Maxwell, Neal A. *A Time to Choose.* Salt Lake City: Deseret Book, 1972.

————. *But for a Small Moment.* Salt Lake City: Bookcraft, 1986.

————. *Deposition of a Disciple.* Salt Lake City: Deseret Book, 1976.

————. *Even As I Am.* Salt Lake City: Deseret Book, 1982.

————. *If Thou Endure It Well.* Salt Lake City: Bookcraft, 1996.

————. *Men and Women of Christ.* Salt Lake City: Bookcraft, 1991.

————. *Neal A. Maxwell Quote Book.* Compiled by Cory H. Maxwell. Salt Lake City: Bookcraft, 2001.

————. *Notwithstanding My Weakness.* Salt Lake City: Deseret Book, 1981.

————. *We Will Prove Them Herewith.* Salt Lake City: Deseret Book, 1982.

————. *Wherefore, Ye Must Press Forward.* Salt Lake City: Deseret Book, 1977.

May, Rollo. *Love and Will.* Scranton, Penn.: W. W. Norton, 1969.

McConkie, Bruce R. *A New Witness for the Articles of Faith.* Salt Lake City: Deseret Book, 1985.

————. *Doctrinal New Testament Commentary.* Salt Lake City: Bookcraft, 1973.

————. *Mormon Doctrine.* 2d ed. Salt Lake City: Bookcraft, 1966.

————. *Sermons of Bruce R. McConkie.* Edited by Mark L. McConkie. Salt Lake City: Bookcraft, 1998.

McConkie, Joseph Fielding. *Here We Stand.* Salt Lake City: Deseret Book, 1995.

————. *Joseph Smith: The Choice Seer.* Salt Lake City: Bookcraft, 1996.

McKay, David O. *Gospel Ideals.* Salt Lake City: Improvement Era, 1953.

————. *Pathway to Happiness.* Salt Lake City: Bookcraft, 1957.

————. *Treasures of Life.* Salt Lake City: Deseret Book, 1965.

Millet, Robert L. *The Mormon Faith: A New Look at Christianity.* Salt Lake City: Deseret Book, 1998.

————. *Selected Writings of Robert L. Millet.* Salt Lake City: Deseret Book, 2000.

Nelson, Russell M. *The Power within Us.* Salt Lake City: Deseret Book, 1988.

Nibley, Hugh. *Old Testament and Related Studies.* Salt Lake City: Deseret Book; Provo, Utah: Foundation for Ancient Research and Mormon Studies, 1986.

———. *Teachings of the Book of Mormon—Semester 1: Transcripts of Lectures Presented to an Honors Book of Mormon Class at Brigham Young University, 1988–90.* Provo, Utah: Foundation for Ancient Research and Mormon Studies, 1990.

———. *The World and the Prophets.* Salt Lake City: Deseret Book, 1966.

Oaks, Dallin H. *Pure in Heart.* Salt Lake City: Bookcraft, 1988.

Old Testament Student Manual: Genesis–2 Samuel. Salt Lake City: The Church of Jesus Christ of Latter-day Saints, 1981.

Packer, Boyd K. "The Law and the Light." In *The Book of Mormon: Jacob through the Words of Mormon.* Edited by Monte S. Nyman and Charles D. Tate Jr. Provo, Utah: Religious Studies Center, Brigham Young University, 1990.

———. *Our Father's Plan.* Salt Lake City: Deseret Book, 1984.

———. *That All May Be Edified.* Salt Lake City: Bookcraft, 1982.

———. *The Holy Temple.* Salt Lake City: Bookcraft, 1980.

———. *Things of the Soul.* Salt Lake City: Bookcraft, 1996.

Parrott, Les, III, and Leslie Parrott. *Saving Your Marriage before It Starts.* Grand Rapids: Zondervan Publishing House, 2000.

Parry, Donald. *Temples of the Ancient World: Ritual and Symbolism.* Salt Lake City: Deseret Book; Provo, Utah: Foundation for Ancient Research and Mormon Studies, 1994.

Pratt, Parley P. *The Essential Parley P. Pratt.* Salt Lake City: Signature Books, 1990.

———. *Key to the Science of Theology/A Voice of Warning.* Salt Lake City: Deseret Book, 1965.

———. *Writings of Parley Parker Pratt.* Edited by Parker Pratt Robinson. Salt Lake City: Deseret News Press, 1952.

Ralph, Margaret Nutting. *The Bible and the End of the World.* Mahwa, N.J.: Paulist Press, 1997.

Rasband, Ester. *Confronting the Myth of Self-Esteem.* Salt Lake City: Deseret Book, 1998.

The Seer. Published by Orson Pratt in Washington, D.C., 1853–1854.

Smith, Joseph. *History of The Church of Jesus Christ of Latter-day Saints.* Edited by B. H. Roberts. 2d ed. rev. 7 vols. Salt Lake City: The Church of Jesus Christ of Latter-day Saints, 1932–51.

———. *Teachings of the Prophet Joseph Smith.* Selected by Joseph Fielding Smith. Salt Lake City: Deseret Book, 1972.

———. *The Words of Joseph Smith: The Contemporary Accounts of the Nauvoo Discourses of the Prophet Joseph.* Compiled and edited by Andrew F. Ehat and Lyndon W. Cook. Provo: BYU Religious Studies Center, 1980.

Smith, Joseph F. *Gospel Doctrine: Selections from the Sermons and Writings of Joseph F. Smith.* Compiled by John A. Widtsoe. Salt Lake City: Deseret Book, 1939.

Smith, Joseph Fielding. *Doctrines of Salvation.* Compiled by Bruce R. McConkie. 3 vols. Salt Lake City: Bookcraft, 1955.

Snow, Lorenzo. Edited by Clyde J. Williams. *The Teachings of Lorenzo Snow: Fifth President of The Church of Jesus Christ of Latter-day Saints.* Salt Lake City: Bookcraft, 1984.

Talmage, James E. *The Articles of Faith.* Salt Lake City: The Church of Jesus Christ of Latter-day Saints, 1975.

Thomas, M. Catherine. *Selected Writings of M. Catherine Thomas: Gospel Scholars Series.* Salt Lake City: Deseret Book, 2000.

———. *Spiritual Lightening.* Salt Lake City: Deseret Book, 1996.

Widtsoe, John A. *Evidences and Reconciliations.* Edited by G. Homer Durham. Salt Lake City: Bookcraft, 1960.

———. *Priesthood and Church Government.* Salt Lake City: Deseret Book, 1939.

The Woman's Exponent. Salt Lake City: The Church of Jesus Christ of Latter-day Saints, 1872–1914.

Woodruff, Wilford. *Wilford Woodruff's Journal, 1833–1898.* Edited by Scott G. Kenney. Midvale: Signature Books, 1983–1985.

Young, Brigham. *Discourses of Brigham Young.* Compiled by John A. Widtsoe. Salt Lake City: Deseret Book, 1941.

about the author

After earning a bachelor of science degree from Brigham Young University and serving eight years as a military pilot, Richard K. Scott earned a master of education degree in counseling from the University of Idaho and a professional level master's degree in counseling from Arizona State University.

He has worked as a marriage and family counselor, and for thirty years he has worked for the Church Educational System. He currently teaches at the Orem Institute of Religion.

Richard enjoys the scriptures and Church history, but his special focus is on preparing young couples to have successful marriages. He has served in six bishoprics, on a high council, and in a stake presidency.

Richard and his wife, Janice, are the parents of thirteen children and have served as foster parents to thirty children. They make their home in Mapleton, Utah.